Days of Our Lives

TOM & ALICE HORTON *loved deeply, devotedly and without reservation. They shared an enormous and rare respect for each other, their marriage and family. In 1980, after fifty years together, they renewed their vows with a love that continued to grow stronger with every year until Tom died in 1994.*

"We had many traumatic times, but Tom and Alice never fought. Originally, we were too busy taking care of the children to argue. Then we simply got into the endearing habit of just not fighting. I think we developed an amazingly similar, and sometimes complementing, view of life. Alice simply adored the man."

—FRANCES REID

Days of Our Lives

The Complete Family Album

LORRAINE ZENKA

A 30TH ANNIVERSARY CELEBRATION

ReganBooks
An Imprint of HarperCollinsPublishers

FIRST EDITION

DESIGNED BY JOEL AVIROM, JASON SNYDER & MEGHAN DAY HEALEY

Library of Congress Cataloging-in-Publication Data

Zenka, Lorraine.
    Days of our lives : the complete family album : a 30th anniversary celebration / Lorraine Zenka. — 1st ed.
      p.   cm.
    Includes index.
    ISBN 0–06–039171–5
    1. Days of our lives (Television program)   I. Title.
PN1992.77.D38Z46   1995
791.45'72—dc20   95-35566

95 96 97 98 99 ❖/RRD 10 9 8 7 6 5 4 3 2 1

Contents

Acknowledgments

Executive Producer Ken Corday for contributing his valuable time and input. Co-executive Producer Tom Langan, head writer James E. Reilly, and Executive in Charge of Production Gary Fogel for their support, contributions, and guidance.

William Bell for his insights and his forethought in creating the William and Lee Bell Television Collection at the University of California, Los Angeles. The extensive treasury of *Days of Our Lives* scripts from the sixties and seventies was precious to this project. And special thanks to UCLA's Special Collections Librarian, Brigitte Kueppers.

Warm thanks and gratitude to the show publicist, Paulette Cohn, and my colleague, Robert Waldron, for cooperation, encouragement, and support. My agent, David Vigliano. The professional and even-tempered staff at HarperCollins, especially editor Eamon Dolan and his assistant, Sarah Polen, and copy editor Erin Clermont, and designer Joel Avirom.

Former head writer Pat Falken Smith and past senior producer Becky Greenlaw for their sense of history and generous spirit. The National Broadcasting Company, Inc., network publicist Charles Riley, and photo librarian Dusty Morales for time-consuming help with current and archival photo access and selection. Production Assistant Stuart Howard for his "Behind the Scenes" expertise. Casting Associate Ron Sperber for research assistance. Janet DiLauro, Kathy Hutchins, Dick McInnes, Arika Mittman, and Roberta Ostroff for editorial and photo assistance. My family and many friends for their patience, kind words, and prayers.

Present and past cast, crew, production personnel, technical and creative staff of *Days of Our Lives*, who have each contributed to the success of a show that touches millions of hearts each day.

TED AND BETTY CORDAY, in creating *Days of Our Lives*, produced more than a daytime drama. With Irna Phillips, they set into motion a living monument to family love, devotion, and traditional values.

Ted Corday began his career in the entertainment industry in the 1930s when he became a stage manager on Broadway. He later directed many theater productions there too, including *Cabin in the Sky* and *Porgy & Bess.* After being discharged from the Army Signal Corps as captain in 1945, Corday took his talent to the national radio networks, where he directed several major productions, including *Gangbusters* and *The Shadow.*

In the late forties and early fifties, Corday became a director for CBS radio and was the first to direct the new radio soap opera *The Guiding Light.* In 1952, Corday directed the same script daily on radio and at the CBS Television Center, where *Guiding Light* aired live on national television. It was during this time that he entered into a working relationship with Irna Phillips.

In 1956, Corday helped Phillips create and bring *As the World Turns* to CBS Television as a half-hour soap opera that he directed and produced. His daily working relationship with Phillips thrived throughout the next ten years. During this time he became acquainted with two of Phillips' brightest scriptwriters, Agnes Nixon and Bill Bell. Each was writing either *Guiding Light* or *As the World Turns.*

The original idea for *Days of Our Lives* was conceived in one of many informal discussions between the Cordays and Phillips on the porch of a Southampton, Long Island, home in the early sixties. At the time, Corday was producing *As the World Turns.* Phillips was head writer on that show and had created *Guiding Light, Another World,* and was co-creating *Days of Our Lives.* (Phillips has been gone twenty years, but one-third of the daytime dramas still on the air are ones she created.)

On November 8, 1965, *Days* debuted on NBC. It was the first soap opera to be broadcast in color, and the first set in the rural Midwest.

Ted Corday died in July 1966, leaving his legacy to his wife, Betty, who had been a producer of the radio soap operas *Young Dr. Malone* and *Pepper Young's Family.*

Betty Corday ran the show from 1966 until she retired in 1985 and stayed with the show until she died in 1987.

Their son, Ken Corday, began working on the show after college in 1980. Today he is the executive producer.

Ted and Betty Corday received the Lifetime Achievement Award for Extraordinary Contributions to Daytime Television from the National Academy of Arts and Sciences this year at the Daytime Emmy Awards ceremony held in New York City. Ken proudly accepted the award on their behalf.

Bill Bell, who was head writer for *Days of Our Lives* from 1966 to 1973, noted: "I worked with Ted and Betty, these extremely talented people, over a continuous span of sixteen years—nine with Ted on *As the World Turns* and seven years with Betty, who carried on for Ted on *Days of Our Lives*. These were very exciting years and *Days* became the top daytime show just four years after its inception.

"I knew Ted and Betty very well," Bell continued. "Ted was a superb producer and director whose unique rapport and sensitivity with actors is legendary. His ability to extract every ounce of drama and emotion from the written word was a writer's dream. Betty, partner of Ted, was an equally dedicated mother and writer and producer and a very powerful force in her own right. Each, the ultimate complement of the other. They were very precious to each other and to all of us who knew them. Betty and Ted, I will never forget you, not ever in all the days of my life."

KEN CORDAY, executive producer of *Days of Our Lives*, has been a part of the show since 1965 on a personal level and an official capacity since 1980.

"I'm extremely thrilled that *Days of Our Lives* continued in the same vein as it began when my father started it," he says with justifiable pride. "And wonderfully, it has grown into the eighties and nineties. My dad died in 1966. My mother shared his outlook and ran the show from 1966 until she retired about 1985 and stayed with the show until she died in 1987."

Only sixteen when his father died, Corday learned his best lessons from his mother, Betty. "My mom would come home at night and talk about this show, which I knew little about, and these characters, and their problems," Corday fondly recalls. "I was her sounding board and perhaps through osmosis I picked up her philosophy. In 1980, I came to the show first as a composer and later as someone who answered fan mail and brought coffee to producers while I absorbed as much as I could for a few years. As an adult, I was able to understand those lessons I had assimilated as a teenager."

It had been very challenging for Corday to get past the stigma of nepotism, to prove himself. "At the time, that was very difficult," he admits.

Days of Our Lives is a living memorial to the Corday family. It is that personal. "This show is thirty years old. I'm forty-five. I look at this show as both a sibling and a stepchild. As a younger brother or sister left in my custodianship.

"I feel as if I'm a curator of a museum where there is a very precious piece of art on the wall and many, many people come through every day. It's important that it's kept in the right light, in the right frame, that it's kept clean, and other people's fingerprints don't get on the picture.

"There was really only one artist on *Days of Our Lives*: the creators then and the head writer today," Corday points out. "Producers interpret the creation, but it really is a writer's and actor's medium. Let the writers write; let the actors act; let the directors direct. The producer should not try to do everything. That would be the downfall of many who want to produce, direct, write, etc. The Executive Producer is only as good as the company . . . the characters and philosophy are the hub of the wheel. My contribution is to stay true to what Tom and Alice would have done in the past. The pace of the show may change, but the philosophy cannot. I believe we have the following we do because our families are still in place, so are their philosophies, and usually good overcomes evil."

Until *Days of Our Lives*, soaps were all based in an urban setting with a vertical layout from penthouse down through corporate offices and basement. *Days* was set in a more rural, middle-American setting. Salem later grew into suburbia, and today has a major airport. The movement and geography are horizontal.

As Tom and Alice Horton, Macdonald Carey and Frances Reid were *Days'* linchpins from the very first episode. Carey was an accomplished film star with more than 500 movies to his credit, and Frances had a list of prestigious theater credits, including several acclaimed Shakespearian productions on Broadway. On *Days*, they provided a foundation, and warm familiarity.

"If Tom and Alice were as comfortable as well-worn shoes, their children were far from broken in," says Corday today. "Tom and Alice never had a major story line of their own. For many years, until the early eighties, the Hortons were the only core family. Other families were in Salem—the Bannings, Andersons, Grants—but they were not the core units like the Horton family and later, with head writer Pat Falken Smith's vision, the Brady and DiMera families. Pat was also responsible for creating a new youth and geography at that time.

"There has always been a core morality based on good family values. Tom and Alice always knew what was right," Corday continues. "Family is the safe harbor when all else fails. Family is there to love and protect. Basically, love and decency win out. If you do something good, it's revisited once. Do something bad and it's usually revisited upon you three times.

"Some people would argue, however, that daytime is amoral. We can do things in daytime that cannot be done on prime time until after 10 P.M. There's a certain amount of passion and romance that others might call sexuality. But we tend not to complete the emotion for the viewer. We start it, and let the viewer complete it. For example, Marlena may have a tear forming in her eye and it may start down the cheek, but we cut away before it falls. Two characters kiss, embrace, and fall down in front of the fireplace while we dissolve and fade into the candle flame. The audience can complete the scene in a way they see fit."

In that sense, *Days of Our Lives* is interactive. It has also kept pace with today's younger audience, which wants speedier storytelling and dramatic dialogue. Still, Corday believes there are three basic concepts at work at *Days*. First, you are only as good as your last episode. Second, you are only as good as your actors and writer who create good characters whom the viewers will know intimately. And third, you must love what you do and love the people you work with. Beyond that, the other elements have importance: 45 percent is casting; 45 percent is story; and 10 percent lies with production and promotion.

As far as the "run and gun" action stories, Corday points out, "We never launch a character on such an adventure unless we completely understand exactly what that character has emotionally invested in the quest."

Corday admits that there were times in the late eighties when he was lured by other projects, like prime-time miniseries, and other occupations. But he recalls, "I would go away for a few weeks and after just one week away I'd start getting itchy. It's something in my blood. I may sometimes think differently, but that would be a lie. When I say I need something new and different in my life I sit on the beach for a few days, and then I miss the show.

"There are likely three or four generations watching *Days of Our Lives*," he realizes. "Daytime dramas, this show in particular, make an important contribution to society. It's studied not only in entertainment courses but in philosophy and psychology courses, too. Yet this is not brain surgery. It's very simple in a very intricate way. It is simple and well woven. We don't want to delve into the violent or overall social issues. It is no longer the place to discuss heavy social issues, illnesses, and politics. People get enough of that in the news. People watch daytime television for the romance, the love stories."

For thirty years, *Days of Our Lives* has been sharing love and finding it in new places, proving love thrives with nurturing, tender care, and devotion.

30 Years of
Days of Our Lives

"Like sands through the hourglass,

so are the days of our lives . . ."

D AYS OF OUR LIVES is the story of the Horton family and all the people who crossed paths with them and their friends over the last three decades.

It all began with Tom Horton, who was born in the Midwest town of Salem in 1910. He so loved and admired his father, a physician in general practice, that he looked forward to being just like him when he grew up. It was no surprise that Tom eventually became a doctor, too.

In high school, Tom dated Alice Grayson, an intelligent, sensitive teenager, a year younger than Tom. She came from a blue-collar family headed by her dad, who was lovable but somewhat irresponsible. He had started out as a fine cabinetmaker, but because of a weakness for drinking, eventually became a handyman. Perhaps a bit of social embarrassment kept Alice withdrawn, buried in books and fantasy. However, with Tom's persistent love, Alice blossomed into an outspoken and handsome young woman. They wed a few years after she graduated high school in 1930.

Tom had been the star pitcher of his high school baseball team and athletic ability served him well. Later, while at the local university and already married, he earned money by playing for a local minor league team. If not for his dedication to medicine and serving humanity, Tom likely would have pursued a professional baseball career.

Tom completed his military service, reaching the rank of captain in active duty in the South Pacific during World War II. Afterward, he began his medical career as a professor of internal medicine at the Salem University Medical School while also employed as a staff physician at University Hospital in Salem.

He was always well-liked as a student, soldier, athlete, and physician. Tom was always ready to lend an ear—or some money when he could. He tried always to see the best in people and let them learn by their own choices, whether he viewed their actions in their best interests or not.

1965

By November 8, 1965, the Hortons' children were grown and several had off-spring of their own. Alice bemoaned her "empty nest" as their youngest planned to wed and leave the Horton household. Alice found it difficult to get used to the quiet of the house and having "five gallons of ice-cream in the freezer, but no one to eat it all." Tom missed the children, too, but tried to console Alice. Now the two would have more closet space, the kids wouldn't be at Alice's apron strings, and they no longer had to go to PTA meetings or sell Girl Scout cookies.

The twins, Tom Jr. and Addie, were born in 1931. Tommy was killed in Korea in 1953. His wife, Kitty, whom he met while in basic training, had their daughter Sandy while Tommy was in the war. Addie, in 1949, married status-conscious Ben Olson, whose father was the richest man in Salem and the president of the First National Bank. They lived in the toniest part of Salem, Wycliffe Heights, and had two children, Julie and Steven, teenagers in 1965.

At thirty-three, Mickey Horton, an attorney, was a very popular bachelor. Although he had his own apartment, he often stopped by his parents' house for dinner, and if a chess game with his dad ran into the late hours, he would stay overnight. Bill, twenty-five, was in his final year at Harvard Medical School. Marie, the baby of the family, born in 1942, was a biochemistry graduate student at Salem University. She was engaged, and plans were being made for her Thanksgiving wedding to neighbor Tony Merritt.

Julie, Addie's daughter, was a rebellious, troublesome teenager. As the first-born grandchild, she had been the prime focus of family attention until her brother Steven arrived two years later. Being cheated of the spotlight was an affront to this spoiled, pampered princess. As Steven grew into a popular young man with an outstanding academic record, Julie found less savory ways to get attention and control.

When Julie tried to impress two girlfriends by stealing a fur piece at Bartlett's Department Store, a store detective saw her open the display case and stuff the fur into her shopping bag. At the police station, Julie gave her last name as Horton, not Olson, and Tom was called. Mickey was visiting at the time and went with Tom as Julie's legal adviser.

At home, Alice continued to discuss wedding plans with Marie and Tony. Alice's only personal request was that Tony's dad, Craig, a handsome airline pilot, wear his uniform on the Big Day, the first real wedding for the Hortons.

Alice recalled, "Addie and Ben got married in Washington right after the war. Poor Tommy married Kitty at City Hall before he was shipped overseas. Of course, your dad and I could never afford anything but a very simple ceremony."

Later, alone outside, Marie and Tony talked excitedly about moving to Boston, where he was interviewing for a teaching fellowship. Marie planned to work part time on campus while finishing her postgraduate studies. During their conversation, Tony hid spells of pain and dizziness from Marie.

Meanwhile, at the police precinct, Julie self-righteously denied trying to steal the fur, which was inferior to any she already had in her closet. It had been only a joke. Mickey let her know this was no joke. Records showed Julie had been questioned about stealing three previous times.

> "You were five. . . . We were at a park and got separated. . . . All you did was yell, cry, and kick up the dirt. You've been doing that ever since—being frightened, scared, running off in ten directions at once."
>
> —TOM HORTON TO JULIE

Since Ben and Addie were still not back from a dinner party, Tom brought Julie home with him until her parents were contacted. When the Olsons, in their formal attire, finally arrived, tension was thick. Ben was furious and concerned about keeping the embarrassing incident quiet. He was certain he could influence the department store manager to drop the charges. Mickey and Ben argued over the best course of action. Addie used the moment to take Marie to task for choosing Tony, only a teacher, over wealthy Rick Butler, whom Marie had been engaged to the year before.

After the Olsons left, Tom noted, "Ben has been so busy making money to be a good father that he's lost the ability to communicate as a father. In order to get love, you have to have the time to give love. Ben has just never made the time. They better wake up to Julie's needs before it's too late."

After the Olsons viewed the surveillance tape at Bartlett's Department Store the next day, it was clear charges against Julie would not be dropped. At home, Ben laid down the law to Julie: more chores, less privileges. But Julie remained defiant.

Visiting Marie without prior permission, Julie broke a wedding gift that she should never have opened. As Craig Merritt helped Julie clean up, the young girl became mildly infatuated. He was strong, handsome, and gently supportive. When she told him it was not likely she would get married because she wanted to travel, meet people, and not be like her bickering mother and dad, he countered with, "People are all different. Your marriage may be the romance of the decade."

Later, after Julie left, Addie stopped by with fabric swatches for the bridal attendants' dresses. She was feeling sorry for herself, annoyed that Julie was getting everyone's attention while no one cared about her problems. Again, she criticized Marie's choice of Tony as a husband, Mickey's attitude toward Ben, and Julie's attachment to Marie. The sisters had a good blowup before Alice succeeded in playing peacemaker.

Unfortunately, at this point Tony had not consulted his future father-in-law for a checkup. Once he was diagnosed with a blood disease that could be fatal, he was overcome with fear for himself and what his death might do to Marie. He kept his illness a secret. Not thinking clearly, Tony broke their engagement the night before the wedding. Stunned and devastated, Marie fell into a dark depression and eventually attempted suicide with an overdose of sleeping pills.

As the Hortons hung their traditional Christmas ornaments with the names of each family member on their tree, it was clear each colorful ball was both strong and fragile, different and similar, and changing in tone with the light or darkness that fell upon it.

"Tom was a father who shared an equal—and sometimes even greater—involvement with the children. He and Alice agreed between themselves how to raise the children and maintained a mutually supportive approach as parents."

—FRANCES REID (ALICE HORTON)

While Marie recovered from her suicide attempt, she found comfort from long talks with and growing fondness for Craig Merritt, Tony's father. He was a lonely widower and had always like Marie. He was not merely trying to make things right when he proposed to the sensitive and vulnerable young woman nearly half his age. He looked forward to true companionship. After a small, quiet wedding, the two settled into what appeared to be a comfortable and stable marriage. This,

1966

in spite of several weeks when Tony was also living in the Merritt home. There were moments packed with tension as the two young people fought their passion and unresolved anger, longing and fears. Marie remained always faithful to her husband, however, and Tony respected his father's wife. In a short time, he took an apartment of his own, in the same building where Laura Spencer, an intern at Salem University Hospital, was living.

Meanwhile, Mickey and Tom got caught up in Salem's ecological crisis. One of Mickey's clients, Woodstock Industries, had allowed poisonous waste to contaminate some of the town's water supply. The problem hit home when Julie was stricken ill. The conflict of interest between Tom the doctor and Mickey the lawyer also caused strife between the two men. Political factions split the town as well, and the Hortons endured several broken windows for their trouble.

The industrial problem was handled in short order. Mickey, meanwhile, began seeing Diane Hunter. He had handled her divorce several years before and the two had developed an easy friendship and drifted into a comfortable affair. Neither had expected anything more. Diane was still healing the wounds of her failed marriage, and Mickey enjoyed his status as one of Salem's most eligible bachelors. The relationship was distasteful to Alice. Tom, although he could not condone the relationship, often pointed out that Mickey was a grown man with natural needs and had to be allowed to make his own choices without parental interference.

Besides, Tom and Alice had their hands full with Julie. She was now living in the Horton household, in her grandparents' care after her parents moved to Europe. The rebellious and outspoken teenager often perplexed the couple and tried Tom's patience as no one else could.

On the sly, Julie began dating somewhat older David Martin. They had found a common bond: both were overindulged, even spoiled, but neither felt they were really loved. Within a few months, the couple became secretly engaged and even planned to elope. However, on the night they were going to cross the state border, Tom, who suspected Julie was up to something, lectured his grand-daughter about her choices in life and love. It made the girl think twice, and she refused to leave with David, who then went off to drown his sorrows in drink. He crossed paths with Susan Hunter, who was feeling lonely and rejected because her parents were divorced. She particularly missed her father, who had moved to New York and was thinking of remarrying.

On that one night of disappointment and frustration, David and Susan found solace in each other. They made love in David's car and Susan conceived. Ironically, it was Dr. Tom Horton, who had unknowingly contributed to Susan and David's night of passion, who several months later entreated Susan to do what she could to give the baby a name and a right start in life. Susan was deeply hurt by David's initial questioning of the baby's paternity. Striking out with a sound slap to his face, Susan insisted he stand by the child. The couple embarked on a loveless and turbulent marriage with the agreement that they would give the child up for adoption, then divorce.

The couple's parents were not aware that Susan was pregnant before the wedding. Julie did know, but believed David still loved her and would follow through on the plan he and Susan hatched. Julie even agreed to be maid of honor at her high school pal's wedding. As had always been her style, Julie spent many lonely hours bemoaning her sad situation and catching stolen moments with

David. She also played confidante to Susan who, at that time, was unaware of Julie and David's true feelings for each other. To quell her fears that David and Susan were really behaving as husband and wife, Julie often found excuses to drop by their apartment unannounced. At one point, she even woke them in the middle of the night on the pretext of being caught in a rainstorm. Her true mission had been to verify their separate-bedroom sleeping arrangements.

While Susan bemoaned her pregnancy at every turn, Marie was enchanted with her baby and plans for its arrival. Tragically, Marie miscarried the child that would likely have given the Merritt marriage its one true chance for survival. Craig sympathetically excused Marie's ensuing depression as postpartum blues. He loved Marie, had pulled her through one depression, and was confident he could do so again. He was there for Marie through bouts of hallucinations, hearing babies cry from rooms where there were none. Craig even excused her withdrawal and avoidance of intimacy, believing they truly had many years together ahead of them.

*"Daddy, I want to be
a little girl again!"*

—JILTED, DIVORCED,
ALONE, MARIE HORTON
AT TWENTY-TWO

About the same time, Tony, who was cured of his illness, finally told Craig why he had so abruptly walked out on Marie nearly a year ago. Suddenly realizing that Tony still loved Marie, Craig saw his marriage as an obstacle to happiness for the two people he loved most.

Hiding his true feelings, and claiming that he never really loved her, Craig asked Marie for a divorce. Marie felt some guilt and responsibility since she had never been able to give herself completely. But Craig insisted the blame was all his. In his forties, Craig felt he should have realized a marriage to a woman in her twenties could never be successful. He offered her the house and alimony, but she refused both.

The Horton household was in turmoil over the news of divorce. Alice knew Craig truly loved her daughter, but Marie, who didn't want to be treated like a child, refused her counsel. Later, as Marie stood with her bags packed at the Merritt home, ready to call a cab to take her to a small efficiency apartment, she was more than a little relieved when her father, Tom, stopped by to visit. Tearfully, Marie admitted, "Daddy, I want to be a little girl again!" She returned to the Horton home.

After Tony told his dad he would be calling on Marie, Craig dealt with his heartbreak by giving up the airfield he had started and going back to his flying career. He took a job offer that would keep him in Asia, China, and Indonesia. On the day of his departure, Marie came to him to say good-bye. He never told her he still loved her. Only after she left and he headed for his plane, did he quietly sigh and say, "I love you, Marie. Darling, I'll never stop loving you. Never." As he spoke he fingered the wedding ring in his pocket.

Tony did indeed start calling Marie who, with mixed feelings, started seeing him again. Rebuilding a trusting relationship would be difficult, but Tony made every effort to recapture the woman he loved, only slowly realizing that Marie had changed quite a bit from the naive young girl he had jilted just one year ago.

Meanwhile, Susan encouraged David to pursue a transfer out of state so that they could have the baby, give it up for adoption, and simply tell their parents that the child had been stillborn. Not anxious to leave Julie, David hesitated but eventually put the transfer into motion. Susan continued to carry the child as

> *"I don't love the man who's going to be the father of this child. He doesn't love me. I did only one thing for this baby . . . it will have a name."*
>
> —SUSAN HUNTER MARTIN

if it were a most unpleasant burden. She often hissed at David: "Once the baby is born, I don't ever want to see you again!" She had grown weary of the marriage that was just a "stupid game."

The only brightness in Susan's life was seeing her parents. Susan nudged things further along by orchestrating a dinner for three at a lovely restaurant, then not showing up so that her estranged parents could have a romantic dinner and evening of dancing as they got to know each other all over again. Richard had almost remarried in New York, but his fiancée did not want a husband who was very attached to his daughter. Diane, by this time, had already stopped seeing Mickey.

Susan's plan to bring her parents back together worked beautifully. Richard and Diane remarried at year's end. Susan even arranged to have an exact duplicate wedding corsage made, based on a photo of her parents' first wedding. It was a lovely touch that totally thrilled Diane. Although Susan's marriage was virtually nonexistent except on paper, she found romantic joy in watching her parents reunite.

Rather than watch David and Susan's masquerade any longer, Julie decided to visit her parents in Europe. She and David exchanged Christmas gifts before her trip. She gave him a gold watch. David gave Julie a locket pin in the shape of a heart inscribed inside: *Darling, I'll never stop loving you.*

Bill, who had been accepted at Johns Hopkins Medical Center, decided to stay in Salem. An important part of his decision had to do with psychiatry intern Dr. Laura Spencer. A bright and attractive woman, sensitive about her position in a man's world, Laura played down her good looks. Bill often teased her with comments about how she would look with her hair down, glasses off, and eyes made up. Finally, after several months of playful sparring, Laura finally agreed to go to dinner with Bill. Eventually, she let her hair down as well.

1967

In early January, Susan Martin suffered severe hemorrhaging and her premature baby boy was delivered by emergency Cesarean section a few days later. Mother and child were in critical condition. The crisis brought Susan's parents back from their honeymoon in Jamaica. It also drew Susan and David momentarily closer, but they were determined to stick with their plan of putting the baby up for adoption and getting divorced.

When Julie heard that Susan was in the hospital, she returned from Paris. They had been best friends, and the sense of caring still existed, especially since Julie believed she would soon be able to marry David.

Susan heard the cries of babies being taken to their mothers at feeding time, and Dr. Bill Horton, who had always had an easy rapport with Susan, encouraged the young woman to see her baby in the nursery. A sense of love and maternal bonding came over her and Susan's defensive anger melted. Her concern shifted to the baby, now named Richard after her father. Susan vowed to protect her son from the pain of loneliness and rejection she had felt as a child of divorced parents. She became determined to provide Dickie a stable home with his natural parents and told David they would make their marriage work for the sake of the child.

Not surprisingly, David resisted Susan's new demand and agreed with Julie to force the issue by going to both Susan's parents and his own with the truth: the wedding took place only to give the baby a name. One step ahead of him, Susan told her parents and won their support. In fact, her dad strongly encouraged David to take responsibility and focus on his family.

At that point, Julie's frustration and anger flared openly and she declared war on Susan. When Tom learned the complete truth of Julie and David's relationship, he wanted to send Julie back to her parents in Paris. But Julie was eighteen and had a trust fund income from Grandfather Olson's estate. Determined to fight for the man she loved, she found an apartment of her own.

Meanwhile, the Horton men had their own conflicts. When Mickey agreed to handle the Martin divorce case before Susan put her foot down, it only fueled the differences between Mickey and Bill, who harbored an ongoing case of sibling rivalry. That rivalry became more troublesome when Mickey noticed Bill dating Laura Spencer, a woman who sparked his interest, too. When Tom tried to step between his sons, Bill rudely pointed out that Tom could be overbearing.

Bill took the occasion to point out to Tom that Tommy likely had left medical school and enlisted in the military to avoid the "trap" their dad had set for the favorite son and his career. Tommy had died escaping from his father's hold, Bill implied. The remarks rekindled the pain Tom felt over the tragic death of his oldest son and provoked deep sadness when Tom realized his thinly veiled favoritism had not gone unnoticed. Bill had gone into medicine by his own choice, but Tommy's ghost constantly hovered between him and his father. These two Horton doctors had developed an abrasive relationship, and even at the hospital, staffers noticed it. Of course, it was assumed to stem from "old school" and "new school" medical philosophies.

As if all this were not enough to aggravate Bill, he quietly but coldly disapproved of Tony Merritt, who had dated Laura during Marie's marriage and was now pursuing Marie again. He was not alone. While Marie cautiously allowed Tony back into her life, Alice let him know that she understood his turmoil at the time he was ill and jilted Marie, but she could not forget the consequences his actions had had upon her daughter. Fueled by her family's subtle disapproval and Marie's conclusion that they could never recapture what they once had, Tony left Salem in early spring. Craig remained in Rangoon, while Marie, sadder but a bit wiser, picked up her life and worked as a technician at University Hospital.

Over the course of several weeks, Bill discovered a nagging ache in his scalpel hand. While several co-workers noticed his new habit of casually rubbing that hand, Bill tried to ignore what seemed to be a minor nuisance until the hand stiffened completely during an operation and another surgeon had to step in. Tests revealed Bill's problem was tuberculosis of the bone and he had surgery to save the hand, but it seemed unlikely he would ever be a surgeon again. Unfortunately, no other area of medicine appealed to Bill and the loss was devastating.

Although he and Laura had decided to marry after each had finished residency, he left town abruptly in late spring. Bill wanted to sort out his future plans away from the influence of his family, well-meaning friends, and even Laura. Without a particular destination in mind, Bill simply left and soon found another position in a small-town medical facility.

While Bill was gone, events in Salem took many lives in unexpected and sometimes tragic directions. While Julie continued to see David at every possible opportunity, he had grown attached to his son and a bit weary of Julie's nagging him about divorce. Julie realized if she had lost David, it was not to Susan, but to the baby. David and Susan had at least a mutual love for their son between them but were diametrically opposed to how the child should be raised. David felt that Susan was overprotective to the point of being neurotic. He started to spend more time with the boy, taking him on outings to the park without Susan.

One early summer day, David took Dickie to the playground. There were other children, new sights and sounds, swings, slides, and a sandbox. Innocently thinking the swing would be safe fun, David placed the baby in the harness that was too big to keep the youngster securely in place. Within a short time Dickie slipped out of the swing and struck his head.

The child remained unconscious at the hospital for over a week while Susan kept vigil and kept David away, often with violent threats. Then little Dickie, the baby Susan had not wanted but who had become the focus of her world, died. In a terrifying calm, Susan finally went home to get burial clothes for Dickie. At that moment, she and David came face to face. He had been responsible for her baby's death. In a haze, Susan took a gun from the drawer, and shot and killed David.

After being arrested, Susan was placed in a psychiatric hospital for observation to see if she was fit to be tried on murder charges. During her confinement there, she escaped and was later recaptured. Finally put on trial, Susan relived the nightmare of her pregnancy, loveless marriage, the joy of motherhood, and heartbreaking loss of her child.

The prosecution presented a strong case. There was neighbor Mrs. Riley's testimony about Susan having a gun, exchanging heated words with David before he was shot, and Susan's confession afterward. Nurse Jean Perkins reported hearing Susan's threats to David in the hospital while the baby remained unconscious. Tom Horton had to admit he found Susan with the gun and heard her admit to shooting David. John and Helen Martin added to the case against the woman who killed their son when each confessed to knowing of the animosity between David and Susan over marriage. Susan had attempted to run away when she escaped the sanitarium, the prosecution reminded jurors. And Julie gladly told the court that Susan had threatened David on many occasions prior to Dickie's death. The police had a confession. The evidence against Susan was very strong indeed.

Susan's lawyer, Mickey Horton, and her psychiatrist, Dr. Laura Spencer, had their work cut out for them. Between them, they were able to discredit the reliability of certain witnesses who were not qualified to judge Susan's state of mind. Unfortunately, in discrediting Julie's testimony, Mickey also revealed that Julie was currently pregnant with David Martin's child. As far as Tom was concerned, that was unnecessary, even perhaps unforgivable. Julie was humiliated by the public admission and left town to have her baby. Laura's expert psychiatric testimony ultimately convinced the court that Susan was not truly sane at the moment she'd shot David. By early October, after a long torturous summer, Susan was found not guilty on the basis of temporary insanity.

Susan's problems, however, were certainly far from over. Shortly after the trial ended, Susan visited Mother Martin to express her personal sympathy and apologize for David's death. In distress of her own, Helen reached into a drawer and turned on Susan, taunting her with, "How does it feel to have a gun pointed at you? Now you know how David felt!" Then she pulled the trigger. After barely surviving surgery, Susan was left a semi-invalid with a serious heart problem.

During her hospital confinement, John Martin visited Susan offering sympathy and compassion. That visit touched Susan deeply. She blamed herself for destroying the man's family: first David, then driving Helen to an insane act. John's forgiveness helped her fight for her recovery.

When Bill came home to Salem about the same time, he discovered Laura no longer wanted to marry him. She had fallen in love with his brother Mickey. Adding insult to his injury, Laura became engaged to Mickey within a month of Bill's return. Bill turned his emotional pain into professional dedication. And there were Dr. Mark Brooks and little Timmy McCall, who came to Salem with Bill.

These three were brought together by simple circumstance in the quiet little town where Bill had taken refuge five months earlier. Bill had rented a room at the McCalls' home and Timmy grew fond of him. Before Timmy's terminally ill mother, Mary, died, she extracted a promise from Bill that he would become Timmy's legal guardian, which Bill did willingly. It was through Mary that Bill met Mark, a well-liked physician with a few problems. A Korean War veteran, Mark had recurrent nightmares of his capture and extreme physical torture. He had no memory of his life prior to the military, nor did he remember what he looked like before extensive plastic surgery reconstructed his severely disfigured face. He drank a little too much, but never so much that he was ever unable to be a good doctor. Mark encouraged Bill to use therapy to regain total use of his hand. He provided the emotional and professional support Bill needed to conquer his fears and refocus on a surgical career. After Bill performed emergency surgery to remove Timmy's appendix, Bill knew he could return to Salem and his chosen profession. He had Mark to thank.

Soon after his arrival in Salem, Mark accepted a position at University Hospital and Marie became his research assistant. A deep respect and caring developed between the two, but Mark was hesitant to pursue a serious relationship because he was still haunted by nightmares and uncertainty about his past. But Marie steadily fell deeper and deeper in love with this handsome, mysterious man, a man who was exceptionally at ease in the Horton home, and with whom Tom felt an unusually fast rapport. Every one of the Hortons found Mark to be so likable he was virtually "one of the family" by year's end.

The holidays were a happier time at the Horton home that year. Bill was back in town and, if not personally, at least professionally back on track. Mickey and Laura wed just after Christmas. Kitty, Tommy's widow, had also come to Salem, and while she set her sights on Dr. Elliot Kincaid, her daughter Sandy began to develop a relationship with her grandparents.

"Mickey enjoyed his bachelor pad and lifestyle. Then he met Dr. Laura Spencer and for the first time in his life, Mickey was completely, wholeheartedly in love."

—JOHN CLARKE (MICKEY)

1968

While Salem was covered in snow, Mickey and Laura enjoyed a wonderfully romantic honeymoon on the white sand beaches of Jamaica. They talked for hours about their future together, raising children while each pursued their career.

Bill, however, was bedeviled by jealousy and resentment. He was still obsessed with Laura. No matter how he tried to put thoughts of her aside, she haunted him day and night. Since both worked at the hospital, it was impossible for him not to see her nearly every day. His passion made it impossible not to want her. It was likely Bill's anger toward Mickey, mixed with too much alcohol and lust, that brought Bill to Laura's hospital quarters late one night when she was on call. In a drunken stupor, Bill raped her. The next morning, with scratches and only a conveniently vague memory of the night before, Bill came to her again. He asked about what had happened. Laura was deeply hurt and humiliated but, seeing Bill's sincere fear and confusion, convinced him that she had successfully turned him away. To admit the truth, she believed, would result in violence between Mickey and Bill. For the sake of family peace, she vowed to put the night out of her mind as best she could.

Not long afterward, Laura discovered she was pregnant but with doubts whether the child was Mickey's or Bill's, she told no one for a few days. Meanwhile, after reading an article about sterility in a popular magazine, Mickey consulted his father and had some tests done. Recently married, over thirty, Mickey just wanted a checkup and reassurance. The results showed Mickey was, indeed, sterile. Shortly after the lab report crossed his desk, Tom happened to see Laura at the hospital and told her about it before talking to Mickey. She suggested she be the one to tell Mickey, and Tom agreed. After all, Laura was not only Mickey's wife, but a psychiatrist. At home that evening, Laura immediately told Mickey she was pregnant. Mickey was certainly no longer the least bit interested in pursuing his sterility test results. Unfortunately, once the news became known to family and friends, Laura had to tell Tom the details of her conception. Stunned, and aware of the havoc the

Laura and Tom became co-conspirators as each kept painful truths from her husband, Mickey. Tom had told Laura that Mickey was sterile. She told Tom the disturbing circumstances of how she became pregnant by Bill. The secrets were kept for years.

truth would create, he felt there was no choice but to keep the secret with Laura to protect the family.

Yet another crisis loomed. Mark's presence around the Horton house had become increasingly unsettling to Tom. Without asking, Mark knew exactly where a closet, bathroom, or the kitchen was; he reached for fireplace matches without a second thought even though they were kept in an odd place. Tom, more than anyone, noticed these things. When Alice innocently commented how easily drawn to Mark she was, how Mark's eyes reminded her so much of Tommy's eyes, Tom was unable to fight the instincts that were nagging at him. As incredible as the thought was, Tom had to admit that Mark was suspiciously very much like Tom Jr., even in the way he walked.

Meanwhile, Marie and Mark became closer as they worked together at the hospital. They felt so at ease with each other, enjoyed talking, laughing. They were in love. In fact, they were moving toward the moment when Mark would soon propose marriage. Realizing that, Tom knew he had to voice his suspicions concerning Mark, as incredible as they seemed, so he turned to Mickey. The circumstantial evidence left the seasoned lawyer dubious, but he fully understood how crucial finding out the truth about this man had become. He made a background check on Dr. Mark Brooks and turned up nothing. Playing detectives, Tom and Mickey managed to have fingerprints taken from a glass Mark handled. Through a friend in Washington, Mickey had the fingerprints checked against those of the many Mark Brookses on file, but none matched. When compared against the prints of Private Thomas Horton, Jr., the fingerprints did match. The Hortons' oldest child was alive, in Salem, and in love with his own sister. The news was staggering to all concerned. Alice needed sedation. Marie retired to her bedroom for weeks. Mark realized he had to stop running, although he had to admit he was not even certain from whom or what.

Through a complicated investigation, the Hortons learned that combat and physical and mental torture had totally erased Tommy's memory. His first memories were contained in his recurrent nightmares of Korean prison and the abuse he suffered there. After escaping, Tommy saved the life of a Soviet military officer, who repaid the debt by providing excellent facial reconstruction and plastic surgery. Eventually, Tommy found his way back to the United States through Canada. But the man had not been anxious to find his past. He feared what he might find. Had he been a deserter? A traitor? He would not have been able to face those possibilities, or the consequences. After being identified by the Hortons, Tommy realized he could run no more. He stayed and, to his enormous relief, discovered that his record vindicated him. If anything, he was a hero.

Not that it helped Marie. As the youngest in the family, Marie was just a child when Tommy was sent to Korea. She never really knew him; in fact, hardly

The Horton men: (CLOCKWISE FROM TOP LEFT) Bill, Mickey, Tom, and Tommy.

Bill had always felt overshadowed by Tommy, so it was particularly ironic that he was the one to bring his older brother back to Salem. Mickey and Tom did the super-sleuthing to verify Tommy's identity. Alice was overwhelmed: "We had just celebrated the date of his death before Tommy reappeared. The shock, the emotions . . . it was like a second birthing, rediscovering him as he learned about himself."
—FRANCES REID

When Susan Martin delivered David's child, Bill helped her accept the baby she had never planned to keep. Then, when Laura gave birth to Bill's child, Susan helped him through the painful time of letting go of the son he could not acknowledge as his own.

remembered him at all. Marie had been through so much already: jilted by Tony, divorced by Craig, and disappointed by Tony again; this final heartbreaking turn of events proved too much for her. Marie withdrew from life in the mainstream world—certainly from men—and went off to work as a medical missionary in Africa. She ultimately joined a convent.

Although the Horton family made a point not to force their relationship, Kitty was still Tommy's legal wife. She was no longer the pretty young girl Tommy had met at a USO dance in 1950, but the security and respectability that came from being a doctor's wife strongly appealed to her. They were complete strangers with one common bond, their daughter Sandy. Kitty played on Tommy's concern for the teenager to maneuver him into picking up a very tenuous marriage relationship. Ironically, it was through Sandy that Tommy gleaned some indication of the kind of woman Kitty was before she came to Salem looking for help from the Hortons. He had discovered his past, and was growing more curious about Kitty's past, and present, shenanigans.

Bill, meanwhile, accidentally discovered that he was the father of the child Laura carried. He had stopped by his father's office to pick up his own medical records for his yearly checkup with another internist. Back at his own desk, casually leafing through the pages, Bill realized the clerical assistant in Tom's office had mistakenly given him Mickey's folder. As he closed the file, a last notation, about the results of a sterility test, caught his eye and left him breathless. It took but moments to recall the unfortunate evening he burst into Laura's quarters and the announcement of her pregnancy shortly thereafter.

In her eighth month, Laura was in an auto accident. Her injuries, primarily internal bleeding, threatened her well-being and her unborn baby. After many tense hours, Laura came through her surgery and the baby was safe, too. Laura remained in the hospital until a Cesarean delivery became necessary. Although the baby, named Michael William Horton, was premature, he appeared healthy.

Bill had been in New York on business when Laura gave birth. During the flight back to Salem, Bill debated choosing to fight for his son and Laura or building a new family with Susan. Could he remain silent about his paternity now that the child was born? Waiting excitedly for his return, Susan fully expected Bill would propose. After explaining about Laura and the baby, Bill did ask Susan to marry him, but she questioned him about the possibility of moving away from Salem and starting a new life with her. Could he forget Laura? Never wonder about his family? Carefully balancing Bill's reactions, Susan told him she needed time to think. It was not long before it was clear to both that marriage was not in their future. Friends for some time, they ended their romance and parted without bitterness. While Bill dealt with his emotional turmoil, Susan found comfort and distraction from her painful disappointment by helping Scott Banning and his terminally ill wife, Janet, care for their infant son Bradley.

Bill had neither Susan nor his son. He realized that confronting Mickey with the truth would do more harm than good for everyone concerned. On the day that Laura and Mickey came to take Michael home, Bill spent a few tender moments with the infant, whispering to him, "This is our last daily visit. I'm going to miss you, my son."

Meanwhile, Tommy's doubts about Kitty deepened and he hired a private investigator to follow her. At first, the reports were insignificant, then Tommy and his investigator devised a plot. On an evening it was certain Dr. Kincaid was not on duty, Tommy made plans to be out with Sandy, leaving Kitty on her own. Kitty immediately called Elliot and they planned a romantic dinner for two at his apartment. She intended to work her wiles on Kincaid and pressure him about divorce, and marriage. He had been hedging on the subject, pointing out that since Tommy was back, she would have to get a divorce first. They were in a stalemate since she was reluctant to divorce Tommy until Elliot made a commitment to her.

Tommy's investigator had followed Kitty to Kincaid's apartment and called Tommy with his report. Within the hour, Tommy knocked on Kincaid's door and confronted the couple. Later, Kitty, who had a family history of heart problems (her father died of a coronary at thirty-nine), faked chest pains. Dr. Tom Horton had her admitted to the hospital and she won her bid for sympathy. Tests also revealed that although there was no immediate cause for alarm, she did indeed have a heart condition and would have to take precautions to maintain her health. The few days in the hospital also gave her a bit of time to come up with some justifications for her dalliance. For the sixteen years of Tommy's absence, Kitty had lived a life of independence. She lied, manipulated, and did what she had to do in order to survive and raise Sandy. Kitty was used to doing things her own way.

So was Julie. Yet, when it came time to decide what to do about her newborn son, Julie did take her grandfather Tom's words of counsel into consideration. Against her own instincts, Julie gave up her child for adoption. As Fate would have it, Janet and Scott Banning started adoption proceedings for that very same infant and unwittingly moved into Salem expecting a fulfilling family life. Sadly, Janet was diagnosed with a brain tumor and her health declined rapidly.

Kitty tried to make Tommy believe that her affair with Elliot Kincaid was her only mistake and begged for a second chance. Not the least convinced that Kitty was being truthful, Tommy had his investigator dig deeper into her past. During the nearly two decades before she came to Salem, Kitty had lived in St. Louis, Missouri, and Dallas, Texas, and had left an unsavory trail, including two rather embarrassing affairs. She had been named as co-respondent in both divorce cases. The report was the final straw. Tommy decided to file for a divorce, a decision that was most painful for Sandy, who had hoped her natural parents would provide the normal family life she longed to enjoy. Alice and Tom were deeply disappointed as well. They had hoped a good marriage would encourage Tommy to stay in Salem. For the moment at least, he did stay, since he wanted to develop a relationship with his daughter. She too wanted to get to know her father, so she stayed with him and Kitty was left alone.

Janet Banning's health was failing quickly and Susan was taking care of Brad more often. Sadly aware of the fragility of life and relationships, Susan wanted to make amends to Julie for taking David's life. She was even willing to give Julie the money from David's estate. Eventually, Julie did stop by, but her

1969

motives were hardly benign. She was far more curious about the severity of Susan's heart problem and the extent of her feelings of guilt than in considering a reconciliation or extending any semblance of forgiveness. During that visit, Brad, in Susan's care, was sleeping. Julie often thought of the baby she gave up, and aware of a baby in the other room, Julie could not help wondering aloud, "He's about the same age as my little David is—wherever he is . . ." During this time, Scott and Susan grew closer, but not in a romantic way. Susan had become a stronger and far more well-balanced woman through her tragedies and intense psychiatric analysis. She was also sensitive, giving, and vulnerable. Caring for Brad, aware of Janet's sad state, Susan and Scott shared many tender moments.

Meanwhile, Kitty and Tommy's divorce had become final. Dr. Kincaid had ended the affair with Kitty so she moved on to another married man, Peter Larkin, whose wife was out of town caring for a sick sister. When his wife returned, he wanted to continue a mutually beneficial arrangement with Kitty and paid her for so-called part-time clerical help. Kitty was indeed brushing up her secretarial skills, doing some tape transcribing for Dr. Tom Horton. Kitty quite accidentally left a machine running on RECORD when she left Tom's home office one afternoon. When Tom and Laura stepped into that room a few moments later and discussed not only little Michael's health problems but the fact that Bill was his father, they had no way of knowing they had just created a time bomb. When later the information fell into Kitty's lap, she immediately began to think of ways she could profit from it. After some thought, she decided that approaching Bill would be her best shot of coming up with some money, maybe even enough to help her leave Salem. She called Bill and suggested that he come to her apartment to discuss some information about Laura that he would find fascinating. So much so that he would gladly pay several thousand dollars for the tape recording she had in her possession. Bill could not believe Kitty had somehow learned the truth, but decided not to take the chance. He rescheduled his flight to New York to a later one and stopped at Kitty's apartment on the way to the airport. He had to find out exactly what she was talking about before he started a new job away from Salem and his past.

When Bill arrived, Kitty was seductive. He was all business. Kitty told him what she had found out and Bill berated her for the kind of woman she was. Their angry voices were loud enough for neighbors to hear the tone, if not the actual words. Bill became determined to find the tape and ransacked the apartment, which infuriated Kitty, who physically attacked him. Still, his only focus was finding the tape. Once he did, he pushed past her and left. The hysteria was too much for Kitty. With severe chest pains, she made it to the phone to call for help, but collapsed and died in the process.

Soon after, Kitty was found dead. Although the coroner declared that the cause of death had been a heart attack, there were bruises on her body and her apartment showed definite signs of a struggle. At first, Tommy was the prime suspect, then Peter Larkin's name came into the investigation. Eventually, the doorman remembered Bill. When detectives eventually tracked Bill down in his New York hotel, he admitted being in Kitty's apartment, and was arrested and charged with Kitty's murder.

Bill did nothing to help his case beyond insisting that he never laid a hand on Kitty. Still, as a doctor and aware of her heart condition, he was accountable for her wrongful death. The judge allowed a lesser charge, involuntary manslaughter, but prosecution pushed for a sentence of three to fourteen years in prison. Mickey sought probation. Bill's refusal to tell anyone the reasons why he was at Kitty's apartment in the first place cast serious doubts on his character, but he realized the explanation would only hurt more people he loved. He would rather live with the speculation that the two of them were having an affair than publicize his paternity of Laura's child. Ironically, Mickey was defending him in court and was livid over his brother's stubbornness. Bill, of course, was angry and frustrated too, often telling his brother to just back off. Laura, Tommy, and Tom were all baffled by Bill's behavior. Only Alice was absolutely unflinching in her support.

Eventually, the New York hotel where Bill had stayed sent a letter to his Salem address regarding possessions left in a safe deposit box. Tom retrieved the contents of the box, which included the tape that caused so much trouble. After listening to it, Tom decided the best he could do, under the circumstances, was to keep it in a drawer.

In the months following Janet Banning's death early in the year, Susan became very fond of Scott, and little Bradley filled the void left by Dickie's death. Scott and Susan grew closer, and likely would have married, but Julie came between them. Finally aware that Brad was indeed her son David, Julie sued Scott to have her child returned to her. After all, Scott was no longer married and the adoption proceedings had not been finalized. The court awarded Julie custody and Julie allowed Scott visitation rights with the boy only if Susan was not with him. Julie was always quick to remind, "She killed the boy's natural father!" and was determined never to allow Susan and Scott to marry. Julie could not tolerate the thought of little David being raised by her most hated enemy. Eventually, although both Julie and Scott shared a mutual distrust at the start, they developed an understanding and respect as they shared moments together with David. They also realized that there was one way they could both share in the boy's life equally: they should marry. It was a mature decision, not lacking in some attraction, but without the fire of real romance. Still, Julie won a double victory. She had David back and had stolen Scott from Susan.

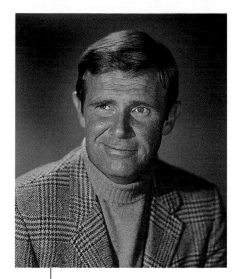

Tommy survived wartime bombing, torture, and imprisonment but lost his memory and former physical features. When he returned to Salem, he unwittingly fell in love with his sister Marie. His father and brothers helped him uncover his true identity and Tommy was reunited with his family, teenage daughter Sandy, and cheating wife, Kitty.

Months after Kitty's demise, Sandy was still having a tough time dealing with the loss of her mother. She was angry that only a handful of people showed up at Kitty's funeral. In her grief, and guilt over leaving her mother alone and defenseless, Sandy lashed out at the Hortons for not helping her mother more. As far as Sandy was concerned, at least her mother had lived openly by her own rules, while most of the residents of Salem were simply self-righteous hypocrites. That certainly included Peter Larkin, who claimed he was bilked for almost $20,000 by Kitty and made a claim against her estate. At the start of the new semester, Sandy left the Horton household and moved into the student dorm, just down the hall from her boyfriend Bruce.

About the same time that Sandy moved out, Sister Marie heard of Bill's troubles and returned to stay with her family during this time of crisis. Mickey continued to encourage Bill to tell him why he had been at Kitty's apartment the night of her death. Consistently, Bill refused, fueling the already existing friction between the two. Their frustrations nearly came to angry blows one afternoon

1970

when Mickey warned Bill to stay away from Laura, and Bill angrily shouted that Mickey could have her, he didn't care at all. Of course, Bill certainly did care about Laura, the love of his life. No one else, not Susan nor the attractive model Janene Whitley who had fallen in love with Bill, could break the hold Laura held on his heart. His silence, which others viewed as self-serving and indicative of guilt, was lonely testimony to his love for Laura and his son—and, in some part, for the love and respect he ultimately felt for Mickey. In mid-February, Bill was denied probation and was sentenced to one to three years in prison.

In jail, Bill worked in the infirmary, but never as a physician. He also developed a friendship with his cellmate, a likable con man finishing up the last few months of his two-year sentence for a white-collar crime. Like Bill, Doug Williams was out of step with the mainstream prison population. He was quite the opportunist, however, always ready to find an angle, a deal, some scheme to make money. In casual conversation, Bill mentioned the various people of Salem, including Susan Martin inheriting $250,000 from her late husband's estate. Bill never realized he was inadvertently setting Susan up for potential trouble. When Doug was freed in early autumn, he headed for Salem with his sights set on Susan. Unfortunately for him, Susan was not the least bit interested in Doug and his smooth-talking ways. She did, however, recognize how his charm and good looks affected most other women. She knew his flair for flirtation would immediately lure Julie away from Scott, and Susan would have the last laugh. So, in her plan to prove the Banning marriage was just another of Julie's manipulations, and to win Scott back for herself, Susan offered Doug what he really only wanted most—money—to have an affair with Julie. As Susan explained to her psychiatrist, Laura, "Julie didn't marry Scott to provide David with a father. She married him because I was in love with him and wanted him. She would do anything to hurt me." But in voicing that rationalization to Laura, Susan chose the wrong sounding board. The next time Susan spoke to Doug, she told him the deal was off. She could not be that manipulative and look herself in the mirror. He told her it was too late.

By early December Doug was already weaving his seductive spell over Julie. Their flirtation had not yet progressed to affair, although Julie enjoyed Doug's company. Unlike Scott, Doug was fun, well-traveled, and exciting. Julie had found a wonderful escape from her mundane domestic routine. Keeping their budding relationship a secret only made it all the more exciting. Doug, being the pro, knew that in order to really win Julie, he could lay the trap, but Julie would have to make the first move.

After Bill was released early from prison and returned to Salem, his presence was often annoying to Mickey. Although neither voiced longings, nor behaved in any inappropriate manner, the attraction between Laura and Bill was evident to the astute observer. Mickey wrongly suspected that Bill and Laura were having an affair. Still, trouble between Laura and Mickey escalated to the point that Laura refused to give herself sexually to her husband. That only aggravated matters further, since Mickey was already doubting that Laura wanted more children, as he did. She, of course, knew the truth of his sterility, a sad fact impossible to share with him. Once Mickey moved out, it didn't take long before Mickey fell into an affair with his secretary, Linda Patterson, who had just said good-bye to a suitor, Jim Phillips, who had taken a job on the East Coast.

Doug was working as a singer at the local cabaret Sergio's and clearly very interested in Julie. While Scott was away on a brief business trip, Julie finally crossed the line of flirtation and went to see Doug at his apartment. After an evening of a romantic dinner, wine, and their special song, "The Look of Love," the couple became lovers. Although Doug did not push Julie in the direction of divorce, after several weeks he implied that marriage would be something to consider after she divorced Scott. The couple did not discuss the matter of Julie's son.

In the Banning household, David was growing especially close to his adoptive dad. One day, while leafing through a photo album containing pictures of Janet holding David as an infant, the boy asked why his real mother gave him away in the first place. Scott, who believed in the permanence of his marriage, did his best to help the boy understand the emotional turmoil unwed Julie was going through at the time of his birth. Still, the question never seemed sufficiently answered for David, who grew more emotionally remote from Julie and more dependent on Scott.

By December, Laura and Mickey had reconciled and Laura believed her marriage was back on solid ground. Mickey, although truly devoted to Laura, found it hard to fight his attraction to Linda, whom he saw daily at the office. When Linda realized she was pregnant she honestly believed Mickey to be the father. Neither lover would have reason to believe that it was not possible. Furthermore, Linda knew how much Mickey wanted more children so she believed her news would be met with joy. Or at least it would be reason for Mickey to move forward with a divorce from Laura to marry her. Coincidentally raising the thin ghost of another romantic triangle, Linda had also casually dated Bill, but had never been intimate with him. She accepted dinner invitations with him because, with Mickey back with Laura, there was no reason not to enjoy his company. In fact, because Linda was friendly to all the Hortons, to decline could have seemed rather odd.

On New Year's Eve, the Hortons gathered to ring in 1971 together. Mickey and Laura, Tommy and Sandy, Marie, and Bill were among those who filled the living room. Alice was encouraged to hear Bill talk of some interest in Linda Patterson at her apartment. However, that same night, Linda was alone, pining for Mickey.

At the first secret opportunity, Mickey and Linda celebrated their personal start to the New Year over dinner at The Embers, a romantic restaurant outside of town. Pregnant and completely in love with Mickey, Linda urged him to start divorce proceedings so he would be free of Laura to marry her. Mickey, still touched by family holiday spirit, had been doing a lot of soul searching and told her he needed more time.

Across the room, Julie was having dinner with Doug and noticed her uncle and Linda holding hands. Julie, being Julie, found the situation even more delicious than her meal. A few days later, Linda expected to have dinner with Mickey again, but Julie had called the office and asked to see her uncle privately. Annoyed that she was again being pushed aside, Linda accepted a dinner date with Bill instead. So, while Linda was off with Bill, Julie confronted Mickey, telling him she'd seen him at The Embers. The two sparred, then agreed to keep each other's secrets.

"Bill went to prison to protect Laura and their son. Mickey too, but that was secondary. There was an *East of Eden*, or *Cain and Abel* aspect to the relationship between Bill and Mickey. Bill was always the rebel brother. He did things his own way and was often misunderstood."

—ED MALLORY (BILL HORTON)

1971

Although Julie kept her relationship with Doug under wraps, tensions and disagreements in the Banning home escalated to the point that Scott decided it was best to take a job offer in another city and take David with him, at least for a while. Julie, certain she would eventually have sole custody of David, allowed the separation, knowing she would enjoy her liaison with Doug all the more without a husband to go home to each night.

The news of Scott and David leaving town had a devastating impact on Susan. Although she felt the Banning marriage would never have lasted anyway, she could not overlook the fact that she had instigated Doug's move on Julie. In a mood of loneliness and guilt, Susan became withdrawn. Depressed, she wandered through a local park late one afternoon. Several hours later, she was brought to University Hospital's emergency room, unconscious but still clutching a button from a man's blazer tightly in her hand. Once she came around, Susan was so distraught that her psychiatrist, Dr. Laura Horton, was called. Still, Susan refused to give Laura or the police any details of what was apparently an attack. Whether because she really did not remember, or because she was too humiliated, Susan refused to explain what had happened to her.

Linda Patterson was going through her own trauma. Mickey finally told her that though he would take financial responsibility for their child's support, he would remain married to Laura. Linda appeared to take the news in stride, but she tried to commit suicide. That turn of events set the Hortons into a spin. Bill discovered that Mickey and Linda had had an affair. Bill and Tom knew that Mickey was sterile, but while Linda was in the hospital, knowledge of her pregnancy became known to all. Laura, who knew that Bill had dated Linda, suspected he could be the father of the unborn child, for certainly it could not be Mickey. Besides, Laura and Mickey had reconciled. Laura, Bill, and Tom each realized individually that only one sperm count had been done on Mickey. There was the remote possibility that Mickey just might not be sterile after all, which cast a shadow of doubt upon Michael's paternity again. Another irony was that the suicide attempt had put Linda in contact with Laura on a professional basis. Meanwhile, Linda's dad, Cliff, returned to visit his hospitalized daughter, and he confronted Mickey. Laura ascertained that Mickey had been intimate with Linda and cautiously told Linda that Mickey was sterile.

After Linda gave birth, Mickey was deeply hurt to find that Melissa was not his daughter. The father was actually Linda's former beau, Jim Phillips. Jim, unlike Mickey, never believed Linda was trying to trap Mickey nor did he know the truth of her child's paternity until the blood test made it clear. Jim, living on the East Coast, was about to marry another woman, but after learning about Melissa, he decided to break the engagement. By the end of the year, Jim and Linda were married and living in Boston. Her father, Cliff, moved in with the couple and their child.

Problems continued to mount for Mickey and Laura. Although Linda and her child had left town, the affair had caused Laura a lot of pain and humiliation. Bill became caught up in the turmoil because Linda's pregnancy came so close to revealing Bill as Mike's father. Given the circumstances, it was no surprise that Laura and Bill found themselves emotionally vulnerable and longing for each other's comfort. Although Mickey was still willing to give Laura a divorce if she wanted it, Laura decided to stand by her man, and her son. Although she could never feel the same depth of love for Mickey she once did, she suggested they

BELOW: **L**inda Patterson fell in love with Mickey and really believed that he was the father of her child. Laura set her straight, and Linda's ex-lover, Jim, came back to Salem to convince Linda to go back east with him. She and their daughter Melissa did just that.

BOTTOM: **D**oug Williams was a smooth-talking opportunist but loved deeply. In spite of circumstances, he often brought out the best in the women around him.

both do whatever they could to make the marriage work, at least for the sake of providing Mike with a stable home.

Julie too was trying to make her marriage work. Or at least, make the masquerade work. After David understood that his parents would be divorcing, he grew closer to Scott. Julie felt her son's attitude could eventually jeopardize their relationship so she orchestrated a reconciliation with Scott. She was never interested in saving her marriage but was setting up good cause to maintain custody of David when she and Scott eventually did split. They muddled through the year, Julie hoping that David would become more emotionally attached to her. But, though never outwardly disrespectful, David felt little love for his natural mother since he was all too keenly aware that she had given him up shortly after he was born.

Meanwhile, Julie and Doug were keeping their affair quiet, but he gave her a sexy nightie for Christmas promising that one day she would wear it for him in Portofino where they planned to escape together.

Julie's mother, Addie, returned from Paris after her husband Ben's death, but their son Steve stayed in Europe to finish his last semester of school. Middle-aged, but not deep in mourning, Addie was lonely. She found comfort being among her family, yet there was a void in her life. Although her marriage to Ben had been a well-made union, it never exuded passion. Addie was the kind of woman who needed a man to help define herself. Her daughter Julie was no comfort. There was a long-standing rivalry between Addie and Julie based on years of jealousy and rejection. Addie had always felt in competition with Julie for Ben's attention; Julie, however, felt she never got enough attention from either Ben or

The Horton women: Addie, Alice, Marie.

Addie first married for social standing then found true romance with her daughter's lover. Alice was the rock of unconditional love, no matter the storm. "Marie, my baby, really had some bad times. She was stood up by her fiancé the night before the wedding. After trying to commit suicide, she later married her former fiancé's father. After a divorce, she innocently fell in love with her own brother. Then she went away and had a secret life in New York . . . I don't think Marie really matured until she went into the convent."

—FRANCES REID
(ALICE HORTON)

Addie. Julie felt rejected when her parents went off to Paris without her and again when she approached them for help while pregnant with David's child and was turned away. Addie suspected there was another man in Julie's life, causing the apparent stress in the Banning marriage. Julie should consider herself lucky a man of Scott's caliber would have anything to do with her, Addie often reminded her daughter. As far as Addie was concerned, it was only marriage to Scott that gave an aura of respectability to Julie's life. As for Doug, Addie haughtily referred to him as "the kind of man I choose to ignore."

Susan recovered sufficiently from her trauma to throw herself into work at the David Martin Clinic, which she had set up with her inheritance money. There she met Dr. Greg Peters and the two formed a sweet attachment and deep friendship. They were moving toward a true romance when Susan became ill and faint one morning. She was pregnant. Repulsed by the circumstance of the conception—clearly the attack in the park—Susan went to New York for an abortion. At the last minute, she changed her mind and chose to keep the child that was growing inside her. The pregnancy conjured many emotions for Susan. Deprived of family happiness twice already, she saw this baby as a focus of love, a reason for being. Besides, she was really quite unsettled about her emotions for Greg. Was it love or friendship that she felt for him? And pregnant with another man's child, she realized Greg's feelings for her could quickly cool.

Around the holidays, Laura, Mickey, and Michael went to Chicago to visit her mom, Carrie, who was in a Chicago sanitarium. Unfortunately, her dementia was so severe, she didn't recognize Laura and her family. It was a heartbreaking encounter, but it gave Mickey new insight into his wife and why she had chosen psychiatry as her medical specialty.

New Year's Eve found Julie with Scott at Sergio's, where Doug was entertaining. Bill was there with his current date, Sheila Hammond. Laura and Mickey shared a quiet night at home, but Laura's thoughts, and her heart, were with Bill.

1972

When Laura learned how Kitty had tried to blackmail Bill with the tape that revealed his paternity of Michael, Laura realized the full extent of Bill's sacrifice. In addition to personal humiliation, Bill quietly suffered the professional blow of having his medical license suspended. As Laura became more emotionally estranged from Mickey, her new insight into his brother only drew her all the more to Bill. She asked for a formal meeting of the medical board and in a confidential hearing, Laura gave them the painful personal information that got Bill reinstated into medical practice. She also planned to ask Mickey for a divorce. But before she could, Michael overheard her and Bill expressing their love for each other and wrongly assumed they were having an affair. Overcome with bitter disappointment, the disillusioned boy ran blindly into traffic and was hit by a car. While recovering in the hospital, Mike made it clear he hated his Uncle Bill and never wanted to see him again. Michael insisted that Bill stay away from him—and his mother. About the same time, Mickey was diagnosed with a heart problem. Laura realized both her son and her husband needed her and could not bring herself to ask for a divorce.

Meanwhile, Julie was keeping up the facade of her marriage. Although she rarely responded to Scott in the bedroom, she made certain to keep her birth control pills in use. She convinced Dr. Tom that it was a precaution until she and Scott were certain their marriage was mended. In reality, she cleverly orchestrated a divorce petition behind Scott's back. On the date her lawyer and Scott's were scheduled to appear before the judge to indicate the reconciliation had been a success, Julie planned to have her lawyer pursue the divorce after all. She was practically counting the days until she would be free to marry Doug.

Meanwhile, Susan was reticent to discuss her past with Dr. Greg Peters, but his patience and understanding won her over. Although Greg had some mixed emotions about Susan being pregnant by another man, once he fully understood the circumstances of her conception and weighed his love for her against any objections that came to mind, he still wanted a future with Susan. However, for professional as well as personal considerations, the couple wanted to wait a while before setting a date for the ceremony. Since Susan had decided to have the child alone anyway, marriage prior to the baby's birth was not an issue for her.

After school was over, Steve Olson popped into Salem to catch up with his grandparents, sister, and mom. But after exposure to Paris, small-town life had lost its hold, at least for the moment, and he returned to Europe. Alice hoped Addie would stay and tried to play matchmaker for her eldest daughter and Dr. Mark Larson, but Addie was distracted by an odd fascination with Doug Williams. She was convinced there was something shady in this slick operator's background and hired a private investigator to look into Doug's history. The report was quite complete. Doug, whose real name was Brent Douglas, had been raised in an orphanage until he ran away at fourteen to live on the strength of clever cons and his inherent charm. Addie learned for the first time about his prison sentence and that he had shared a cell with her brother Bill. Addie also discovered that Doug had been seeing a young married woman, Julie Banning. Mulling over the report, Addie debated whether she would expose Doug for the flimflam man she always knew he was. In the end, she confronted him privately. Addie fully expected to have the upper hand, but her assault on his character was nothing compared to the painfully incisive truths Doug showed her about herself. Although their first encounters were quite hostile, Addie soon had to admit to Doug that he had been right. Her marriage to Ben had been an unfulfilling farce for the sake of social status. She also discovered she was not immune to Doug's easygoing charm. He had an impact on her she never expected. In the following weeks, Addie found plenty of reasons to spend time with Doug. She consulted him on investment matters and found herself opening up to him on a personal level. She felt differently around him—vibrant, alive. Others saw a change in her, too. She was suddenly happier, dressing younger, wearing a more current hairstyle. Addie had become a new woman. Doug had empathy for Addie and became her confidant while deftly keeping her at a seemingly safe distance.

By late June, Julie and Doug were ready for their Portofino escape. Their dream adventure would have become a reality just one day after her divorce petition was filed, but suddenly Julie insisted that David come with them. Doug, who had never expressed desire to be a step-dad, was stunned by Julie's stubborn ultimatum. He was also shocked by Julie's nonchalant attitude about taking David away from Scott. The two had a heated quarrel before Julie left Doug's apartment. Julie's pique was so dramatic that Doug never suspected she had been bluffing. She privately had already determined she would do anything rather than lose Doug. Unfortunately, Doug took her at her word. While still reeling from

Dr. Greg Peters offered Susan Martin respect, understanding, and marriage, but she often wondered if her own feelings were genuine love, friendship—or need.

the confrontation with Julie, Doug was paid a visit by Addie who boldly asked him to marry her. Displaying that impulsiveness that made him so appealing to many women, Doug accepted. The two eloped and, using the tickets he already had in his pocket, Doug and Addie took off at midnight for their honeymoon in Portofino. Addie called her parents from the airport, and although quite surprised, Tom and Alice were delighted for the newlyweds. Except for the late hour, Alice would have called Julie that night. Instead, she called her granddaughter in the morning. In total shock, Julie seemed strangely withdrawn for several days. She remained married to Scott, who never did find out about the divorce petition, which, no longer necessary, was set aside.

When Doug and Addie returned to Salem, Julie and her mother were more estranged than ever. Julie maintained a steely composure but was deeply wounded that Doug had chosen Addie as his wife. Addie, on the other hand, had never been happier. She flowered into a fulfilled and loving woman. And, having inherited Ben's sizable estate, Addie could provide a very nice lifestyle for herself and Doug. In fact, she bought Sergio's and renamed it Doug's Place as a wedding gift. She often played hostess there while Doug and another singer, Robert LeClair, entertained. It was clear to everyone that Doug had deep compassion and respect for Addie. That turned to love and their relationship was truly rich and devoted. Of course, Doug would always have longings for Julie, but he was loyal to Addie.

Susan, far along in her pregnancy, got quite a shock when she ran into the man she had encountered in the park, the father of her child. The chance meeting in the hospital cafeteria was so brief and unexpected that Susan was not totally certain that he was indeed her unborn baby's father. She looked at him and asked if he remembered her. He looked her up and down and dismissed her with, "No, should I?" But that was not the end of it. Weeks later, Susan was invited to dinner at Greg's parents' home. The situation was already tense, since Greg's mother Anne had plenty of reservations about her son the doctor being involved with a young woman who had little education, a troubled past, and a future involving another man's child. Things went from bad to worse for Susan when Greg's brother Eric, a struggling writer, arrived and she recognized him as the man she had run into at the cafeteria. Both Susan and Eric ignored any mention of ever having met anywhere before. Greg thought it was his mother's attitude that kept Susan so off balance that evening.

Over the course of several days, Susan casually questioned Greg about Eric. She learned that he lived in an apartment in a seedy part of town among drug users and hookers while writing his novel, but he still kept many of his things in his old bedroom. The next time Susan and Greg, now engaged, were invited to the Peterses' home, Susan made an excuse to go lie down in one of the spare bedrooms upstairs. She slipped into Eric's room and in his closet found a blazer. Except for one replacement button, the others matched the button Susan still had from the night of her encounter in the park. Susan no longer had any doubt that Greg's brother had been her attacker.

When she and Eric met again and were alone enough to talk frankly, Susan confronted him about the rape. He was totally taken aback by the accusation. When they came upon each other in the park, Eric had been going through some emotional turmoil. He was not estranged from his family, but apart from their traditional lifestyle. He was a sensitive creative type, withdrawn from the world in many ways, including experience with women. As far as he was concerned, what happened in the park had been an odd, but mutually agreed upon, encounter. In fact, he bluntly pointed out, Susan had been the instigator. It was only toward the end of their anonymous lust that Susan seemed to panic and pull away from him. He considered her at the time not only a slut but quite neurotic, and now she had proven herself highly unbalanced again as she rattled on and on about rape. Susan came close to a total breakdown and resumed counseling sessions with Laura while she and Eric kept their encounter a secret from Greg.

Anderson Manufacturing was one of the largest and most successful operations in Salem. Bob and Phyllis Anderson had one daughter, Mary, who had a casual relationship with Bill Horton. Through Bill, Scott, an architect, was introduced to Bob and was considered for one of Anderson's biggest projects. Julie understood how important the high-paying deal would be. She made certain to have Bob and Phyllis over for dinner and used her social graces to create an image of domestic stability and happiness. The four became friends and Scott landed the project. As the work progressed, the Andersons and Bannings became like family to one another.

Late in the year, Susan delivered a healthy baby girl, and named her Annie after Greg's mother. Sadly, Susan had also learned from Dr. Tom Horton that she had cancer of the uterus. Although the baby was unaffected, it would be her last. Susan had a hysterectomy. She realized this could change Greg's mind about marriage since he had always wanted a large family. However, Greg was still in love with her and they planned a Valentine's Day wedding.

At Christmas, since Scott was doing so well at Anderson, he gave Julie a mink coat. Julie, still unforgiving of her mother and in love with Doug, presented her step-dad with a portrait of himself. It was a gift Addie quickly but privately told Julie she found quite inappropriate. Clearly, their animosity was not lessened by holiday cheer.

1973

Early in the year, while working for Anderson Manufacturing, Scott Banning was seriously injured by a falling beam at a construction site. He was rushed to the hospital and lingered for several days before he died, never knowing that Julie had finally decided to divorce him after all. Bob and Phyllis Anderson, feeling genuine concern and a sense of responsibility, were exceptionally helpful to Julie in the aftermath of Scott's death. They offered her financial help, the use of their lake house, and moral support. It was a complex emotional time for Julie, who felt guilt over not giving her marriage a real chance and realizing that she was now free, and Doug was not.

In fact, Doug and Addie were more deeply united when Addie, who thought she had already gone into menopause, found out that she was pregnant. The joy she and Doug shared was quickly dampened, however, when doctors found Addie had leukemia. Chemotherapy was the logical choice of treatment, but rather than risk danger to the baby, Addie opted not to take medical measures. She placed her faith in God's will. While the rest of the family gathered around Addie, Julie only knew of her mother's pregnancy, not her terminal illness. When

Julie needed maternal comfort she turned to Phyllis, who had become her best friend. Bob's support, however, became attraction. Julie, emotionally needy, encouraged him with words and gestures that seemed innocent to the casual observer, but not to middle-aged Bob, who longed for his long-faded youth.

Susan and Greg were in the middle of plans for their February wedding when Susan suddenly balked and left town after putting her baby Annie in the care of Greg's mom. In a letter she left for Greg she said, "Don't search for me . . . only I can find myself. I'm searching for life, not death. Don't worry about me." She needed time away to decide whether to tell Greg the entire truth of the encounter in the park. Would he still want to marry her when she told him it had not been rape? Could she marry him without sharing her mind and soul with him?

During Susan's absence, Laura explained the circumstances and background of Susan's traumatic amnesia to Eric, who finally recognized his impressions of her were totally incorrect. Susan had been devastated by losing Scott and baby David to Julie. In the park she was lonely and disoriented. Clinging to the stranger she met, she longed for closeness and emotional intimacy. As her mind and body got away from her, she was caught up in the sex act that was only the second in her life. At some point, she opened her eyes and saw David Martin, not Eric. It took some questions and sorting through the answers before Eric could fully understand what had actually happened. He realized how bitterly wrong he had been about Susan.

Eric's novel, *In My Brother's Shadow*, was accepted by a publisher in New York. Although the characters are supposedly fictional, the chapter titled "The Girl in the Park" was a thinly veiled report of Eric's encounter with Susan. Anyone knowing the Peters family could see that. Now that he understood Susan's state of mind, Eric asked to have that chapter deleted. However, when Greg heard of Eric's concern about the so-called rape chapter it spurred his curiosity and he read it. Realizing that it was written before he had introduced Eric and Susan, Greg reached his own conclusions. When he confronted Eric about being the man in the park, the writer said not a word in his defense. Literally blinded by rage, Greg beat his brother so savagely Eric was hospitalized.

Secrets and misunderstandings led to tragic consequences elsewhere in Salem. Laura and Mickey's marriage was at least tranquil, if not truly happy, but then Michael overheard a conversation that revealed to him

Susan Martin married Dr. Greg Peters in a sweet and touching ceremony about six months after delivering a baby fathered by his brother Eric, who did not attend the wedding.

that his father had had an affair with Linda Patterson, his former secretary. The boy was shaken as he finally understood the reason why his mother had talked about divorce—it had not been her desire for Bill. She had been wronged and Mickey had let Michael believe a lie. The boy kept the information to himself until his restlessness became obvious and Mickey asked what was eating him. Michael spewed such contempt for his father's weakness that the tirade caused Mickey to have a massive coronary. The boy was so stunned he was motionless, then remorseful, as Laura hurried from the bedroom and attempted to resuscitate Mickey. Meanwhile, Michael called the fire department and then his grandfather.

Once at the hospital, the drama continued as doctors Tom and Bill Horton watched Mickey flatline. That's when Bill literally pushed his dad aside and took over his brother's emergency care, knowing it was impossible for a cardiac surgeon to get there in time. In spite of his emotional turmoil, and fully aware of his vulnerable professional position, Bill courageously performed the life-saving operation.

Laura stayed in the lounge with the tormented Michael, who confessed about the circumstances of his father's heart attack. The boy was flooded with emotions of guilt and deep sadness for the way he had treated his Uncle Bill over the last months. It was also apparent that Michael would never feel the same devotion and trust toward the man he still believed to be his father. When Bill joined them, the trio kept a vigil together, joined as family more than ever before. Mickey survived the triple-bypass operation but required a lengthy hospital stay.

Susan returned to Salem about this time and heard what had happened between Greg and Eric. Her visit to see Eric in the hospital was touching—the two now understood better than anyone the fears and vulnerabilities they shared. She was overwhelmed with compassion for Eric, who had protected her confidentiality during the confrontation with Greg. She told Eric that she herself would have to tell his brother the true details of that evening. The next time Susan visited, she brought Annie along as Eric had asked.

After Susan explained, in detail, what happened in the park, Greg was utterly shocked. He left her without a word and went to Eric. Through the trauma, the brothers found a new level of communication and awkward, but heartfelt, emotion. Greg had his doubts about Susan for a while, and his mother did what she could to dissuade Greg from seeing Susan, but with Eric's insight and encouragement, Greg decided to let love rule his senses. Greg and Susan married a few weeks later in a lovely ceremony. Susan had, at last, a husband who loved her, a baby, and a family of her own.

While the Hortons were at the wedding, Mickey was still in the hospital making considerable progress in recuperating from his surgery. Emotionally and psychologically troubled, Mickey was filled with haunting memories of his son's indictments and fears about his future as a husband, father, and lawyer. Then he suffered a stroke. A blinding head pain came on suddenly, and almost as quickly disappeared, taking Mickey's memory with it. Disoriented, but having no physical symptoms beyond minor numbness in his left hand, Mickey found his clothes, dressed, and simply walked out of the hospital. By the time family and police were alerted, Mickey had disappeared from Salem without a trace.

Dr. Bill Horton's desire for Laura never stood in the way of his oath as a surgeon and enduring love for his brother. He skillfully performed the heart operation that saved Mickey's life. That trauma brought Bill and Laura even closer together.

After weeks of ambling through small towns, Mickey wandered into a farmhouse where he sought a glass of water and relief from the July heat. Maggie Simmons, a lovely young woman on crutches, welcomed him. She was hungry for the conversation and companionship, however brief. Raised on the farm, Maggie had been left crippled in the same collision between pickup and big rig that killed her parents, Elmer and Dorothy. Simple and sweet but no willing victim, Maggie hired men to tend the livestock and the fields. Otherwise, she took care of the household herself. When Mickey felt weak and faint, Maggie let him lie down. His bandaged chest needed care. He needed food, comfort, and rest. Luckily, he had knocked on just the right door.

The rapport between Maggie and Marty Hansen—as Mickey called himself, based on initials on his belt buckle—grew quickly. Enchanted by the countryside's clean air, easy pace, and warm company, Mickey realized he was short on memory but was not particularly eager to disturb his haven with intrusions of the past, whatever they might be. He was filled with a sense of peace and contentment. That was quite enough. As for Maggie, who had resigned herself to a lonely and loveless life, all the stranger at her door would have needed was a white horse to complete the romantic image.

While efforts to find Mickey continued, Mike was depressed and moody in his guilt. Laura and Bill, though they refrained from physically making love, grew closer and more devoted. They also wondered when Mickey would be found alive, or dead, or at all. Without wishing Mickey harm, they also wondered about the painful limbo of waiting seven years before Mickey could be declared legally dead, and they could marry. Laura consulted a lawyer before the end of the year to find out her options.

1974

Julie's love life was still stuck on a rollercoaster. Successful attorney Don Craig and Julie had been dating for several months so she was not surprised when he asked her to marry him. She accepted for many reasons: strong physical attraction, loneliness, and mounting bills. However, Julie had never stopped loving Doug, and Addie was, after all, dying, as Julie had found out. So she broke her engagement to Don.

Mother and daughter made a deeply moving deathbed reconciliation just before Addie slipped into a coma. Addie evoked a willing promise from Julie that after she was gone, Julie would take care of Doug and their child. Doug and Julie kept their daily vigil at Addie's bedside, still praying for a miracle and the healthy birth of the baby that Addie so desperately wanted to carry to term. Both blessings arrived within a short span of each other. Hope was born, and Addie, alone with Doug at her bedside, opened her eyes and called out his name. She was out of her coma, and the leukemia was in remission. Julie, already bonding with the newborn she had imagined she would raise with Doug as her own, was pulled between happiness for her mother and self-pity. Doug's words of heartfelt thanks for her support during the hospital vigil carved deep into Julie's heart, but she kept a calm exterior despite her emotional torment.

Steeling herself, Julie tried to pick up with Don, but the smart lawyer realized he would be only a rebound romance for Julie and gently turned her away. Meanwhile, Bob had left Phyllis and asked for a divorce without ever making it known that Julie had caused his marital discontent. Resigned to the cynical conclusion that money, not love, was the only thing she could count on, Julie turned to Bob. As she had expected, he impulsively proposed and she took the opportunity for a marriage that offered security and companionship, if not passion. Phyllis was thoroughly stunned to realize there had been attraction between Bob and Julie for some time. When they announced they were going to get married, Phyllis, already unbalanced by divorce, became totally unglued at the thought of being replaced by a much younger woman, a woman she thought of as her best friend and confidante. Blinded by betrayal, Phyllis set out to murder Julie and ended up shooting her own daughter, Mary. Although Mary recovered, the emotional wounds for Phyllis were deep and never really healed.

Julie became the pampered new bride and delighted in the role. Her marriage to Bob was filled with dinners at the best restaurants, unlimited wardrobe allowance, travel, and entertainment. They enjoyed the good life, and Julie, in her whirlwind of constant distractions, was placated at least for the time being. Bob was tired out almost immediately. Marriage to a young and vibrant woman only made the contrast of years more apparent. A demanding business and packed social calendar tired Bob, and once in the bedroom, his lack of sexual vitality often left Julie restless and unsatisfied.

Susan and Greg's marriage predictably suffered a slow deterioration. Susan was content with her work at the clinic, home, family, and quiet nights at the piano. Greg, however, needed more. When roguish Dr. Neil Curtis, an internist with an upscale private practice, asked Greg to become an associate, he liked the idea and the increased income, but Susan disapproved. Differences in background, education, goals, and attitudes began to erode the foundation of the Peters marriage. Occasional social visits from Eric stirred unspoken discontent, too.

In contrast, Doug and Addie were truly happy with their baby and dreams of their future. Addie was absorbed in motherhood and domestic bliss. Doug was a doting dad by day and successful entertainer by night. Their happiness would not last. Addie was crossing the street with Hope when a speeding car made a turn and would have struck the carriage had Addie not thrust it forward. The move put Addie directly in the path of the car, which killed her on impact. Doug was so grief stricken he was unable to reach out to anyone, even Julie, for solace. She, of course, was bitterly aware Doug was free, and she was not.

In the country, Marty (Mickey) continued to make Maggie's romantic dreams come true, and when he asked her to marry him, she wept tears of joy. Hank the farm manager gave the bride away as the minister's wife played the organ at the small rural chapel. Maggie, her crutches set aside, looked radiant as she sat in her summer wedding dress, reciting marriage vows she had written herself. Maggie and Marty were a perfect match, as long as they remained in their harvestland haven. But the outside world had a way of intruding.

Marty read a medical story in a magazine about new surgical techniques being done at University Hospital in Salem for injuries such as Maggie's. On the day of the appointment, he had a problem to tend to on the farm, so Maggie went alone. She spent hours at the hospital for consultations, X-rays, and tests. While

Don Craig would have been a more satisfying mate for Julie, but he wisely recognized she was driven by money, not love.

ABOVE & RIGHT: Julie Olson became the pampered young bride of Bob Anderson and, if not happy, was at least pleasantly distracted by an active social life and unlimited wardrobe allowance. However, Julie's nights were long and lonely with a man past his prime.

doctors gathered facts about Maggie, she found much unrequested information herself. She was unnerved by a photo on one doctor's desk. It was a clean-shaven man who looked a lot like Marty. Later, Maggie overheard bits of casual conversation and she learned that Dr. Laura Spencer's husband, Mickey Horton, had disappeared after heart surgery about the time Marty showed up at the farm. Shaken, Maggie left without making any follow-up appointments. At home, she dismissed thoughts of Mickey Horton, and told Marty the operation would not work for her. She did, however, want to start the family they'd talked about, the sooner the better.

Coincidentally, another photo had sparked attention. A feature story about a country fair turned up in a Salem newspaper. When the Hortons noticed a man who looked like Mickey had won a farming prize, they followed up on the lead that brought them to the Brookville farm. The first encounter and many that followed were awkward for everyone. Mickey recognized no one. The Hortons were relieved and joyful to find Mickey alive and happy. But Michael in particular was devastated when his father showed no recognition and only shook his hand when they were brought together. There were mixed emotions for Laura and Bill, but Mickey was willing to give her a divorce. After all, as he was told, he had been a jealous and unfaithful husband. He had no feelings for Laura now and simply wanted her to have a chance for love and happiness as he shared with Maggie. However, because of the loss of his memory, a simple divorce became complicated and time-consuming. Neither desertion nor insanity were technically valid in this case. But Mickey and Laura did divorce, and by the end of the year Laura wed Bill.

Although Mickey had no memory of his past life, he saw the sincerity of the Hortons' entreaties. Mickey felt no attachment to Salem, no sudden flood of memories, and so opted to stay with Maggie on the farm. Tom and Michael sometimes visited, often hoping it would spark father-son memories. Mickey declined the operation that might have restored his memory. Maggie eventually agreed to undergo the surgery that could restore the use of her legs so she could better fight to keep Mickey, who because the bigamous marriage was invalid, was not really her husband. She was also disappointed that she had not become pregnant yet.

Entertainers Jeri Clayton and her daughter Trish preferred singing under a spotlight to sleeping under starlight. These ladies had left their rural roots for the glamour of city life. Once in Salem, Jeri made an immediate hit at Doug's Place, where she always seemed happiest. At home, her musician husband, Jack, was often brutish toward her and overly affectionate toward his stepdaughter Trish.

Meanwhile, Julie's mercenary marriage to Bob had gone from bad to worse. Phyllis continued to make emotional demands on him as she dealt with the aftermath of nearly killing their daughter. His guilt over divorcing Phyllis in the first place continued to interfere with his sexuality, and because he assumed his young wife needed more intimacy, Bob became irrationally jealous, suspecting Julie was having affairs with younger men behind his back. In truth, Julie enjoyed the flirtations, but remained physically faithful to Bob even while her heart never stopped longing for Doug. By the end of the year, Julie considered divorce again.

Julie's old nemesis Susan was not having any better luck with own marriage. As Dr. Greg Peters became more involved with the care of his patient Amanda

Maggie Simmons had little contact with the outside world until a stranger came to her farmhouse door. She found new hope, and love. But every happiness exacts a price.

Jeri Clayton was an ex-prostitute married to an abusive husband. She and Doug Williams shared a friendship based on their other-side-of-the-tracks background and love of music.

Howard, he grew more distant at home. Amanda had been deeply troubled after her husband died. Her depression was not only the result of grief, but guilt over the affair she was having with Neil Curtis even at the time her husband was hospitalized. Because Neil asked her to, Amanda kept the identity of her lover a secret even from her psychiatrist, Dr. Laura Horton. That selfish request did nothing to help Amanda's state of mind. Although Greg remained faithful to Susan, his coolness further damaged their marriage. Eric, who continued to hide his deep and growing feelings for Susan, began to spend more time with her and Annie.

1975

Unlucky in love and luck, compulsive gambler Neil Curtis continued to sink further into debt. Totally self-absorbed, Neil had little regard for the harm he had done to Amanda's mental state. He made matters worse when, with any eye on her money, he proposed. Then, the night before the wedding, Amanda found him in bed with a prostitute. Her already tenuous balance crumbled and she tried to commit suicide. Greg Peters found himself even more drawn to the vulnerable woman, but because of his marriage to Susan and Amanda's history, he kept his interaction with her on a professional level. Amanda was developing some feelings for Greg too, but kept her distance, learning what she could about him by reading Eric's novel, *In My Brother's Shadow*. Meanwhile, Greg's concern over Amanda's emotional and physical welfare caused constant friction with Neil. Eventually, Neil's callous attitude toward Amanda brought them to physical blows.

Trish, anxious to get away from her stepdad Jack and her mom Jeri's dark moods, took an apartment with young adult Mike. He wanted to escape family upheavals and disappointment. When Mickey refused the operation that might restore his memory, Mike felt rejected. He also felt alienated when Laura and Uncle Bill no longer had a need to disguise their devotion. So Mike and Trish found themselves kindred souls in a platonic relationship, each emotionally vulnerable, afraid of the pain a sexual relationship might bring.

Julie had filed for divorce from Bob and hoped that now she and Doug would be able to reestablish their romance and pursue the dreams she still held in her heart. Although Julie and Bob had not had a particularly passionate sex life, she was pregnant with his child. Julie did not let that sidetrack her plans for divorce, but Doug found out about the pregnancy and, without letting Julie know that he was aware of her condition, told her the one lie that could send her back to her husband. In a self-sacrificing move, Doug told her that he did not love her and the best thing she could do was reconcile with Bob. That was not something Julie felt she could easily do, even though Bob wanted her to come back.

Luckily for Julie, who needed more to think about than learning to knit baby booties, David Banning chose this time to return to Salem. He wanted to collect his inheritance from the estate of his grandmother Addie and, secondly, he was at least open to soothing some of the hurt that estrangement from his mother had brought them both. David had been something of a playboy, but he planned to marry his current girlfriend, Brooke Hamilton, once he got his money. Brooke was a street-smart young woman raised by her alcoholic mom, Adele, who had once had a brief affair with Bob Anderson when they were in high school together.

While the women got together for Laura's wedding shower, the groom-to-be Bill shared a bonding moment of beer and sports telecast with his dad Tom and friend Bob.

After a decade of bittersweet romance and tears, Bill and Laura wed in mid-1975. They had a daughter, Jennifer Rose, the following year.

Dr. Bill Horton was to perform Maggie's operation. Unfortunately, when Mickey overheard the rather intrusive questions Bill asked Maggie about his relationship with her, familiar animosity surfaced between the two brothers. When Maggie still could not walk after the grueling operation, Mickey blamed Bill's ineptitude. Mickey still had no memories of the past, but old emotions were coming to the surface. Laura explained that Maggie now suffered psychological paralysis out of fear of losing Mickey and guilt over stirring problems between Mickey and Bill. While Maggie recuperated in the hospital, Mickey was devotedly at her side. He constantly brought her gifts to lift her spirits and inspire her courage. There was the wind-up walking doll, flowers, and candy. But the most significant symbol of hope were the red shoes and dress that hung in the closet. When the two talked of their dreams, romantic images of the waltzing, whirling couple came to life. He promised Maggie that one day they would really dance that way.

Once home on the farm, Mickey and Hank made certain that Maggie's therapy was constant and complete. Equipment was brought in, but the atmosphere was never sterile. Mickey delighted in playing the guitar and singing for Maggie. They'd share duets along with their dreams. Mickey was devoted to Maggie—they shared a sweet and innocent love that was, at least within the confines of the farm, untouched by manipulations, jealousies, and greed. But then trouble-making Linda Patterson Phillips, who'd had an affair with Mickey years ago, returned to Salem with her daughter Melissa. She decided to take full advantage of Mickey's memory loss to rekindle a relationship with him. She and Melissa spent a few days on the farm and Linda tried to tell Mickey that Melissa was his daughter. Luckily, Linda's ailing and estranged husband, Jim, wrote Maggie a note warning her about Linda and her devious ways. Maggie showed it to Laura and wanted further explanation. Laura, now pregnant with Bill's child, explained about Mickey and Linda's past relationship, which thwarted Linda's lying plan in a hurry. Still, Linda stayed in Salem and eventually caused trouble for others.

When Doug finally emerged from mourning, he had Doug's Place remodeled. There was a new sense of joy as Robert and Doug sang together. The club's customers loved classics like "Singing in the Rain" and melted when the duo sang

Paul Grant took David Banning into his home after David drove his car into the river. David almost married his daughter Valerie.

"Oh, You Beautiful Doll" to little Hope who, although being raised by Tom and Alice, was often around for early evening shows. When Doug finally felt emotionally strong enough, he decided to take Hope from the Hortons' care and raise her himself with the help of a housekeeper-nanny. He hired Rebecca North in midsummer and celebrated a festive "Welcome Home, Hope" party at Doug's Place. When Doug decided that Hope needed a little brother or sister, he went to see Dr. Neil Curtis, who had started a surrogate mother program at the hospital. For a substantial amount of money and a sperm donation, Doug was promised an anonymous surrogate mother would bear his child. Neil chose Rebecca, who wanted the money to send to her boyfriend, Johnny Collins, an artist studying in Paris. When her pregnancy became obvious, everyone assumed Johnny was the irresponsible father. Robert offered to marry her to give the baby legitimacy, but Rebecca insisted she loved Johnny and that he would be coming back soon. In fact, she had led Johnny to believe the child was his.

After losing Amanda, Neil tried to get help with Gamblers Anonymous, but he was not committed to recovery. As his debts continued to mount, he put his charm to work on Phyllis. He proposed marriage and gave her a diamond ring. Although in love with him, Phyllis was smart enough to draw up a prenuptial agreement. Neil did his best to dodge signing it, but she insisted. Their tug of war on that issue continued for several months.

Julie was still separated from Bob and stayed in Doug's guest room for a time. Brooke, who was never happy unless she was stirring up gossip and trouble, saw a perfect opportunity. She was jealous over the renewed relationship between David and Julie, so she maliciously spread the lie that Julie was actually pregnant by Doug, not Bob. This caused a rift between Julie and Alice, who was led to believe that Julie's affair with Doug had continued even after Doug and Addie were married. At first David refused to believe a word Brooke said. Then he overheard a loving conversation between Julie and Doug. Fueled by Brooke's lies, David's doubts turned to conviction about his mother's infidelity. His feelings of distrust for his mother returned to erase the renewed love that had started to grow. He and Julie argued, then, disillusioned and feeling foolish for having been

Dr. Neil Curtis had a bedside manner that worked magic on many women. He and Amanda Howard had an affair while her husband lay dying. Gambling debts and other women came between them.

vulnerable to his mother again, David got into Doug's car and sped off. He didn't care if he lived or died as the car careened off a bridge and plunged into the river below. Although a body was not found, David was presumed drowned; when all hope for his body being found faded, a memorial service was held in Salem for him. Distraught by David's death and filled with guilt over her part in the scenario, Brooke took an overdose of sleeping pills. She survived and recuperated at the Hortons' home while only occasionally visiting her mom, who had come back to town.

For the last few months, David had been living with the Grants, a black family who had taken him into their home after he stumbled out of the river. He had been happy with them, in an environment of loving family warmth and support that had never been part of his background. Paul and Helen Grant had two children—Danny, who worked in his father's diner, and Valerie, who was a student looking forward to a medical career. The friendship David and Valerie found soon turned to romance. Eventually, Paul accidentally found out the truth about David's identity and went to Julie, who was ecstatic that her son was alive. Unfortunately, in her excitement to rush to David, she tripped and tumbled down a flight of stairs and suffered a miscarriage.

Brooke was pregnant with David's child, but when she realized he was no longer in love with her but cared for Valerie, she refused David's offer of marriage. When David brought Valerie home to Salem at Christmas, family and friends welcomed them both and Valerie took a part-time job working in Laura's office.

Horton family love and loyalty was tested when a tragic accident led to a devastating revelation and anguished response. Mike had been spending a lot of time at the Brookville farm and one day while he was helping with the haying the flatbed truck broke down. A mechanic by trade, Mike was underneath, fixing the truck, when the jack gave out. The truck nearly crushed Mike to death. He was rushed to the hospital for massive blood transfusions. Naturally, Mickey immediately donated blood, but when it was typed, neither his blood nor Laura's matched the boy's. The sudden reality that he could not possibly be Mike's father shocked Mickey, and in those electrifying moments he regained his memory in a violent flood of images and emotions. In torment, Mickey had to find out the truth immediately, that night. First he checked Bill's file to find his blood type, which turned out to be the same as Mike's type. Then Mickey went to Linda's apartment and learned that Laura had told her he could not be Melissa's father because he was sterile.

Outraged by years of betrayal and lies, Mickey bought a gun and went to the house he once shared with Laura to wait for Bill to get home. Meanwhile, as Laura was trying to reach him, Bill was performing unscheduled emergency surgery. So when Bill arrived home, he had no warning that his brother intended to kill him. Mickey confronted Bill and spewed forth all the memories of conflict, rivalry, and pain he was now remembering. He accused Bill of stealing everything of value from him—his wife, his son, his pride, and manhood. He had been made a fool of, lied to, deceived by those he loved and those he believed loved him. Enraged, he was about to shoot when Bill lunged for his gun. It went off and wounded Bill in the arm. Tom arrived, having gotten a frantic call from Laura, and had to break a window to get inside to his sons.

Clearly in mental collapse, Mickey was hysterical. The Hortons, devastated, had to commit Mickey to Bayview Sanitarium where he experienced hallucinations and became uncontrollably violent. He kept seeing Laura's face everywhere and actually tried to strangle two blond nurses. He also attacked Dr. Powell, one of his three therapists, which also included Laura and Dr. Marlena Evans.

Mike, meanwhile, was in critical condition and felt abandoned again by his father. As his status improved some, it was hard for him to understand why Mickey had not come to see him. His family told him that Mickey's memory had returned very suddenly and he was having a problem dealing with the overwhelming amount of information. Still, Mike wanted to see his father. In hopes that it would help the boy's recovery, Mickey was medicated and allowed a supervised visit. Mickey had to agree that he would not tell Mike the truth about his parentage. But in an irrational moment, Mickey blurted out the truth, which enraged Mike against Bill and Laura.

Laura and Bill were on the drive back from one of their many visits to the sanitarium when they were caught in a snowstorm and Laura went into labor. They became parents of a baby girl, Jennifer Rose, in a delivery at a nearby farmhouse. After all the trauma of the last few weeks, Laura's postpartum blues gave way to full depression and she withdrew from everyone for a while. Dr. Evans eventually helped pull her through the rough time, and Laura and Bill established the family life they hoped would last the rest of their lives.

Neil married Phyllis and paid off most of his gambling debts. But he never would have married her if he'd gotten Amanda's telephone message professing her continuing love, or if he had known about her condition: she had a brain

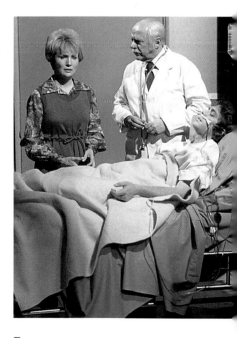

Laura's world nearly shattered when her son Michael almost died in a farm accident and, at the same time, the secret of his paternity became known.

tumor and only six months to live. Worse, she refused to have the operation that could possibly save her life. Because her mother had died recently from a similar procedure, Amanda was too terrified to have surgery. Neil really loved her and, with Greg Peters's help, eventually convinced her to have the surgery. She survived, but temporarily lost her memory and speech. Amanda even forgot which man she had loved, Neil or Greg. Since he was married, Neil made a point of stepping aside and encouraging Amanda to allow a relationship with Greg to grow.

Robert LeClair, unaware that Rebecca was a surrogate mother, heard that Rebecca would be giving up the child soon after it was born. He wired Johnny in Paris and, thinking the child was his, Johnny came back to marry Rebecca. When she told him the truth about the baby, he had a hard time handling it. It was on her wedding day that she found his good-bye note in their new apartment. A month later, in July, Robert married Rebecca in a simple ceremony hoping that she would grow to love him. Meanwhile, Julie and Bob had divorced. She and Doug reconciled. Doug was hoping to have children with Julie and told Neil that he no longer wanted the anonymous surrogate's child. Rebecca, happily, could keep the baby. Shortly after little Dougie was born, Rebecca received a note from Johnny and it was clear she still loved him.

Parents and offspring elsewhere in Salem were having a hard time. After her step-dad Jack told Trish that her mother had been a prostitute, Jeri left town and Trish became determined to find her father, James Stanhope. She did, and he came to Salem, but even when Jeri returned to help things along, there was no emotional reunion. Although Trish took the revelation about her mom's past and her dad's current rejection in stride, her wounds were deep.

Kim Douglas arrived in Salem looking for her husband Brent Douglas, whom everyone in town knew as Doug Williams. She claimed that she never signed their divorce papers. The bombshell meant not only that his marriage to Addie had been invalid but put a quick damper on his engagement to Julie.

Linda often visited Mike at the hospital as a way to gain the boy's trust and eventually bring her closer to Mickey, whom she still wanted to steal from Maggie. After Mike was discharged, he left Trish after an unsuccessful attempt to make love to her. He went to Linda and told her of his sexual confusion. He was attracted to Trish, but uncomfortable about sex with her. Was he homosexual? To find some quick comfort for herself, Linda took him to bed and cured him of his sexual doubts. Mike then became obsessed with her. Linda tried gentle ways to dissuade him, then finally told him she always closed her eyes and saw only Mickey when they had sex.

Kim, after tormenting Doug for several months, finally admitted that she had lied about the supposedly unsigned divorce papers. She and Doug had been legally divorced years ago. Doug and Julie immediately finished their wedding preparations. On the day of the garden ceremony, Kim was melancholy, playing "Second Time Around" with one finger on the piano in an empty room. Clearly, seeing Doug again had rekindled her love.

On their long-awaited wedding day, Doug was a most handsome and happy groom. And Julie was a radiant bride. Addie was there in spirit. Her memory was honored by Julie, who tucked her mother's clown pin inside her bag. Hope was the flower girl for the double-ring ceremony. After years of heartaches and obstacles, the wedding day was grand and glorious. Afterward, the newlyweds took off for a month-long honeymoon starting in Italy and winding through Europe.

Brooke had made travel plans, too. She took her mom Adele on a cruise through the Greek islands after stealing checks from Anderson Manufacturing. She knew her mother's health was failing rapidly after the last emergency surgery. Adele was a hopeless alcoholic, and no matter what love and support Brooke and the Grant family showed her, she backslid into drinking. Before the cruise ship sailed, Bob flew to New York to confront Brooke and found Adele in a hospital, near death. Before she died, Adele confessed that Brooke was actually his daughter but made Bob promise to keep it a secret. He forgave Brooke the theft and gave her a job in the company so she could repay the money in small increments. He also lavished her with gifts and his daughter Mary became suspicious.

After spending most of the year in the sanitarium, Mickey was released. Maggie, recovered and able to walk again, had stayed patiently by his side the entire time and the two were able to rekindle the love they had before his breakdown. Although it would never be quite the same, the couple had a solid basis for their relationship that overcame Mickey's recent problems. Also, they lovingly added an adopted daughter, Janice, to their home and became a true family.

Phyllis became pregnant but believed Neil was totally unhappy about it. So, even though she was far along, she went to Chicago to have an abortion. When doctors told her it was impossible at this point, she almost took a drug overdose but Neil arrived just in time and brought her back to Salem. However, when he learned Amanda had accepted Greg's marriage proposal, Neil got sloppy drunk. He was embarrassingly rude to Phyllis and put the moves on her daughter Mary before passing out cold. Lifting drunken Neil caused Phyllis to go into labor. She delivered a tiny premature baby boy, Nathan, who died within a few days.

Susan had divorced Greg so he would be free to marry Amanda and had left for California with Greg's brother Eric. When Greg married Amanda, they went on a honeymoon in Mexico. At the reception, Marlena Evans, who had been dating bachelor lawyer Don Craig, caught the wedding bouquet.

Although her parents were concerned about the complications of an interracial marriage, David Banning and Valerie Grant became engaged. However, David started to feel himself more attracted to Brooke than Valerie. He also had a brief one-night stand with Trish. The thought of a marriage commitment to anyone had David unnerved.

Johnny Collins returned briefly to Salem and then went to Chicago and encouraged Rebecca to join him there. But she had a nice life with Robert, who had adopted Dougie. When Robert gave her a lovely engagement ring that he could not afford earlier, she decided to stay with him in Salem.

Distraught over the years of deception, Mickey turned his anger against his brother Bill, bought a gun, and headed to his house.

1977

OPPOSITE: **A**nother star-crossed couple, Julie and Doug, were finally married in 1976 and spent a month in Italy touring on the *Honeymoon Express* with stops in Rome, Florence, Venice, and Naples.

As the year began, Trish was finding disturbing notes under her door, a frightening omen that had started a few weeks earlier. They were from her unbalanced stepdad, Jack Clayton, who knew Trish slept with David during a stormy time in his romance with Valerie. Jack was fixated on Trish. At his apartment he had photos of her, over which he had scrawled: "A hooker just like her mother!" One evening he went to her apartment and terrorized her. While Trish ironed the dress that Jack insisted she wear, he continued to ogle her and down tumblers of bourbon. Then he took a knife and cut through the telephone cord and started to attack her. Outside her apartment, Mike heard the scuffle and broke down the door. As he and Jack struggled, Trish took the iron and smashed it into Jack's head, killing him. Trish immediately went to pieces. Mike gently soothed her before leaving as the police and ambulance arrived. Later, he confessed to killing Jack to protect Trish from further turmoil.

Trish, displaying two imaginary personalities—Cynthia and baby Lisa—remained sedated at the hospital in Laura's care. Eventually, Trish was regressed to her childhood and her abuse came through. It took Trish about a month of intense therapy in the hospital before she was ready to leave. After discharge, she continued counseling with Laura, and Trish's mom, Jeri, took part in the sessions, too. David, although still engaged to Valerie, offered emotional support. Unable to live in her old apartment anymore, Trish moved in with Brooke.

Karl and Sharon Duval, who had arrived in Salem late the year before, hired Julie to redecorate their home and paint Sharon's portrait, which was near completion. Troubled and lonely, Sharon was showing sexual interest in Julie. So was Karl. Happily married to Doug, Julie was not interested in either of them. By the end of March, Sharon had taken an overdose of pills. Now, a few months later, Sharon was rushed to the emergency room with another suicide attempt. This time she had slashed her wrists. After a stay in the psychiatric wing, she recovered and the Duvals left Salem. Before they went, Sharon left Julie a touching note and a gift of a favorite cameo.

At Doug's Place, Doug and Robert often practiced their new musical numbers while Hope played with her dolls and playmate Dougie. When Johnny again returned to Salem it caused trouble in Robert and Rebecca's marriage. Rebecca still had strong feelings for Johnny and over the course of several months went back and forth between him and Robert before finally she took Dougie and left town.

Mike, cleared of any wrongdoing in Jack's death, worked as a mechanic at a garage. He realized he still cared deeply for Trish and the two shared several quiet nights over dinner, but Trish soon learned she was carrying David's baby. Meanwhile, there was a lovely wedding shower for Valerie at Doug's Place—David and Val were still planning to marry. After some long, soul-searching conversations, however, the couple broke their engagement and Valerie went to medical school in Washington, D.C.

Linda was still trying to win Mickey away from Maggie. Although Mickey and Maggie were not completely happy, Mickey's occasional evenings at Linda's apartment were not enough to move him away from Maggie. Even when Maggie

Linda came back to Salem with her sights still on Mickey, but when she failed with him, she turned to twice-divorced Bob Anderson.

Samantha Evans was a medical school dropout and wannabe actress who brought together skills from both those fields to impersonate her twin sister Marlena for the biggest, baddest role of her trouble-making career.

forced the issue of separation and took her own apartment, he could not imagine a future with Linda. So when Bob Anderson offered Linda a job as his executive assistant, she happily set her sights on her new boss. Bob's daughter Mary was rightly suspicious as she watched Linda provoke Bob's interest and flaunt the attention she was also getting from Tommy Horton.

Meanwhile, Mary's mom Phyllis had gotten over her depression after losing baby Nathan. She turned all her emotional focus on Neil and continued to shower him with expensive gifts: first a Mercedes, then a very fine gold watch. However, Neil and Mary continued their dangerous liaison. When Phyllis was in town, Neil would bring her a single red rose from the garden on her breakfast tray. Whenever he and Mary had the opportunity, they enjoyed picnics in the park, amorous nights, and breakfast in bed. When Phyllis went off to a lengthier out-of-town meeting, Neil and Mary took off for a mountain lodge.

Also in spring, Dr. Tom Horton was honored with a formal dinner. While speaking at the event at University Hospital, surrounded by family, friends, and colleagues, he had a heart attack. He was rushed to Emergency and stayed in the hospital until early June.

Manipulative schemer Brooke Hamilton slyly sold copies of Anderson Manufacturing documents that she photographed from the files in the Plans and Operations room. Then Mary, who had earlier seen Brooke's tiny camera in a drawer, saw Brooke snooping. As Brooke's industrial espionage came to an end, nearly exposed, she packed her bags just in time and left town. Soon after, someone driving Brooke's car was involved in a high-speed chase with police. Within hours, a badly burned young woman wearing Brooke's locket was taken to Emergency. Later, a newspaper headline declared: BROOKE HAMILTON BURNED TO DEATH. Her memorial service was held in the middle of July.

About this time, Marlena's twin sister Samantha came to Salem. The aspiring actress had a serious problem with alcohol and drugs. She also harbored plenty of jealousy and resentment for Marlena's success and comfortable lifestyle. Soon Samantha stole blank prescriptions from Dr. Evans's pads, and as her addiction became worse, she stole pills right out of Dr. Evans's office cabinets. By the time Marlena realized what was happening, Samantha had also stolen her checkbook and jewelry. In early September, Samanatha managed to knock Marlena out, drugged her, and called an ambulance to haul her off to Bayview Sanitarium. Impersonating Dr. Evans, Samantha managed to get Marlena committed. As an actress, Samantha played her most important role. After reading volumes of psychiatry texts, Samantha took over Marlena's office and life in Salem. Marlena—drugged, but experiencing lucid moments and plenty of frustration—managed to escape. She called Don to pick her up, but she was caught and returned to the sanitarium before he could reach her. Samantha, who convincingly impersonated Marlena, convinced Don the call had been a ploy. She also realized that Marlena had gotten too hard to handle and signed the forms that authorized shock treatments to keep her sister docile.

Toni, Trish's friend from the Sherman Home for Unwed Mothers, brought trouble around, too. In Trish's apartment, Toni's gun-toting boyfriend Kenny tried to steal Toni's purse. Trish was hurt in the altercation and hospitalized. When Mike came to visit Trish, David was already there. In a fit of hurt and jealousy, Mike threw away the flowers he had brought for Trish and left without saying a word. Mike decided it best to put hopes of being with Trish behind him and started dating other women.

Although Trish had not gotten over Mike, she and David had their baby to think about. Several weeks after Trish was out of the hospital, they shared a weekend together. After a night at the Stonybrook Inn in separate beds, Trish and David enjoyed an idyllic picnic lunch by a stream. Trish wore flowers in her hair, and before long, the couple made their way to a lovely little wedding chapel and got married. Later, back in Salem, David moved into Trish's apartment. In late September, Trish went into labor, had some problems, but delivered a boy, Scotty.

Neil was drinking more, and after Phyllis found out about his affair with her daughter Mary, they separated. Phyllis made life miserable for Mary, who had started to date Chris Kositchek, a foreman at Anderson Manufacturing. Phyllis even tried to bribe Chris with $1,000 to stop seeing Mary, but he tore up her check. Phyllis eventually left Salem and embarked on a world tour. Finding out about Mary's affair with Neil did not dampen Chris's ardor. However, Mary and Chris's romance remained turbulent.

After Linda told Bob about Tommy Horton proposing marriage, Bob gave Linda an expensive necklace. Linda, disappointed by Bob's lack of commitment, accepted Tommy's engagement ring.

ABOVE & BELOW: Valerie Grant was engaged to David Banning, but her parents' concerns over interracial romance made the couple reexamine their relationship. Valerie went off to medical school and David married troubled Trish Clayton, who was pregnant with his baby.

Chris Kositchek and Mary Anderson had a turbulent romantic relationship. Neither ever found lasting love in Salem.

Finally, in early October, Don started to get suspicious about Marlena and Samantha so he compared Marlena's current signature to one she had written in prior months. Meanwhile, Samantha got a call for a movie and prepared to leave town. Don and Laura searched for Samantha when they realized she had made a switch. Luckily, they managed to find her, convinced Dr. Powell of what had happened, got Marlena released and Samantha arrested.

Salem's new residents, Fred and Jean Barton, had an abusive, co-dependent relationship. After several months of counseling with a battered wives group, Jean finally left Fred. Within a short time, Jean agreed to a trial weekend with her husband. Unfortunately, during an argument, Fred tripped over a suitcase and fell down the stairs. In spite of emergency brain surgery performed by Dr. Bill Horton at the hospital, Fred remained paralyzed. Fred decided to serve Bill with a malpractice suit. Jean stayed with him to care for him while he was disabled.

When Bill and Dr. Kate Winograd, an anesthesiologist, became romantically involved, it didn't take long for Laura and Bill to start arguing over her. He felt Laura had been spending too much time and attention on her work and clients. Still, she felt that was no excuse for Bill to take up with Kate.

After Marlena got back on an even keel, she called her parents in Denver and explained Samantha's problems. Once released on bail, Samantha went to stay with the Evanses until the hearing date. During the hearing Samantha cracked up and was placed in a mental hospital in Colorado. There had been too many arguments between Don and Marlena over Samantha, and how she had completely duped him. They split up until things were finally settled between them in early December.

Doug lost the liquor license for his club and was forced to close it. Julie decided to help him redecorate and turned it into Doug's Coffee House. After Julie bought the club, she was able to get a temporary liquor license. When Doug left for business in Detroit, Julie and Robert often disagreed over the management of the club. Larry Atwood, a sculptor and schemer with crime organization ties, new to Salem, orchestrated problems for Doug so he could get close to Julie. He then helped her get through the labor strike and advised her on other management issues. Jeri, fed up with discord at the club, and siding with Larry at every turn to win his romantic favor, asked to be let out of her singing contract.

In December, Bradley asked Don to run for the state senate. After several weeks of deliberation, Don announced his candidacy and plans to marry Marlena. While Don tended to his new career, Marlena visited her parents and childhood home in Denver. In the bedroom she had shared with Samantha, Marlena grew melancholy. Eyeing the posters of Elvis and Simon & Garfunkel on the wall, their twin beds still made up in the linens she remembered, framed photos of both Samantha and Marlena in riding clothes on dresser, Marlena's heart melted. She loved her sister and sorely missed her. The next day, Marlena visited Samantha in the Hillcrest Sanitarium and they shared a touching reconciliation.

After recuperating from his heart attack, Tom Horton decided not to retire after all and was reinstated at the hospital. Larry and Jeri started a romance that Jeri took more seriously than Atwood ever intended. And in Wisconsin, Doug was picked up on a drug charge. It was a frame-up, arranged by Atwood who wanted to keep Doug away from Salem and Julie for as long as possible.

Doug Williams made the first Salem headline of the year with: LOCAL ENTERTAINER HELD IN DOPE BUST. He hired Mickey, who flew to Wisconsin for the hearing and managed to get Bill back to Salem, but not before Larry Atwood caused devastating problems for Julie. Before Doug returned, Larry took Julie out to dinner and told her that he loved her. Jeri saw them and absolutely seethed with jealousy. She continued to spy on them and, days later, saw Julie go to Larry's studio. Heartbroken and angry, Jeri drove away before Julie was raped by Larry, who was a complete scoundrel. Julie suffered the secret trauma in silence and withdrawal from everyone.

Just prior to this, Julie fired Arlo Roberts, who had been working for Atwood, spying on Julie and the workings of Doug's Place. Chris and Mary found Roberts battered and bleeding. They took him to the hospital, but as soon as he was fixed up, he disappeared without explanation.

When Doug returned and Julie rejected him, he thought it had to do with his arrest. However, Julie insisted that was not the case, but refused to say more. So, when Jeri sent Doug a letter laying out what she believed was an affair between Julie and Larry, it almost seemed to make sense. When Larry threatened Julie, she finally broke down and told Doug about the rape. At the same time, Jeri confronted Larry about his relationship with Julie. Then, shortly after Doug went to see Larry, Atwood was found dead. In no time at all, Julie was arrested. Julie got some counseling from Laura to help her get over the trauma of the rape, Doug's emotionally cool reaction to it, and the homicide arrest. During Julie's courtroom testimony, details of her rape came out. Shortly afterward, private investigator Ted McManis found Atwood's henchman Arlo and, after meeting with Julie, he confessed to killing Atwood. Jeri, fully understanding the facts, tried to kill herself with an overdose, but Marlena and Don found her in time.

Fred Barton was actually able to walk after his fall down the stairs, and though he was always looking for a quick buck, he finally dropped the malpractice suit against Bill Horton. Jean went back to group counseling, and dropped him once and for all. But a lot of damage had already been done. Bill, suspended from the hospital because of the suit, was drinking more as unpaid bills mounted. Then he walked out on Laura and moved in with Kate. After only a few weeks, Bill realized he still loved Laura and began to repair their relationship.

Smearing Don's public image, columnist Arlene Harris ran the story of Don's relationship with Marlena and her trouble-making twin Samantha. Realizing he was now a public figure, Don moved out of Marlena's gatehouse, but the two became engaged. Not long after that, Harris had more to write about. When Don's former girlfriend Lorraine Temple saw Don's picture in the newspaper, she flew to Salem to talk to him about the daughter, Donna, he never knew he had. This caused some friction between Don and Marlena, but they got over it. Then Lorraine brought the girl to town and contacted Harris, who broke the story of Don's past affair and

1978

Larry Atwood was a sculptor and a schemer who caused legal problems for Doug and raped Julie before being shot to death.

daughter. Marlena stood by him through the bad publicity. After Lorraine left Salem, Donna stayed and had trouble adjusting. The Craig-Evans wedding came to a halt when Marlena left Don at the altar because someone was threatening to jump off the hotel roof. When it turned out to be Donna, Don also rushed to the scene and fell while pulling her to safety. Luckily, he survived after emergency surgery and an adverse reaction to medications that left him temporarily deaf. Donna went into counseling with Laura and eventually went to live with the Hortons. Meanwhile, between personal and recurrent health problems from his fall, Don was knocked out of the state senate election race.

Bob's heart problem was worse so Linda took more control of business matters at Anderson Manufacturing. After a clash with David, she had him transferred. She then promoted Chris to have more control over him. Whether it was love of Bob or her need for power, Linda married Bob at the end of April and the couple honeymooned in Italy. Shortly after their return, their new house burned down and, at Neil's suggestion, they moved into the lake house.

By late spring, Maggie and Mickey's marital problems had eased, but they had new woes over their foster daughter, Janice. Joanne Barnes, her natural mother, came to Salem and, after manipulating the child into keeping their chats in the park a secret, kidnapped her. Luckily, Janice had mentioned her "fairy godmother" and their planned trip to Disney World to Hope, who told Laura. Hank, Maggie and Mickey's farmhand, remembered a woman he'd run into at the general store. Armed with a composite sketch, the search began. Meanwhile, Joanne had a heart attack in her Florida motel and was taken to the hospital where the FBI caught up with her. Maggie, Mickey, and Janice were reunited, but Joanne came back to Salem for the operation she needed. When she was fully recovered, Mickey asked her to leave town, but Hope had told Janice that Joanne was her real mom and the child became curious to know her better. After Joanne left the hospital, she stayed in Salem and often talked with Janice on the phone. When she was stronger, she took a job as housekeeper for Linda and Bob. That put her in proximity to Janice through Linda's daughter Melissa. The situation was too much for Maggie, and drove her to drink.

While Doug and Julie visited Paris, they saw her brother Steve, who immediately hit up Doug for a loan, then returned to Salem with them. At Doug's Place, Steve skimmed the till and made it look as if the waitress Theresa did it. When Julie thought about starting her own business, Steve encouraged her. When she opened an antiques and gifts shop in the fall, Steve went to work for her and used every trick possible to make money for himself. For starters, he had cheap, fake antiques made and sold them to Julie at a high price.

Trish left David a letter and took off with Scotty earlier in the year. Then Jeri left town and joined them. Finally, in August, private investigator McManis found them in Los Angeles. By the time David got there, he had missed Trish who had gone to do a movie in Italy, but he brought Scotty back to Salem with him. Once home, he got help baby-sitting from Julie and Amy, Chris's niece.

Margo Anderman, whom Mike had been dating since late last year, was hospitalized for tests and diagnosed with leukemia. Mike proposed marriage and they wed in July. Mike, however, was in denial about the prognosis of her illness.

By September, Maggie's drinking was out of control. She had a small kitchen fire, then a car accident. Janice was with her and was brought to the hospital unconscious, and Maggie was arrested and booked. Arguments with Mickey mounted. The accident made the newspapers and Joanne visited Janice in the hospital. Seeing her daughter's safety jeopardized, Joanne went to Legal Aid and started proceedings to regain custody of Janice. Even though Joanne had the kidnapping charges against her, she built a case pointing out Maggie's drinking, kitchen fire, drunk driving felony, and Mickey's mental breakdown. Joanne used Janice's innocent conversations to check on whether Maggie was still drinking. Although in counseling with Laura, Maggie was still unable to stay away from liquor.

Neil's distant cousin Pete Curtis came to Salem and dated Donna. After a few weeks, she was spending nights and weekends with him while lying to Alice about her whereabouts. When she became pregnant and confronted Pete, he suggested an abortion; when she refused, he left town. Soon after, she stole some pills from Dr. Tom Horton and she disappeared, too. When she returned, Don threatened to put her into Juvenile Hall as a wayward minor. When Donna explained she was pregnant, he finally told her he believed she was his daughter and pulled out a birth certificate he'd hunted down after he heard Lorraine's story. He postponed his wedding to Marlena to focus on Donna's problems. By December, after Don confronted him, Pete had returned to Salem with the promise to marry Donna.

At Anderson Manufacturing, Linda's management style and the ecologically questionable Greenoaks project caused dissension. Chris left to start his own busi-

Don Craig's wedding to Dr. Marlena Evans was interrupted when his daughter Donna threatened to jump off a building. She was talked down. He fell down and had a prolonged stay in the hospital after a bad reaction to medications.

David dated Stephanie Woodruff, a truly two-faced troublemaker, after her brief fling with Chris fizzled.

ness, and Mary helped him out at his company while their romance continued its turbulent course. A new face in Salem, Stephanie Woodruff, was hired at the Anderson plant and David started dating her. But after a TV debate with Chris Kositchek over Greenoaks, she set her sights on him. Meanwhile Bob, in the hospital after a severe heart attack, told Chris he wanted him back in charge of the plant; Chris refused at first, then came around. Bob managed to talk his daughter Mary into returning, but then gave his power of attorney to Linda. While Bob was still hospitalized, Linda started a not terribly discreet affair with Neil. Mary and Stephanie became immediately suspicious, but kept the truth from Bob to spare him stress. Besides, they were involved in their own tug of hearts over Chris. When Mary refused to go off to a convention in Dayton with him, Stephanie showed up unexpectedly and joined him for dinner and dessert in his hotel room. When Mary got wind of Stephanie's plan, she took off for Dayton, but it was too late.

Dr. Greg Peters and his wife, Amanda, left Salem when he landed a chief-of-staff position in a Chicago medical center. Then, after some Horton family concern and disagreement, Tom accepted the position of University Hospital's chief-of-staff and gave Bill the chief-of-surgery post.

Maggie had made some progress with her drinking problem, but as the custody hearing approached, she skipped her Alcoholics Anonymous meetings and fell off the wagon. Worse, she tried to leave town with Janice. When Maggie failed to show up in court, a continuance was issued, but the following day the newspaper headline read: MOTHER RUNS OFF WITH ADOPTED DAUGHTER. A photo with the story alerted a gas station attendant who, recognizing Maggie, called the Horton house. Tom headed to the nearby town of Fairfield and brought them back. But that crisis was no sooner settled when another tragedy struck. While Janice was visiting Melissa, she fell off the dock and nearly drowned; Chris pulled her out. Janice remained in a coma with possible brain damage, and Maggie and Joanne had an emotional confrontation at the hospital. Afterward Maggie went off to a bar, but left without taking a drink. Instead, distraught and out of control, Maggie tore in to the judge's chambers to plead her case. Although under the circumstances it could have been worse, the judge awarded Joanne custody of Janice—for a six-month period. Maggie became depressed and rejected Mickey sexually. Luckily, to help keep her mind off the loss of Janice, Doug asked her to help him produce the charity benefit show. Although emotionally fragile, Maggie agreed to do all she could.

Mike showed Mickey support by having a heart to heart with him and explaining that he still thought of him as his father, even though Bill was undoubtedly his biological dad. Meanwhile, Mike was optimistic about Margo because her leukemia was in remission. Then, near the end of the year, Mike told Chris he was concerned about the safety of a particular construction site. When the two went to inspect it, the sub-basement collapsed. After many hours of near-fatal danger, they were rescued.

There was plenty going on behind the scenes at Anderson Manufacturing. Linda had secret talks about a possible merger. Stephanie, who continued to date David, tried to sell Chris's carburetor design; then she told Bob and Linda that

Chris himself was trying to sell his plans elsewhere. Linda wanted to fire Chris immediately, but Bob held off. When Mary told Bob about Linda and Neil, he withdrew his power of attorney and hired McManis to investigate his wife's activities.

No one had investigated Steve yet, and he was nose-deep in fake antiques . . . and worse.

Blackmail, greed, pornography, and drugs added to upheavals in the heart of Salem.

With his investigator's report in hand, Bob confronted his wife Linda as she was about to knock on Neil's door. She became so agitated and befuddled that she fell down the stairs. After Dr. Bill Horton performed emergency surgery, Linda conveniently suffered selective amnesia and claimed not to remember her affair with Neil. Bob made Stephanie his executive assistant, replacing Linda, and Mary noticed how much Stephanie reminded her of Brooke. When Bob later ordered a security check at Anderson, it worried Stephanie, who was really Brooke, so much that she burned her hands so she wouldn't be fingerprinted with the rest of the employees. At home, Bob still had warm feelings for Linda, but little trust. Hoping to work things out for Melissa's sake, Neil said good-bye to Linda.

When Trish returned to Los Angeles and found that Jeri had gone back to Salem, she headed back there, too. Almost immediately, she had a major blowup with David over Stephanie and considered kidnapping Scotty. David talked about divorce, but Trish took an apartment across from David's and he backed off from his relationship with Stephanie. By summer, the couple were reconciled and living together again.

Marlena and Don were wed on March fifth and honeymooned in California. First they went up the coast to Carmel then visited Samantha in her show's Los Angeles studio.

Mickey and Maggie, seemingly through their marital problems and together again, got a letter from Joanne relinquishing custody of Janice since the court-ordered six months had passed. However, several close friends counseled Maggie to give up Janice and let her remain with her natural mom.

When Rebecca died, Robert LeClair went to Japan to retrieve Dougie. In Rebecca's safe deposit box Robert found a letter she had written to Doug Williams explaining that he was Dougie's father by artificial insemination performed by Dr. Neil Curtis. Doug later told Robert he had loaned Rebecca $5,000 not to reveal that information, but Neil, who performed the insemination, told Robert that Doug's sperm didn't take.

Mike, blinded by his love for Margo, refused to see the extent of her illness and how dangerously in debt he continued to sink. With a loan from his parents, Mike bought a house. Then he was fired from the garage, but was given a job at Anderson. He immediately bought a new car, even though he was now in debt to more than a half-dozen friends and relatives. Because Trish had once been followed home, David hired Mike part-time to see her home after singing at the club. Still, Mike was often overdrawn at the bank. When a co-worker turned him on to a loan shark, he borrowed enough to pay back some loans and then bought Margo a fur coat.

1979

When a flood devastated nearby Cadensville, Bill and Kate Winograd volunteered to help. Their professional camaraderie only fueled Laura's growing suspicions that something more was going on. Since the first of the year, Laura had been showing signs of severe stress that could not be traced to a physiological cause. She'd been paranoid, alternately snappish and distant, and her work suffered. After her mother, Carrie, committed suicide, Laura started seeing her ghost and hearing her voice. For a time, Laura held herself together just well enough to keep her job, but people were beginning to notice her odd behavior.

Bob's blind trust of Stephanie Woodruff grew. He gave her some Anderson stock never realizing she was the source of a damaging article that had cost Bob a government contract. When she moved into the Andersons' lake house studio, Linda felt threatened and seduced Bob, who told her nothing between them had changed. Linda went to work for Mickey and Don at their law office.

Julie was badly burned when she opened a malfunctioning oven at Maggie's farm. Bill raced to Brookville Hospital and had her transferred back to Salem's University Hospital. While taking care of Julie, Laura, who was becoming more irrational every day, insisted no one else come near her. Laura only made matters worse for vulnerable Julie, who became hysterical when she finally saw her face. Julie was convinced Doug would have nothing more to do with her, and Laura encouraged Julie to leave town. After stealing some pain pills, Julie slipped out. After a call to Steve, he brought her back.

Early in the year, Donna had a miscarriage and was brought to the hospital where Pete Curtis and Don had a confrontation. After saying good-bye to Donna, Pete left Salem and went back to school. Months later, it was clear the experience had disturbed Donna. She gave Tom and Alice some small but expensive pieces of jewelry as gifts. A few weeks later, Donna stole a ring from Chez Julie and gave it to Marlena as a birthday gift. After Steve recognized it, Don and Donna had a confrontation. She promised to clean up her act and make money baby-sitting.

Separated from Dr. Greg Peters, who was in Chicago, Amanda moved in with Chris. Greg visited Salem hoping to mend his marriage but left disheartened when Amanda started divorce proceedings. But as Chris and Amanda became closer, Mary realized that turning down Chris's marriage proposal had been a mistake, and she decided to fight for his love. After an argument, Chris accidentally hit Mary with his Jeep. Amanda wanted no part of the mess and moved into the Salem Inn.

Julie had reconstructive surgery, but the skin graft failed. Despondent, she went to Mexico and got a divorce. When she returned, Dr. Jordan Barr, a new arrival at University Hospital, was aggressive in his approach as a psychiatrist and knocked Julie out of her self-pity.

Meanwhile, Laura's sanity had slipped away to the point of making her dangerous to her daughter. In a mental haze, she put little Jennifer Rose on a bus alone. She accused Marlena of stealing files, demanded money back from Mike, and finally became totally psychotic. With Carrie's ghost urging her on, Laura took an overdose of pills and tried to hang herself with a bathrobe belt. Bill broke down the door and saved her but committed her to Lakewood Sanitarium.

Robert took Dougie on a trip to Paris. Steve joined them, and at an auction met Byron Carmichael, who turned out to be Doug's wealthy half-brother. They talked on the phone and looked forward to getting together in Salem. Unfortunately, Byron died before making the trip. When Carmichael family bar-

Little Jennifer Rose was not anchor enough to keep Laura's mental health from drifting. Years of secrets and fears took their toll on this seemingly strong woman, especially after Bill had an affair with a hospital co-worker and Laura's mother Carrie died in a sanitarium.

rister Desmond read Byron's will to his gold-digging girlfriend Lee, she discovered Byron left his entire fortune to Doug.

Marie Horton was back in Salem. Before she entered the convent in New York, she'd fallen under some bad influences. Unfortunately, one of them, Alex Marshall, also came to Salem and was working at Anderson. Seeing him around town brought back memories about drugs, sadomasochistic behavior, a pregnancy, and the death of Harley, Alex's brother, who fell from a balcony during a heated argument with Alex.

Trish had some diamonds and an unquestioning Margo agreed to hide them for her. Meanwhile, trying to work off some of his own loan, Mike made collections at work for the loan shark, Earl Roscoe. When Mike fell behind in payments, Margo borrowed a diamond to loan Earl as collateral against Mike's debt. Unfortunately, Steve learned from Durand at the Blue Cat nightclub that a singer named Trish Clayton had made off with his gems.

Alex recognized Stephanie as the woman featured in a successful plastic surgery story in a magazine he'd read and invited her to dinner to blackmail her into helping him gain control at Anderson. Although he knew of Bob's serious heart problem, Alex constantly reminded Bob of problems at the plant and pushed him harder. Through Stephanie, Alex also got his hands on a new solar device the company had developed. When Bob suspected Linda of stealing it, he cut her out of his will, leaving everything to Mary. When Linda found out, she pretended to be pregnant.

Marlena and Don were delighted when Marlena became pregnant.

Amanda, also pregnant, went to Chicago to get a divorce from Greg, but he refused, saying the baby was more likely his than Chris's. By late summer, Amanda learned she had a tubal pregnancy and malignancy. After a hysterectomy, Greg gave her a divorce and, although Chris wanted to marry her, she set Chris free as well.

Samantha, who had visited a few times this year, took Donna to Los Angeles for a visit. When the teen returned, she was starstruck and talked about becoming an actress. Samantha had a serious kidney problem and before long needed dialysis and a transplant.

When Simpson, sly drug dealer Durand's henchman, came to collect the canes Steve had brought from Paris, Steve found out Maggie had sold several and had a fit. The canes had been hollowed out and carried cocaine. In a panic, he managed to get them back. He also demanded the diamonds he knew Trish had, but she refused. When Simpson tried to break into the shop's safe, Maggie struggled with him and shot him with his gun.

Margo paid Earl for the one diamond so she could return it to Trish's cache, but what she didn't know was that it was a paste copy. When Mike became further indebted to Earl but refused to make deliveries for him, Earl came to Mike's house and threatened to burn it down. Mike continued to get deep into Earl's illegal dealings. When Earl thought Mike had stolen money from him, Earl fired a shot into the house while Margo was home. Later he had her pushed down the stairs at Anderson.

Cathy, a troubled young friend of Jeri's, came to Salem and quickly became infatuated with Alex. She went to work for him as a maid despite warnings from Maggie and encouragement from Tom to study nursing. When Alex fired her, she went to Chris's apartment, where Stan, Chris's visiting father, seduced her.

Hope wanted Doug and Julie to stay together. Steve also encouraged Julie to stay married—because of Doug's inheritance. Crafty Lee cozied up to Doug, and he promised to share some of the cash after probate. In the interim, she stayed at his apartment, and in a short time they were lovers. Julie casually dated Jordan Barr, but Doug thought it was more serious. By autumn the rest of Julie's surgery was complete. She was shocked when Lee and Doug married on November fifth.

Donna, whose head was filled with dreams of glamour, called a photographer about modeling. Terry Gilbert, who worked for Earl, was soon taking topless shots of her and tried to get her to pose naked. When she refused, Earl had her head superimposed on the photo of another nude model's body. Meanwhile, her father was back in politics, vowing to break up a porno ring that was operating in town.

As the year came to an end, Marie, overcome by all the bitter memories evoked by Alex, was happy to be called back to other duties at the convent.

Melissa overheard Linda trying to convince Neil to put her in the hospital and fake a miscarriage so she could cover her lie to Bob, but Neil refused to be her accomplice in the deceit.

When Robert wanted to take Dougie to Paris, Doug insisted he really was Dougie's father and the two friends argued. Eventually, Robert decided not to take Dougie to Paris. Steve, meanwhile, left Salem after Mary refused to marry him.

Phyllis spent the holidays gambling in Las Vegas, losing her money alongside handsome Corley Maxwell. Back in Salem, Alex kissed Mary at his New Year's Eve party and started another seduction.

Mary and Alex began a romance that left Phyllis out in the cold, and although Mary felt guilty over taking Alex from Phyllis even more successfully than she'd once stolen Neil from her, she and Alex decided to marry. Of course, Alex had his sights on Anderson Manufacturing. Meanwhile, Bob, who provided in his will for Linda and her baby, had found out she was never pregnant and had tried to stage a miscarriage. Bob, in failing health, decided to train Mary to take over greater executive power at Anderson Manufacturing but refused to fire Stephanie, even though she was getting high on the job. Bob gave Chris the go-ahead on the solar project even after Alex told Bob another company was making a similar generator. Phyllis moved back into the Anderson house to take care of Bob, and he proposed they remarry. About the same time, Stephanie confessed to Bob that she was Brooke, his illegitimate daughter; she had not died in the fiery auto crash a year and a half ago. He changed his will: he excluded Linda but provided a settlement for her as long as she and her daughter Melissa left town; they did. He included Stephanie, but she had a car accident and suffered a brain hemorrhage. Mary went to comfort her half-sister in the hospital before she died.

At Alex and Mary's wedding in late March, Bob had a heart attack and died. After Mary accused Phyllis of ruining Bob's life, Phyllis left town. Mary was totally depressed and unable to respond to Alex for weeks.

Anderson Manufacturing, the biggest single industry in Salem, became the focal point of schemes and conflicting activity. One of Alex's former associates,

1980

At first, Neil Curtis may have considered Liz Chandler just another rich and beautiful woman. The affair they began would eventually bring them each much joy, pain, and a daughter.

Ray Stone, wanted a piece of Anderson and blackmailed Alex by threatening to reveal that he had bilked Magnus Enterprises out of $4 million. Bob had left Anderson to Chris, so Alex convinced Chris to make him a partner. Leslie James came to Anderson to work as Chris's assistant. Mary was jealous to see Chris was quite taken with this woman, who soon became his lover.

Wealthy politician Kellam Chandler moved into a large mansion in Salem, then called his daughter Liz to return from Paris. When his campaign manager Maxwell Jarvis offered Don a job with the Chandler Corporation, Don accepted it, even though Marlena felt uneasy about it. At a Chandler party soon after, it became clear that Kellam had his eye on Marlena. That very same night, Liz wasted no time before making a pass at Don. Kellam hired Don and Marlena to work on his campaign staff with every intention of breaking them up. Jarvis and Kellam also planned to take over Anderson through a merger. They helped Alex and David conspire against Leslie and Chris, making certain that the first shipment of the solar generators Chris had designed was forced off the road and missed delivery deadlines.

Six weeks early, Marlena had a two-pound, ten-ounce baby boy, Don Jr., who they called DJ. Three months later, while Don had dinner with Liz, with whom he had a brief affair, Marlena found DJ dead in his crib. It was a case of SIDS, Sudden Infant Death Syndrome. Don and Marlena grew more distant, and separated after grief-stricken Don repeated his verbal attacks against Marlena for not taking better care of herself during her pregnancy. If she had been more responsible, the baby would not have been premature. It would have been strong and survived.

Don also thought he had more problems with his daughter. He got a nude photo of Donna in the mail. When Donna showed her father her portfolio, he was convinced the nude shot must be a faked composite and confronted photographer Terry Gilbert, who denied any knowledge of it. Meanwhile, trying to generate a new look, Trish had Terry take new promotional photos for her. Trish knew he had taken the photos of Donna and bought the negatives from him, but Terry still had a "screen test" Donna had made. In a few days, Don met with Earl, who wanted $5,000 for the film, which Don paid. After one of his legal clients, Lester Hall, told Don about porno theaters showing films to minors, Don considered using Donna's picture as an example in his political campaign against pornography. Don was stunned when the mayor told him to back off his cleanup campaign.

Mike told Mickey all about his involvement with Earl, then he and Margo went to hide away at the Brookville farmhouse for a while. Also, Mimi Grossett came to Trish to get the diamonds for Durand. When she discovered one diamond was fake, she told Trish, who figured out Earl's scam in conning Margo out of money and a gem. Trish confronted Earl who, afraid one of his many illegal operations would land him in jail, burned his office and left Salem in a hurry.

Robert and Doug resolved their battle over Dougie when Robert made Doug the boy's guardian in the event of Robert's death. The one condition: Doug would never reveal his paternity. Eventually, Robert placed Dougie in a boarding school and went back to Paris.

Others left Salem as well. Cathy, who was pregnant by Stan after his attack, went to Chicago where she became engaged and settled down. Donna went to live with her Grandma Craig. And Bill, saddened by Laura's mental collapse and haunted by so many memories in Salem, took a position at Lakewood. He left his daughter Jennifer Rose to be raised by his parents. Dr. Tom Horton returned to private practice. He and Alice celebrated their fiftieth wedding anniversary with a renewal of marriage vows. Laura was allowed to leave the sanitarium for the Horton party.

Just before returning to Salem earlier in the year, Sister Marie approached Mother Superior and asked her for information about where her baby daughter had been placed after she gave her up at birth. Mother Superior refused to tell her. Then Marie tried, on her own, to find information about Angelique Horton in the Canadian hospital's records office. Unfortunately, she found nothing. Months later, Marie got a letter regarding a Jessica Blake who was to interview for a student nursing position at the hospital. Jessica passed the enrollment test, and when Alex learned she was adopted but now alone, he secretly sponsored her tuition through Tom. Marie, however, knew that Jessica was the daughter she had given up at birth.

Doug closed Doug's Place and opened a casino at the old Chisholm mansion, which Julie redecorated. Elderly Mrs. Chisholm, who'd known the Chandlers for decades, was allowed to continue living in one of the wings of the house. She often seemed frightened, as if threatened by someone, but refused to explain. When an intruder was discovered in Mrs. Chisholm's wing of the mansion, Joshua Fallon threw the stranger down the stairs. Soon after, Joshua found evidence that his father, Kellam Chandler, was involved in the death of his mother, Sunny. Josh also discovered that spoiled, troublesome Tod Chandler was actually his full brother.

By then, Joshua had started dating Jessica. They met in the hospital when he had a near fatal attack of recurrent malaria, a remnant of his military service in Vietnam. Once he recovered and was discharged, he and Jessica often double-dated with Cassie, Jessica's new friend, and Tod.

Alex and Marie had a confrontation over money he was giving Jessica, and Tom added the girl to his will. But Alex remained in the dark about his paternity for many months, even though he noticed how much attention the Hortons showered on this shy young woman. Jessica was also the one subject Alex could discuss with Marie that brought willing response. He was still very attracted to Marie and even confessed to her that she had been the only women he had ever really loved. Although she discouraged Alex in every way possible, Marie still had deep feelings for the scoundrel.

In midsummer, after a series of unsuccessful chemotherapy sessions, Mike's wife, Margo, died of leukemia. And Samantha, who had been in Salem on and off through the year, had a serious kidney problem. When a suitable donor was found, she was rushed to the hospital for a kidney transplant. She survived and went back to acting within a few months.

The affair Liz had with Don was brief, but quite taken by Neil, they became lovers. Liz actually proposed to Neil, but Kellam bribed Neil to stay away. Although he took no money, Neil encouraged Liz to help her father in his campaign. Neil was very upset after losing Liz, but he turned back to his favorite compulsive pastime, gambling, and got himself deeper in debt.

Jarvis considered Leslie's influence an obstacle to his goals at Anderson, so he planned to get rid of her. He had her assaulted during a fire in the machine room of the plant. Later, she got threatening phone calls in her hospital room. When she recovered, Leslie had no intention of leaving town. Instead, she moved in with Chris and they became engaged. But continued pressure from Jarvis interfered with her relationship with Chris and she abruptly left town after all.

Doug started to doubt Lee's sincerity and told her he thought the marriage had been a mistake. When Julie decided to fight to win Doug back, Lee never stood a chance. Soon Doug realized he still loved Julie; they wanted very much to get married again, but Lee refused to give Doug a divorce. In fact, Lee hired her ex-lover, Brent Cavanaugh, to come from Atlanta and murder Julie. He followed

Gold digger Lee Dumonde came to Salem to get her hands on the money Doug inherited from his half-brother Byron Carmichael. She hired a hitman to kill Julie, but he failed, only wounding her.

her for several days and then lay in wait at the darkened club one night. He shot her in what looked like a robbery attempt and immediately left town. After emergency surgery, Julie survived. Lee's anger over the failed plot pushed her to put herself in potentially fatal danger. In a ploy to win Doug's sympathy, Lee mixed her medications, accidentally had a stroke, and was left partially paralyzed. Lee turned her defeat to victory by convincing Doug her stroke was the result of loving him so much and fearing she was about to lose him. Doug told Julie he could not possibly divorce Lee while she was ill.

David and Trish had been arguing over her desire to more aggressively pursue her career. Their marriage was turbulent, but David, with his bonuses for spying on Kellam for Alex, always managed to come up with an expensive bracelet or other special surprise to make up for their disagreements. Eventually, Mary opposed the Chandler takeover of Anderson and kicked Alex out and sought a divorce. She also told David to get out of town when she discovered he had been working for Alex. Because he realized he had failed some dangerous people, David feared for his life. He deserted Trish and left Salem.

Lots of new faces appeared in Salem this year. And so did plenty of deception
and danger. Renee Dumonde, Lee's estranged younger sister, arrived in town
soon after Lee had her stroke. Brent, after cosmetic surgery, came back too. Using
the name Brad, he intended to finish his contracted killing of Julie and collect the
$150,000 Lee promised him for the kill. As Lee recuperated, she began to walk
but kept it a secret from Doug. Julie, meanwhile, had been on several casual dates
with Brad, whom she considered just a bit odd. She certainly didn't recognize
him as Brent, the man who shot her. When he tried again to kill her, Julie was
shocked to see Lee walk, then actually leap, at Brad. Lee was knocked unconscious. When Doug arrived on the scene, Brad was going to kill him too, but Lee
regained consciousness and killed Brad. For all her trouble, Lee was put into
Bayview Sanitarium while Doug and Julie moved in together.

Chris signed away his rights to the solar generator design and left
Anderson. He and Josh Fallon became partners and opened a health club, The
Body Connection.

Unaware he was her natural father, Alex legally adopted Jessica before
Marie told him Jessica was his natural daughter. Marie made him promise not to
tell Jessica the full truth. Meanwhile, the attraction between Marie and Alex
remained undeniable, so Marie went off on retreat. When she returned, Alex
made her admit that she had missed him. He wanted her to leave the convent so
they could be together again, but Marie refused. She did agree to go with Alex to
the orphanage where Jessica was originally placed to learn more about how she
was raised. They took off for Montreal in a small rented plane and it crashed.
When they survived and found refuge in a mountain cabin, they reminisced
about a ski trip they once took. To keep warm, they slept in the same small bed
and soon exchanged "I love you's" but before they could consummate a new commitment, rescuers arrived. Back in Salem, Marie told her family about her relationship with Alex and that Jessica was their child.

Alex found out the plane had been sabotaged, blamed Kellam Chandler,
and assaulted him. Kellam had even bigger troubles. He argued violently with Liz
until Don intervened, then tried to make Tod believe Liz had also turned against
him. Later, at Marlena's, Kellam was still enraged over his family. When Marlena
refused sex with him, he raped her. Josh, meanwhile, had followed Kellam wanting revenge for his role in his mother's suicide. Josh held a gun on his father but
could not pull the trigger and dropped the gun. Kellam picked up the weapon
and had pointed it at Josh just as Tod came through the door and lunged at his
dad. When the gun went off in the struggle, Kellam was killed. Tod explained to
Don how Kellam's death came about and they all agreed to keep the rape a secret.
Later, Marlena told Tod that he and Josh were half-brothers. He was hurt that
Josh had not told him the truth as soon as he found out. In Kellam's will, the
estate was divided equally between Tod and John Talbot, Jr., who is Josh.
Chandler family attorney Jarvis, however, tried to have the will declared invalid
because he had been given false information about John Talbot, Jr., whom he
believed to be eight years old.

Trish, back from several out-of-town singing jobs, tracked David to San
Diego where she was appalled to find him carrying a gun. She stole Scotty back
from him and returned to Salem, staying with Julie and Doug while she sought
full custody of Scotty and a divorce. David came back too. He turned down a job

with Alex, choosing to stay employed by Stuart Whyland, who was the new administrator of Salem's University Hospital.

Although she'd divorced him, Mary hated seeing Alex and Marie together. She orchestrated a scenario in which Marie saw her wearing only a sheet when she arrived at Alex's place. Alex set the record straight, but Mary was not about to give up.

In spite of Marie's protests, Alex told Jessica that he was her natural father. She happily accepted him but swore never to forgive Marie for giving her up and keeping the truth from Alex. After a confrontation with Jessica, Marie went to Montreal and came back without her habit and planning to marry Alex. However, Jessica left town and Marie insisted they wait until she returned before marrying. Mary found out that Jessica had entered a convent, but after Marie visited Mother Superior, Jessica was dismissed.

Maggie decided she wanted to bear a child through Dr. Neil Curtis's surrogate mother program. Marie warned her about the pain of giving up a baby and, at first, Mickey was resistant to the whole idea, but gave in. Soon, Maggie was pregnant.

Lee was discharged from the sanitarium in time for Doug and Julie's second wedding. She lurked in the background unnoticed as guests arrived at Doug's house, then managed to detain Julie in the den. Doug found them, locked Lee inside and she watched from the window as Doug and Julie were wed. The couple took off for a fun and romance-filled honeymoon in Japan. On their return, Lee apologized for her behavior, but she had managed to turn Hope against Julie. Hope chose to live with Tom and Alice rather than with her dad and Julie.

There was other trouble in Salem. Marlena received the first of many unsettling phone calls from a mystery caller to her radio show. She also started to receive threatening letters, and a young woman was found strangled. And Jessica became busy enough for three people: Jessica, Angelique, and Angel, her split personalities. In counseling with Marlena, the Jessica personality usually maintained tight control. Angelique was a taunting and negative influence. When she prowled the seedy bars at night, she called herself Angel and attracted Jake Kositchek's attention. Jake, Chris's brother, came to town when he read of Chris's health club success.

Stuart Whyland bought the Chandler mansion and the marina and showed interest in Chris's inventions. He also started to date Lee. His son Evan, a sullen widower, came to town and became friends with Maggie. That concerned Dr. Curtis, who knew Evan was the sperm donor for Maggie's surrogate baby. Before long, Evan learned Maggie was carrying his child and doted upon her.

Although Marie and Alex planned to elope, Mary made sure Marie saw her kiss Alex. Infuriated,

OPPOSITE: **A**fter their sabotaged plane crashed on a mountaintop, Alex and Marie spent the night together in a single bed in a cold cabin. She could no longer deny she wanted to rekindle a romance with her daughter's dad.

BELOW: **D**oug and Julie wed for the second time in a lovely garden setting while his exwife Lee was locked in a den in the house.

Women were being strangled in Salem and Dr. Marlena Evans got disturbing phone calls at her radio talk show and at home. Eventually, she was terrorized by a more graphic threat.

Marie told Alex he would never make a fool of her again and rushed out of his office. In a short time, Alex was found shot—Renee walked in just as David was picking up the gun and he was arrested.

In the hospital, when Alex woke from his coma, he had no memory of who shot him, and he was paralyzed from the waist down. Once home, Marie moved in with him but refused sex and postponed the wedding. Angel (Jessica) began a campaign of harassment. She left graffiti on their door and made late-night phone calls.

While David was out on bail, Mary gave Don Alex's file on David Banning. Don asked David about the judge who was bribed to get David off drug charges in Los Angeles, but David refused to tell him because of threats against Trish and Scotty. David was convicted and sentenced to seven years in prison. Harry, David's cellmate in the local jail, caused the car taking them to the state penitentiary to crash and David escaped, then hid in the basement of the radio station where Renee found him and kept him hidden. A thug was following Trish and, posing as a detective, he arranged a meeting. Mike, who still cared for Trish and kept an eye on her, arrived in time to keep him from kidnapping Trish and Scotty.

Angel turned against Jessica and threatened to kill her and Angelique. Hope, curious about Jake's girlfriend, found out Angel was really Jessica and told Marie. At the same time, Jake proposed to Angel and they took off for Las Vegas, after Jake took care of some "personal business" he kept secret from Angel. When Jessica called Alex, Marie rushed to the Vegas wedding chapel and stopped the ceremony. Jessica fell apart.

In Salem, a second woman was found strangled, and Marlena, showing signs of deep stress, got a letter saying the woman's death was all her fault. Soon after, Tod forced his way into her apartment and pulled the phone from the wall. Don came to the rescue and Tod, who had no memory of the event, was arrested. In a few days, Marlena got another call. Tod had problems, but he was not the person harassing Marlena—he had an alibi for the nights of the stranglings.

David, disguised and with his hair dyed, went to see Trish and Scotty. Later, back at his own place packing, someone tried to shoot him. When Mickey and Mike arrived, they found blood on the windowsill, but not David, who had made his way back to the Twilight Bar where Nick Corelli removed the bullet then called Julie for $50,000 to guarantee David's safe return. Nick got intern Valerie Grant, David's former fiancée, to treat David's wound then threatened her with a gun to get David to his feet and to the warehouse for the exchange. Valerie hit Nick with her medical bag and his gun went off. When police responded, they found Nick drugged on the cellar floor. Valerie hid David at her apartment and brought him the $10,000 from his mother, Julie, so he could buy whatever he needed to be safe or leave town.

The son of crime boss Stefano DiMera, Tony, came to Salem because he wanted his wife Liz back. He also intended to further his business holdings, which had been managed by Stuart Whyland. Tony immediately found a $25,000 error in Stuart's hospital financial records. Around the same time, Eames, one of Stuart's employees, went to Stuart's office to demand more money for mysterious "services rendered." Alex, who was at the hospital for more surgery, recognized him as the man who shot him and confronted Stuart. But Stuart blackmailed Alex with threats to his family if he didn't help him acquire Anderson Manufacturing and tell police that David—now also suspected in the stranglings—was the person who shot him.

Marlena continued to get threatening phone calls and then a graphic message: a doll with a broken neck hung by a silk scarf from her curtain rod. The strangler struck again, killing Lori, who had started dating Evan. Salem police officer Roman Brady and Don were with Marlena when she got still another call. Roman camped overnight on her living room floor as part of his police assignment.

Valerie confronted Neil about a patient who died on the operating table. Neil denied his drinking and gambling to Tom, the chief-of-staff. Neil told Valerie to go to Tom and clear him or he would expose her involvement with David and ruin her career. Valerie told Tom the truth, however, and that Neil had tried to blackmail her.

Tony DiMera overwhelmed Renee with flowers for her birthday. Lee was furious and warned her to stay away from Tony, but he then gave Renee a diamond necklace. While bathing after the party, Renee was grabbed by the strangler and left unconscious when Lee happened to walk into the room, interrupting his attempt to kill Renee.

David, tired of running and hiding, went to Mickey's office and gave himself up. Meanwhile, Alex admitted to Tony that David hadn't shot him. Stuart left town and Tony took over Stuart's business interests, which were actually all backed by DiMera money. Tony also became the new owner of the Twilight Bar and made Trish the manager. Danny Grant was hired as bartender.

Dr. Evan Whyland was unaware that his father, Dr. Stuart Whyland, had made a $25,000 "accounting error" with the hospital's funds. It would come back to haunt them both.

Meanwhile, Maggie delivered a baby girl. Mickey overheard Neil and Evan talk about the daughter that Maggie bore Evan and realized Evan was the father. When Maggie told Mickey she wanted to keep the baby, Mickey said he would help her.

Don, who had married Liz only a few months ago, agreed to divorce her after seeing her in a robe at Tony's place. A few days later, Tony happily threw a gala New Year's Eve party with Liz as hostess. As the festivities began, at the hospital the strangler ripped the IV from Renee, but was interrupted again, this time by hospital personnel, and didn't kill her. And Jake, claiming he had a flat tire, finally picked up Jessica to take her to the party, a bit late.

1982

Stefano DiMera changed everyone and everything he touched. With the world as his oyster, Salem became the pearl born of grit, pressure, and constant irritation. He played with it, worried it, and could dispose of it with the flick of his little finger.

The Salem Strangler continued to terrorize the town, but the arrival of Stefano DiMera changed many residents forever.

Don and Officer Roman Brady found Marlena's client Eugene Bradford's apartment walls covered with newspaper clippings about the stranglings while Eugene was kidnapping Marlena at knifepoint. After Roman and Don rescued Marlena, Eugene confessed to the stranglings, but phone calls and murders continued while Eugene was hospitalized in the psychiatric ward.

Since their divorce had never been finalized, Tony and Liz were still married and her wedding to Don Craig was invalid. Tony forced Liz to live with him at the DiMera mansion. They kept separate bedrooms and Tony set his sights on Renee. Stefano insisted that Tony wait before letting Liz go because she would be useful in helping him get Doug's Place. Stefano threatened her with harm to Neil and Don if she refused to spy on Doug for Stefano. Liz did manage to help Neil. At the casino, Liz slyly dropped her purse and Neil picked up the $50,000 that fell out to pay gambling debts.

After Lee introduced Stefano as an old friend from Europe and they renewed their lusty liaison, Lee told Marlena that Renee was her daughter by Stefano. She also told Tony to stay away from Renee, but he would not, so Lee told Stefano that Renee was his daughter.

A secret room in the DiMera mansion set Julie and Doug on a mystery adventure. After Julie showed Doug the hidden chamber they found Horton and Brady family trees, a detailed history of Anderson Manufacturing, aerial shots of Salem, and a picture of their friend Robert LeClair stuffing money into a sack. Later, Robert told them he'd made Swiss bank deposits for Stuart on several trips to Europe. It had been the money Whyland stole from the hospital.

Stuart, out of town but still orchestrating events in Salem, ordered Eames to kill David, who'd escaped from jail. However, Stefano was attracted to Julie, so he spared David, knowing it would please her, and put a hit on Eames. After a bloody gunfight between hitmen and police, Officer Abe Carver was critically wounded, but he survived. Meanwhile, Renee, out of her coma, cleared David of accusations of assaulting her and charges against him were dropped.

After Mary was strangled, Linda and Phyllis came back from

New York. Melissa ran away from school and returned to Salem as well. Mary had left Anderson equally to Phyllis and Melissa. Evan wanted to keep Sarah, but Maggie and Mickey won custody of the girl. Later, the couple also got custody of Melissa. Mike thought about going to medical school and started to make plans. Hope also thought it best to leave Salem for a while.

Jake, prowling in many Salem homes, discovered the DiMeras' secret room and also found the passage from there to the wine cellar in Doug's Place. He again tried to kill Renee, and this time she saw his face, but her memory suppressed the image. Fearful she was in danger, Tony took her into hiding.

Doug and Julie duplicated the coded geological maps they'd found and located the map-maker's wife, Mitzi Matuso, who thought her husband's suicide was really murder. Doug and Julie pretended to separate so Doug could lead Mitzi on to get more information. But she and her cousin Hal planned to get Doug's money and the goods under the casino for themselves. Mr. Matuso had told Stuart about titanium deposits under Doug's Place. Stuart lied to Stefano, and killed Matuso, wanting the mineral money himself. Unfortunately, there was no titanium.

Jessica, who was recovering her mental health, decided she really loved Josh and broke her engagement to Jake. Shortly thereafter, she became engaged to Josh.

When Marlena planned a trip to Mexico, Jake found out and planned to follow. He also stole Marlena's housekey from Salem newcomer Gwen Davies

David Banning escaped from jail after being arrested for shooting Alex. Renee helped him with food and clothes until she was attacked. David was then suspected of being the Salem Strangler.

Hope wanted to find out about Jake Kositchek's new girlfriend Angel, and discovered it was really Jessica. However, Hope did not learn about Jake's own deadly secret until much later.

who had been staying with her. When Jake realized Marlena hadn't taken the flight, he went to her apartment and strangled Samantha, thinking she was Marlena, who had actually gone to visit her parents in Boulder, Colorado. When she returned, Jake cornered Marlena at gunpoint at her home. Roman saw the situation from outside, and in the struggle that followed, Jake shot himself. Marlena went into shock. Chris blamed himself for the way Jake turned out. Roman grieved too, since Jake was his first shooting as a police officer.

Roman and Marlena went to Mazatlán, but at first Marlena backed away romantically, feeling she wasn't emotionally ready. She felt responsible for Jake's victims, especially Samantha. Back in Salem, Roman asked Marlena to wait for him while he cleared up something from his past. He asked Mickey to have his missing wife declared dead, a procedure that would take at least a month, then he told Marlena of his plans to be legally free to wed again and asked her to marry him.

After Tony proposed to Renee, she read Lee's letters and learned the truth. Heartbroken, Renee kept their genetic relationship a secret and told Tony she felt gratitude, not love. Tony was devastated and blamed Stefano for not controlling Lee, who Tony felt influenced Renee. Tony went to Lee's penthouse and read her letter but refused to believe it. But Renee showed him Lee's diary and her birth certificate. Tony acknowledged Lee as Renee's mom but refused to believe that Stefano was her father. Stefano had told Renee to keep the secret and, alone, exploded over Lee's deception. Blood tests seemed to prove that Renee and Tony were siblings. Stefano threw a coming-out party for Renee and his announcement shocked everyone. He gave her his mother's pearls and insisted that both Tony and Renee, his children, stay in Salem. When Tony refused, Stefano collapsed, faking a heart attack.

On the rebound from Tony, Renee gave in to her attraction to David, who turned his back on Kayla, Brady Roman's sister. Kayla then found solace with Chris. Trish took up with singer Woody King, who used her to further his own career.

Anna Brady suddenly turned up in Salem, saying she was back to divorce Roman and leave their four-year-old daughter Carrie with him. Anna claimed she had been forced into white slavery and kept prisoner on a yacht owned by European drug dealers. Carrie was taken from her for six to twelve months at a time. Roman's police partner and friend, Abe, didn't believe her and when Roman later found cash and a Swiss bank deposit slip with Anna's name on it, he had doubts as well. But Roman saw the scars on her back from beatings and swore to kill the people who had done that to her. Anna hid the secret that she had multiple sclerosis.

When Liz pressed Tony for a divorce and threatened to leave, Stefano arranged to have a bomb blow up in Neil's hotel room. Then Tony slapped Liz around and raped her. The terrorized Liz then told friends that Neil's gambling was the reason she'd turned him away and went to Tony. Neil, in his hospital bed, vowed to kill Tony for stealing Liz's love. Don confronted Liz about the arrangement and promised to help her prove that the DiMeras were responsible for the explosion that injured Neil.

Melissa's boyfriend Oliver Martin told her he'd used a computer to steal money from the bank he worked for, but had now gone straight. He showed Melissa a secret passage from Doug's Place to the DiMera mansion that he helped

build when the mansion belonged to Stuart. He used the secret room to spy on the DiMeras and gain stock tips. He also got a job working for Chris at Anderson.

When Evan visited Maggie and baby Sarah, he took the opportunity to hide a safe deposit key in her home. Stefano, who had spied on Evan, was suspicious and sent his employee Delia Abernathy to be the new nanny and secretly keep tabs on Maggie for him. Evan showed Stefano a letter that incriminated DiMera in money laundering and Stuart's untimely death and blackmailed Stefano into buying the ring Evan gave Sandy Horton, now a doctor like her dad Tommy Horton, in Salem, for their engagement. Sandy soon overheard hospital gossip about Evan and other women and told Maggie she would kill him if it were true. When she learned it was, Sandy had Maggie return the engagement ring to Evan who, wanting Maggie, told her he was Sarah's biological father. In Evan's car at the time, Maggie almost got killed when it went off a cliff because Stefano's henchmen tampered with the brakes.

At the hospital, Sandy had to operate on Evan, whom she hated. Alex, working for Stefano, switched medical charts so that Evan died on the operating table as a result of an allergy to penicillin. But Sandy was blamed, placed on probation, and lost her surgical privileges until police finally cleared her. When Evan's last words were about Stefano and Caracas, Mickey and Don figured out there was

At Shenanigans, everyone gathered for opening night fun and festivities but outside in the dark the strangler claimed his latest victim, Mary Anderson.

Blue-collar Roman Brady and Dr. Marlena Evans left tragedy behind and enjoyed the early days of their romance in Mazatlán.

some blackmail going on. They also learned that the car's brakes had been disabled. Mickey went to Caracas and when Stefano found out, his men followed. They retrieved Evan's papers, which Stefano later destroyed. They held Mickey prisoner on the DiMera island, but made it look as if he were killed in an accident. They taunted Mickey by showing him photos of his memorial service in Salem.

In mid-November, David and Renee married. Tony, armed with new lab tests, tried to stop the wedding, but he burst into the chapel just as they were pronounced husband and wife. He covered his abrupt entry by saying he had been in an auto accident. Later, Tony told Renee that they were not siblings and kissed her. Unbelieving, Renee left with David for their honeymoon in Paris. While they were gone, Tony told Liz he would give her a divorce but he wanted to keep the baby. Liz, however, realized she was pregnant with Neil's child. Meanwhile, Neil checked hospital records and realized he could be the father of Liz's baby. Liz continued to push him away for his own sake. Marie Horton offered him comfort and they became lovers.

Daphne DiMera, Stefano's ex-commonlaw mistress and Tony's mother, had come to Salem and threatened to sue Stefano for palimony but he ordered her away. She told Marlena that if she turned up dead, it would be Stefano's doing. At least she felt she could help Tony clarify his relationship to Renee and be near him.

After Renee and David came back, Tony made Renee look at the lab results, which contradicted the first set. They were not siblings. But Renee told Tony to leave her alone, even though it was clear she was still attracted to him.

Roman and Anna divorced. Roman and Marlena went on a late November trip back to Mazatlán to celebrate and Anna went to work as Tony's secretary. She had been working for Stefano all along. Except for her illness, which she continued to keep a secret, everything she had said was a hoax. Stefano told her that Roman was an important member of an international crime fighting organization and was dangerous to him. For $1 million, Anna agreed to discredit, but not harm Roman. She then hypnotized Carrie to have her plant deposit slips in Roman's apartment to make it look as though he were a cop on the take. Roman knew he was being set up but played along. He was called before a hearing board, found guilty, and suspended from the force. Realizing Carrie had been used against him, he vowed vengeance. Meanwhile, the International Security Alliance (ISA) still believed in him. Anna's plan hadn't worked and she could not leave Salem until Roman was firmly discredited.

Both Abe and Danny were infatuated with the new police secretary, Nikki Wade. After dinner with her, Danny thought she was a kept woman, but discovered her dad was wealthy Preston James Wade. Nikki asked Abe to take her to the debutante ball and Danny was disappointed. Nikki was too, when Abe left her at the cotillion without a presenter to head off to a drug bust. Unfortunately for all concerned, the drug dealer turned out to be Roman, undercover. The two friends argued because one didn't tell the other their plans. Alex and Stefano focused revenge on Roman.

Orby Jensen, involved with Alex in drug dealing, tricked Danny into making deliveries. Woody, Gwen, and Oliver each had a shady past, but until they decided to band together against their abusive dad Orby who tried to cash in on their success, no one knew they were siblings. Woody was angry that his father had let their mom Esther take a stolen credit card rap for him. Trish felt betrayed by Woody, deciding she no longer wanted to manage Shenanigans and left town for a singing gig.

Through the holiday season, Don had spent a lot of time with Maggie. By Christmas, he realized he was in love, but spent a lonely New Year's Eve watching Maggie with Stefano, who tried to find out if Mickey had managed to contact her. Eugene was with Gwen, and Chris with Kayla. Later, Don went to see Maggie at the lake house and told her of his feelings, which left Maggie bewildered.

1983

Roman Brady and Stefano DiMera were at war. Roman wanted to bring down DiMera's crime organization and sought revenge because DiMera had used Roman's ex-wife Anna, and daughter Carrie, against him. Likewise, DiMera was determined to eliminate trouble-making Brady, and get to him through others he loved if necessary. Roman pretended he'd left Salem Police Department, but he continued to work for the ISA.

Roman's sister Kayla was almost killed after Alex used a robot to poison her. She went into a deep coma, but recovered. Alice Horton was to be the next vic-

Tony was duped into marrying Anna. Renee married David on the rebound because she thought Tony was her brother. The foursome had to live under the same roof to earn Stefano's inheritance.

tim, but Chris came upon Alex tinkering with the robot and Alex backed off. Later, Gretchen, a nurse, was poisoned with the dose intended for Alice after Alex realized she'd overheard his plan.

Liz, still under DiMera control, tried to get evidence that Tony was having an affair with Renee, hoping the proof would help her get a divorce. She took plenty of photos, including a warm kiss Renee had given Tony after he gave her a horse. However, nothing Liz did could win her release from Tony's control.

After his divorce became final, Roman and Marlena planned their wedding, but Alex also had a scheme. Sending an assassin to the tuxedo store was part of it, but Roman recognized the man's face from a mug shot and, after a struggle, the thug was shot dead. At the church, there was another attempt on Roman's life from the choir loft, but after the interruption, the couple succeeded in getting married. Afterward, the new bride went off on her honeymoon with her ex-husband, Don Craig in disguise, while Roman, further enraged by Stefano's latest tactics, went underground to get DiMera.

Roman succeeded in getting evidence about Stefano's criminal activities, then heard that Liz and Marlena had disappeared. An angry Stefano was having them held hostage at his mountain hideout while he made plans to leave Salem by helicopter. Roman and Abe found them just in time. But as the rescue was under way Liz went into labor and delivered a baby girl, but she fell into unconsciousness before she could tell Neil, who had joined the rescue, that he was the father. When Tony found out, he got a fast divorce. Stefano, who had been captured, was in prison when he had a massive stroke and died. Meanwhile, Neil and Marie Horton were having their own affair for several months, and were wed at the Greenbriar Inn.

Don and the apparently widowed Maggie had fallen in love. Then Mickey finally, after repeated attempts, managed to escaped his island prison. When he returned to Salem in March, Mickey found his wife and best friend telling each other of their love. He had a heart attack, but recovered.

When Anna and Tony went to Las Vegas for Woody's opening, Woody helped Anna drug Tony and, with the help of a corrupt justice of the peace, Anna married Tony DiMera. Meanwhile, in Salem, Renee fell from the horse Tony had given her and miscarried David's baby. Lawyers arrived from Paris and read Stefano's will. In order to inherit their due millions, Stefano had stipulated that Tony and Renee had to live together under the same roof for the period of one year. Furthermore, Renee had to stay married to David, whom she had wed on the rebound when she thought she was Tony's sister. There was also a clause that whoever—Tony or Renee—had a child first would receive another $5 million. After seducing David into a brief reconciliation, Renee, David, and Scotty moved into the DiMera mansion with Tony and Anna.

Hope, homesick and in the throes of late-teen rebellion, left school and returned to Salem. When she fell out of her drunken date's car, Roman found her and took her to safety. She immediately became infatuated with him. Later, while baby-sitting for Carrie Brady, Hope became reacquainted with Bo Brady, Roman's younger brother, and the two were amazed to see how each had grown.

Marie and Liz were at open war. Hope overheard Liz tell Neil how much she hated Marie, and at one point Marie and Liz got into a catfight. Neil planned to be loyal to Marie but Liz had other plans when Marie was away. Liz slipped into Neil's place with her own key, got into his bed, and waited. When Neil came home, he was at first angry, but soon they made love. When he was called back to the hospital, Liz, now alone, heard glass break downstairs. With a gun in her hand, she went to investigate. She shot the prowler who turned out to be Marie. Liz called the paramedics and ran away before anyone got there. Daphne helped her ditch the gun in the river. Eventually, Marie recovered but was temporarily paralyzed. Later, Neil vowed his love to Liz when they happened upon each other at a resort and renewed their relationship. Unfortunately, Liz was arrested and tried for attempted murder. Convicted, she was sentenced to five years in jail.

As the struggle over the DiMera millions continued, Renee rigged a boat to sink and kill Anna. However, Tony was also in the boat and was knocked unconscious. David saved both Tony and Anna, who lost the baby she carried. Woody threatened to blackmail Anna over the circumstances of her marriage to Tony. When Tony found out, he divorced Anna, who was truly in love with him.

Eugene started dating Trista, a sweet girl who had troubling, vague childhood memories of seeing her mother murdered. She was being stalked by someone who tried to steal her old letters and other personal items. Bo, now a full-fledged P.I. with Howie Hofstedder's detective agency, continued to investigate the murder of her mother, Barbara Talmadge, and Trista finally remembered hiding the murder weapon. At the moment she retrieved it from inside the grandfather clock, Alex appeared and took it from her. Luckily, Bo happened by at the same time and overpowered him. Eugene later found Alex's former lover, a woman named Nora, who as it turned out, was the one who had killed Barbara in a fit of jealousy over Alex. Eugene and Trista were in love, but the Bradford Curse proved to be a serious obstacle. When Eugene's grandfather died in Haiti, the curse was inherited, seemingly causing people around Eugene to die.

Roman and Marlena's wedding was almost brought to a halt by Stefano's assassins, who tried twice to kill the groom.

Meanwhile, Hope learned Roman was going on a fishing trip. Her friend Jane delayed Marlena, keeping her from joining Roman, and Hope delivered his forgotten rod to the cabin with intentions of seducing him. Roman had in fact just given her a thank-you kiss for her kind deed when Bo and Marlena arrived. Bo impulsively punched his brother, but denied his own attraction to Hope.

Feeling rejected by Tony, and already divorced from David, Renee married Alex. Afterward, she realized Daphne had found a second Stefano will that left her substantial DiMera money without any stipulations. She realized that Alex had known about this and had used her. Renee decided to expose his scheming ways in grand style during a gala at the DiMera mansion. From the staircase, she made the announcement that her new husband was an opportunist who would never touch her again. Then Renee took apart every one of the people she felt had wronged her: Alex, David, Doug, Julie, Anna, Daphne, and the whole Horton family. Her only true love was Tony, and even he had turned her away.

Tony was so impressed by Renee's spirit that he gave her white roses and confessed he still loved her. They made love upstairs befor he rejoined the party. In the stables, meanwhile, Eugene proposed to Trista. But suddenly screams came from the house. Delia was hysterical, crying out "Murder!" Renee was found with a knife in her back, and a large black feather in her hand. Julie immediately confessed, thinking David might be suspected. He was picked up, but didn't even know Renee was dead. Ultimately, the real cause of death turned out to be poison. The knife wound had not been fatal.

Liz slipped into Neil's bed and then accidentally shot his estranged wife, Marie, thinking Marie was an intruder.

Soon after Renee's murder, nurse Kelly Chase, who had evidence of Alex's connection to Stefano and some of the killings, was found dead. Eugene, thinking the Bradford Curse was still at work, went to Haiti to find answers. While there he and Trista got married in a romantic ceremony, but Eugene was grief-stricken when she was found murdered, also holding a black feather.

Back in Salem, Gwen was attacked, escaped unharmed, but a black raven's feather was found at her bedside. Suspicion fell on Eugene and police were after him, but his eccentric cousin Letitia, who had a raven as a pet, took him in. That was a mistake. She too was murdered, and Eugene was taken into custody. But other women continued to be threatened. Sandy was accosted by a would-be rapist, and Pete Jannings, who happened to be nearby, was held for police by Roman.

Neil and Marie divorced. While serving her time, Liz and Neil planned a prison wedding but several other prisoners—Charlene, Gail, and Billie—plotted to use the wedding as an escape. In the melee, Liz was shot. She recovered, but her injury brought on a bout of amnesia that made her think she was married to Don, who was currently with Maggie.

Sandy and Marlena saw a man murder a woman named Daisy. Shocked, they had to admit they had seen Roman. Reluctantly, Abe arrested him, even though Roman vehemently insisted he was being framed.

Tony's mother, Daphne (above), thought Stefano might kill her for coming to Salem. Eugene's Aunt Letitia (left) was the one who turned up murdered.

Marlena stood by her husband in spite of the growing evidence against him. He escaped jail with the help of Alice Horton's famous homemade doughnuts this time, spiked with drugs that simulated heart attack symptoms. Paramedics arrived to take him to the hospital. Then Alice helped block the road, and, unrecognized, Bo drugged the medics and Roman got away to find the real serial killer.

Anna was trying to get out of Salem because Alex was after her for snooping into his connections with Stefano. She had found a letter from Kelly to her sister incriminating Alex, written just a day before Kelly was killed. In Los Angeles, Roman saved Anna from a warehouse fire and they teamed up.

When Melissa found Pete Jannings stealing canned goods from the pantry at Shenanigans, he took her hostage and left town but a snowstorm stranded them alone at the Horton farm. After a hostage drama with police, Pete was arrested for kidnapping. While together at the farm, Pete had confided his troubled youth to Melissa and she grew fond of him. He was eventually released in Chris's custody.

In Salem, Carrie stayed with Marlena. When Carrie slipped on the ice, broke an arm, and was knocked unconscious, Roman managed to sneak into the hospital to see his daughter. Unfortunately, a Salem police detective, Joan, was there, saw Roman, and reported to Alex. Later, back at the cabin, Anna accidentally set off Roman's gun. A ranger came by, but the couple had already left.

Hope and Bo had grown closer, but Bo continued to fight his feelings; however, he did agree to take her to her eighteenth birthday party. He gave her a book of poetry that his father had given him as a sentimental gift. After Bo left the party, Hope followed him back to his place and the two fell onto the bed in a flood of kisses.

1984

On the night of Hope's eighteenth birthday, she and Bo were about to make love when her father came looking for her. Doug was so furious, he had a coronary. At the hospital, Doug asked Hope to stay away from Bo Brady. It was painful for both, but since Bo worked with Roman, who was an escaped murder suspect, he feared for Hope's safety. Bo asked an old friend, Diane Parker, a prostitute, to make it look as if he was Diane's lover. Diane even moved in with Bo to dissuade Hope. Soon Salem's D.A. Larry Welch went to Diane and told her he would call her pimp if she let Hope near Bo. Then Larry made his move and proposed to Hope. On their wedding day, Bo showed up at the church, proclaimed his love, and the couple ran off together, but before they made love, Larry's thugs got to Hope and threatened harm to Bo and Hope's family unless she wed Larry.

Bo continued to help his brother Roman, who had been framed for murder. Meanwhile, Anna, learning that tapes proving Alex's involvement in the killings had been destroyed, returned to Salem. Without proof, she was no threat to Alex. Anna became Tony's secretary and Alex had her copy Tony's financial records for him. Meanwhile, Delia Abernathy, Tony's personal manager, also spied on Tony and reported to "Phoenix."

Stefano DiMera was Phoenix, and the mastermind behind most of the raven feather killings. On the night of his presumed death from a massive stroke, Stefano paid nurse Kelly Chase to find a corpse to tag with his name and then had her killed. When Trista, Eugene's wife, uncovered some discrepancies in lab reports, she was killed. Now, Tony DiMera's cousin Andre was masquerading as Tony while the real Tony was chained in a room in his penthouse. Andre, as Tony, wore a finely crafted mask of Roman whenever he killed. Eventually, Anna discovered the real Tony and was imprisoned with him.

Roman made it look as if he had been blown up in an empty house. Even his friends and co-conspirators thought he was dead. On the day of his memorial service, Roman, in disguise to look like Don, revealed himself to Marlena and several others. He had to stay out of sight while he proved his innocence, so he hid in Eugene's basement. When Eugene had visions of Trista's ghost, Roman realized

OPPOSITE & ABOVE: **B**ehind the glamour there was danger. Marlena was one of many Salem residents duped by evil Andre impersonating Tony DiMera. While Al Jarreau and Liz Chandler dazzled the benefit concert crowd, a bomb was about to clear the theater.

Although hesitant at first, Pete became a skillful dancer at Beefcakes. He was trying to make money so he and Melissa could leave town together.

they were computer-generated projections—the entire house was wired. Roman realized Stefano was in Salem and that Eugene's "baka," a talisman, figured into Stefano's plans.

Meanwhile, Alex donated $1 million to the psychiatric wing of the hospital as the kickoff to a spring charity event. Stefano planned to have Andre, disguised to look like Roman, kill Marlena at the televised benefit and blow up the theater as well. When Marlena told Roman she was pregnant, he insisted that she leave town, but Stefano found out. DiMera tricked her into staying and played cat and mouse with Roman. Stefano made Roman watch a video monitor that showed Marlena in the penthouse with Tony and another monitor that showed the real Tony in chains.

Stefano allowed Roman to escape, knowing he would go to the benefit to save Marlena. First, Roman released Tony and Anna, and reached the police computer. Meanwhile, people filled the theater where the Vipers did a break dance, Al Jarreau sang with Liz Chandler, and Billy and the Beaters performed. The theater was evacuated and the bomb defused by Eugene's baka, which once belonged to his distant cousins, the DiMeras. As chaos reigned, Stefano got into his limo, driven by Petrov. With Roman and police helicopters in pursuit, Stefano's car plunged into the icy waters of the Salem harbor. Neither Stefano nor Petrov were found. Andre, after being injured in a sword duel with the real Tony, escaped from the hospital.

Meanwhile, Liz, released from prison, still mistakenly thinking she was in love with Don until an attempted holdup at Doug's Place and the sight of guns dispelled her amnesia. Shortly after that, Liz and Neil married. Maggie stopped seeing Don, even though her divorce from Mickey was final.

Melissa dated Viper gang member Pete Jannings on the sly. In June, during a Warrior and Vipers rumble, Pete's friend Speed was shot and Pete accidentally shot Mickey, who'd been caught up in the situation. Mickey recuperated in Maggie's lake house while Melissa was sent to summer camp. Of course, Pete followed her, and they were discovered. When he went back to Salem, Speed got him a job at Beefcakes, a male stripper club. Pete wanted to make money so he and Melissa could leave town, but he kept his job a secret. Calliope, a costume designer who also worked for Liz, gave him some helpful hints and they became friends.

Megan Hathaway, Bo's ex-girlfriend, returned to Salem with her father, wealthy New Orleans banker Maxwell Hathaway, determined to have Bo. She even told Bo that a little boy named Zachary was their child. She'd given him up at birth, she told Bo, but together they could get him back and live happily ever after. Bo was on to her, however, and soon discovered that Zachary really belonged to his friend Diane. Megan invited Bo to a party that turned out to be Larry and Hope's wedding reception, making it clear Maxwell had control over D.A. Larry.

Bo went to work for Maxwell but to prove his loyalty was told to kill Diane. She faked her own death in a way that made it seem Bo had carried out Maxwell's orders. Then, in New Orleans, Bo stole the much-coveted prism from the art show, but Howie, Bo's PI buddy, trying to figure out the importance of the mysterious prism, dropped it in the bayou and an alligator swallowed it. Amid the danger and deception, Bo and Hope managed to have some romance. They made love for the first time in the historic Oak Alley plantation house and vowed their love in their own "wedding of the hearts."

Linda Anderson was back in Salem, staying out of sight as the mysterious and very wealthy Madame DuPrix and buying up several local businesses, including Beefcakes and Melissa's shares of Anderson Manufacturing. After a major theft at Anderson, Alex, who was missing money from Swiss accounts, realized someone was trying to financially destroy him. Maxwell wanted to buy Anderson for a rock-bottom price, just enough to cover Alex's donation check to the hospital and not much more. Linda suggested he torch the plant for the insurance money.

Roman and Marlena became the parents of twins, Eric and Samantha.

Zany Eugene Bradford met his match with zanier Calliope Jones.

Eugene found out there were three prisms in all and several international figures vying for them. The value and importance still eluded him and Bo. One prism was in the belly of the alligator, another looked like a piece of jewelry in Daphne's treasured gem collection, and another in the USSR. Melissa borrowed Daphne's prism necklace unaware of its value and wore it at a dance recital. When Melissa took it off, she put it in her costume pocket where wardrobe mistress Calliope found it and claimed it as her own.

After Hope saw the name *Chorvat* in Larry's Bible, Bo and Eugene traced the name through the computer to an old Russian spy case Meanwhile, Andre went to Stefano's compound to get what was rightfully his. Megan was Stefano's daughter, and Andre was Stefano's nephew. They planned on getting the prisms for themselves.

At Linda's suggestion, Alex, Anna, and Tony decided on a tropical locale for a photo shoot for Anna and Alex's fashion company. Stefano planned to get everyone to his island where his army would capture them. Eugene, Calliope, Bo, Hope, Anna, Liz, Carlo, Daphne, Andre, and Tony were on their way to Haiti. Roman would have been with them too, except that Marlena had given birth to twins, Eric and Samantha, and when one became ill, the baby needed Roman's blood for transfusion. The plane crashed, after co-pilot Andre caused the pilot to have a heart attack when he pulled a gun and demanded a change in course. On a deserted island, Daphne died in Andre's arms. Only Anna realized Andre was not really Tony, who, separated from the group, was with a native girl in the jungle. He named her Jasmine and gave her the crystal necklace he had taken from Calliope while they were on the plane.

Before disabling the radio, Andre sent a message to Stefano, who headed for the island with Roman on his trail. When Tony found out that his mother had died in Andre's arms, Tony fought Andre and drowned him in quicksand. Meanwhile, Stefano found Jasmine, took the prism necklace, and returned to his inflatable boat, a Zodiac, but found Bo had taken it to save Hope from Stefano's men. From afar, Bo had seen Stefano and Roman struggle on a cliff and Bo returned to the beach, but it was too late. Roman had been shot, and he died in Bo's arms. Enraged, Bo tried to find Stefano but couldn't, and when he came back to the beach, Roman's body was gone. The radio was repaired and the Coast Guard arrived.

Back in Salem, Larry Welch had won the election and had spent half of Hope's estate, and Alex had sold Anna's company. Marlena and all the Bradys were devastated by Roman's death, especially Bo, who had a hard time dealing with his guilt. At Roman's wake, Eric Brady showed up and his niece Kimberly Brady recoiled, remembering that her uncle had sexually abused her as a child. Later, she ran into him at Marlena's where he was baby-sitting Carrie. She berated him, but he remained defiant. Soon after, Eric was arrested for molesting a ten-year-old girl. Kimberly was the only one who was not surprised. She was rather distant from her family and never told them about Eric, or that she had been a prostitute in Europe, sometimes working for the ISA.

Shane Donovan, who had worked undercover as Larry Welch's butler, tracked Kate Honeycutt, Stefano's henchwoman and private nurse, to Louisiana where she retrieved the first prism from poachers who had cut it out of an alligator's belly. With two prisms in hand, Stefano took off for Russia and the third prism. He needed all three to heal his brain tumor.

At a press conference, Hope exposed Larry and the lieutenant governor as corrupt and they were forced to resign. She also publicly announced her love for Bo, who remained withdrawn. Larry had had enough of Hope and turned to Gwen Davies. While Bo dealt with his grief, Hope, almost on a dare, went into police officer training.

Neil wrongly accused Liz of having an affair with shady Carlo Forenza, who had planted a romantic note to make Neil suspicious. His ploy worked, however—Neil's accusation sent tipsy Liz into Carlo's bed for a one-night stand, and Neil caught them. After a cooling-off period, Neil and Liz reconciled and he told her of his past as Allen Jackson, who owed the syndicate a large gambling debt. He and Mario Forenza, Carlo's dad, turned state's evidence. Mario was dead and the syndicate wanted Neil dead too. Chris and Neil faked Allen Jackson's death, but when Liz and Neil tried to leave town, Carlo cornered them and Carlo died after a fight with Neil.

Bo discovered Megan was actually Stefano's daughter and that the ISA knew Stefano's whereabouts. Bo wanted to avenge his brother Roman's death, so Shane finally convinced him to join forces with the ISA. Meanwhile, Marlena was being followed and gave Jimmy Porterfield a ride home from the hospital when his car would not start. She had no idea at the time she was in danger.

Melissa fell for Barry Reid's nice-guy routine and took a job at his flower shop, not realizing it was a front for drug dealing. Pete tried to warn her, but she was angry with him after she found him in bed with her mother. He had no memory of that because Linda, as Madame DuPrix at Beefcakes, had drugged him first. Linda, angry that Melissa had sold her shares in Anderson stock, was trying to drive Melissa insane.

On New Year's Eve at Shenanigans, Melissa and Pete kissed at midnight, and Tom and Alice danced to rock and roll. But then on the way home, Tom and Alice saw Anderson Manufacturing explode and a man on fire running away.

1985

Many Salem residents earned plenty of frequent flyer miles credits as adventure took on an international dimension.

Ruthless Megan was still determined to have Bo. She planned to kill Hope by electrocuting her in the hot tub at The Body Connection. The plot backfired when she overheard Larry Welch and his Russian contact Bronsky discussing how one prism could blow up and destroy all of Salem if its container defrosted. Larry was the son of Victor Chorvat, who had invented the prisms. Larry and Megan got into a pushing and shoving match that left Megan accidentally dead. He threw her body into the hot tub, and when Hope discovered it, she was the prime suspect. At Megan's funeral, her father Stefano dressed as a woman, calling himself Mrs. Lafferty, and, disguised, cornered Bo Brady. Stefano threatened to kill Hope if Bo could not find Megan's killer for him.

Meanwhile, Larry blackmailed Alex and Linda because he knew they had torched the Anderson factory. He had planned to leave for London with his lover, Gwen Davies, but discovered she had a tape of him confessing to Megan's murder in his sleep. He slowly poisoned her with arsenic and she went into a coma. Ironically, Larry's guilt did not matter to her, and during her hospitalization, she promised him never to reveal his secret. She later left town without him.

Calliope and Eugene's engagement was sidetracked when, in order to collect an inheritance, he had to find a bride his mother Vanessa could approve of, a cultured society woman. Liz helped Calliope pass the test on a ploy, but it turned out Vanessa had already illegally spent the inheritance and would be jailed if discovered. To help his mom, Eugene married Madeline Rutherford and made money writing an advice to the lovelorn column under the name Bettina Lovecraft. At a charity event, Eugene, dressed as Bettina, revealed his true identity and love for Calliope. Madeline left him, but Linda, owner of *Salem Today*, hit him with a lawsuit for fraud. What little remained of his inheritance went toward the lawsuit, but Eugene and Calliope were together again. Eugene did come into money when he won a lottery. He went on a spending spree, then donated the rest to a child abuse center.

When Melissa blew the whistle on Barry Reid's drug dealing from his flower shop, where she worked, he tried to kill her. When he was picked up and questioned by police, he feigned innocence and insisted any drug dealings were Melissa's doing. On the run, Melissa hid in the remains of the Anderson Manufacturing plant where she discovered in overheard conversation that her mother, Linda Anderson, was the mysterious Madame DuPrix involved in financial dealings with Alex. With Pete's help, she planned to leave town but ended up

"**C**aroline and Victor met and fell in love in Salem before Victor went away to Europe to make his fortune. It had been love at first sight. We danced. I got pregnant. I guess that's why I married Shawn, the fisherman, for security." —Peggy McCay

in a flophouse and befriended by Ivy Selejko. When Bo eventually found her, a lenient judge gave her probation. But Pete had been Ivy's lover and she was pregnant. So in spite of his love for Melissa, Pete married the mother-to-be. Pete and Melissa agreed to stay away from each other, which was nearly impossible especially after Pete opened the dance club JUMP! To assuage her hurt, Melissa developed an attraction to her parole officer, Ian Griffith, who turned out to be married. Pete did his best to be a good husband, but eventually, the two made love.

Bronsky smuggled the third prism from the USSR through a touring ice-skating troupe and when Shane found out, he had Hope get a job as a security officer at the rink. She and Bo got their hands on the prism for a short time but, chased by Stefano's men, they lost it and it became embedded in the rink ice. Bo was held captive for a short time but escaped.

Stefano ultimately blamed the Brady family for the death of his daughter and decided to take vengeance against Marlena. After playing cat and mouse with her for weeks, Stefano decided she was "a more worthy adversary" than Roman ever was. Stefano nearly kidnapped Marlena as she stepped from her shower. He told her she would be his wife and the twins would replace Megan as his children. Meanwhile, Bo rescued twins Eric and Samantha who were already being taken to the airport and would have been flown to Caracas. Afterward, he raced back to the ice rink to keep Stefano from getting the prism. Amid the chaos, Marlena shot Stefano, who fell from a catwalk.

Marlena was charged with Stefano's death and at her trial, two DiMera employees, Jimmy Porterfield and Kate Honeycutt, testified that Marlena had been Stefano's lover, vengeful that he was going to Caracas without her. In an odd twist, the prosecutor, Bennett Hart, openly acknowledged Marlena's innocence. The judge declared a mistrial and Marlena was free.

Kimberly Brady fell for Shane Donovan, but he was still getting over his first wife's death—and her resurrection. Kimberly, an ex-prostitute dealing with international intrigue and family estrangement, was blinded by stress.

Savannah Wilder brought porno, drugs, and passion in her bag of tricks.

Alex stole Anna's dress designs while she was off on a romantic whirlwind trip with Prince Nicholas Arani II. When she found out, she had Eugene create a formula to make Alex's fashions disintegrate at the fashion show. In the middle of the festivities, the Prince was murdered by The Dragon, an anti-monarchist thought to be responsible for the death of Shane Donovan's late wife, Emma. Hope was the only one to see his face, but Shane recognized a description of the ring he wore. Realizing The Dragon planned to kill British Lady Joanna, Bo, Hope, and Shane went to England. Kimberly was having attacks of blindness she kept from Shane, but they were in love, and she joined him on the mission. After much chaos and many chases, Bo and Hope captured The Dragon in the Tower of London and were rewarded with a wedding fit for a king and queen, with all expenses paid by Lady Joanna. Friends and family flew from Salem for the incredibly beautiful late-May wedding at St. Mary's Church in the Cotswolds. The grand event went off smoothly only after Bo evaded arrest for stealing a milk wagon and, in handcuffs, stole a horse to ride to the church barely in time.

Meanwhile, Donovan was stunned to find Emma alive and programmed by The Dragon to kill Bo and Hope at the wedding. Shane foiled that attempt and had Emma deprogrammed. The Dragon, who turned out to be Shane's old friend, the Duke of Earl, escaped from prison and returned to the States. He eventually fell to his death after trying to kill Shane at Shane's apartment.

With Emma in Salem, Kimberly, whose blindness was stress-related, pulled back from Donovan and sought refuge with Victor Kiriakis, a wealthy businessman who donated $1 million to a charity auction on arrival in Salem. Caroline Brady, mom of Roman, Kayla, and Kimberly, soon told Kiriakis she was glad she had chosen her husband Shawn and never wanted their past mentioned, so their connection remained a secret. However, Victor helped the Brady family whenever he could. He turned out to be a powerful crime boss who oversaw Savannah Wilder's operations. Kimberly eventually regained her sight and resumed her romance with Shane, who had been assigned by ISA to nail Kiriakis. Shane had a new house complete with a high-tech communications room. An old ISA buddy, Livinia Peach, came to live with him as his maid.

Liz was happy when her brother Tod came home. But Tod was secretly involved with Savannah Wilder's crime syndicate. Unknowingly, so was Liz. While being promised great music video contracts, Liz innocently delivered illegal pornography and drugs in cassettes, not promotional copies of her work. When Tod tried to dissuade her, Savannah kidnapped Liz's daughter Noel, who had developed diabetes, for a few hours to remind Tod who he was dealing with. Later, Liz was shot in the throat by crooked cop McBride during a drug bust at her record party.

Meanwhile, Bo was surprised by the arrival of Steve "Patch" Johnson who now worked for Kiriakis. He, Bo, and a woman named Britta were once best of friends in Stockholm. The trio even had matching tattoos. But after Patch had sold bad drugs to a friend who died, he and Brady got into a knife fight, which was how Patch lost an eye. Now Patch constantly threatened to kill Bo and the two came close to a showdown several times. Patch tried to retrieve film that Kimberly never realized she had. The prints from that film fell into Melissa's hands, and Pete went to Kiriakis for help when it was clear someone was after her for them. It was clear that Victor was also a threat. Melissa had violated parole by missing a weekly report to her parole officer. Pete and Melissa were on the run from hitmen and cops for many weeks, which eventually led to the resolution of a mystery in Miami.

Marlena dated Richard Cates, the Salem police chief and an old friend of Roman's. Unfortunately, it turned out he was one of the honchos in Savannah's drug operation and was responsible for Theo Carver's and likely Danny Grant's deaths. He was also going to kill Hope because she was suspicious of his activities, but he was killed first. After his death, Marlena took his son, Kevin, into her home.

Mike Horton had become a doctor, like many before him in his family, and had returned to Salem just in time to keep his younger sister Jennifer out of trouble. She had become a rebellious runaway and compulsive liar. She, like Marlena and Maggie had been, was being stalked by a rapist.

Anna and Tony endured a fire and ice relationship that was concurrently frustrating and filled with steamy excitement. Even their wedding plans were bizarre. Their first ceremony was a hoax put together by Alex who hired an actor, not a minister. When the couple went to Bangkok for a honeymoon they found out they were still single. Calliope and Eugene joined them and planned to witness their marriage there. But Anna was kidnapped by Baba, an Asian potentate, and Calliope was nearly added to his harem as well before the quartet regrouped and got back to Salem. There they did finally wed at Tony's penthouse before going to Paris on a honeymoon.

After Anna and Tony returned, Anna was broke and sold some art. Soon she was arrested for the murder of Claus Van Zandt, an art dealer who had bilked her out of several hundred thousand dollars. Tony disappeared on a fog-shrouded pier while trying to clear Anna's name. He was held captive by Claus, who was alive after all.

In Miami, Bo, Hope, Shane, and Kimberly tried to destroy Kiriakis's domain in a mystery plot involving the purse—Kiriakis; the power—DiMera; and the pawn—an unknown element. It turned out Petrov and corrupt ISA chief Nickerson were also involved. Later, with Shane trapped in Victor's study, Kimberly was forced to sleep with Kiriakis in order to save Shane's life. Shane escaped in time to rescue Bo and Hope from an exploding sunken treasure. Victor, Savannah, and Patch were arrested, but Larry Welch was blackmailed by Kiriakis to take the fall as head of the crime syndicate. Victor knew Welch had killed Megan, and the threesome was released. Kiriakis wasted no time, and with Alex's help, bought up much of the property and business on the riverfront.

As the year came to an end, Kimberly, engaged to Shane, told him she was pregnant. Pete, divorced from Ivy, and Melissa became engaged. Mickey asked Maggie to remarry, but she refused, at least for now. Eugene and Calliope wed on New Year's Eve.

The mysterious Pawn turned out to be an unidentified man who escaped his captors.

1986

Marlena was kidnapped and Orpheus led the chase to Stockholm where he wanted Roman to turn over treasury bonds. Bo, with Patch and Kayla, joined the hunt. Marlena was returned safely but enraged Orpheus plotted more revenge.

The Pawn escaped from Patch's apartment before Patch could get a large sum of money from Kiriakis for the man. The Pawn eluded everyone and, after unraveling the bandages from his extensive plastic surgery, came up with the name John Black. He took a job in hospital security and found a friend in Dr. Marlena Evans. As certain Salem residents crossed his path, he was enveloped in cloudy images but no solid memory.

While Eugene and Calliope enjoyed their honeymoon in Finland, their best buddy Anna was cleared of murdering Claus Van Zandt when the victim turned up alive. Unfortunately, Tony remained missing and divorced his wife without coming back to Salem. He had been forced to end it with her by Emma Donovan, who hatched the plot to fake Claus's death, again escaped imprisonment, and married Alex who was now working for Kiriakis.

A rapist was still attacking women in Salem. When Kristie, a nurse at the hospital, was raped, she remembered that her attacker wore a lab coat with Dr. Mike Horton's name badge. Mike was under suspicion for several months. Then, in the honeymoon suite on Melissa's wedding night with Pete, her new husband was knocked out and she was almost attacked but got away. Several weeks later, she realized who the would-be rapist was: her former parole officer, Ian Griffith. His frustrated obsession with Melissa had driven him over the edge.

Recovering alcoholic Tod fell off the wagon with a nudge from Savannah.

The same night he had a fatal car crash. As he lay dying in the hospital, he begged Liz to sing to him. As she tenderly sang a favorite song from childhood, he died in her arms. Eventually, she handled her own drinking problem, got through her tragedies, and her singing voice returned. But the stress had taken a toll on her marriage. When she landed a movie project in late summer, she and Neil divorced.

After building fears that Kiriakis would reveal their affair of several decades past, Caroline Brady agreed to meet with Victor at a hotel. She brought a gun, unaware Bo had followed her. Caroline held Kiriakis at gunpoint, but when she fired, could not bring herself to aim. Bo witnessed the scene and learned the truth. He was Kiriakis's son. The news certainly shocked Bo and Shawn most, but everyone in Salem was surprised that Caroline had had an illicit affair, and stunned it had been with a man like manipulative Victor. He still had a special place in his heart for her and again offered her a life in the Kiriakis mansion. She again chose Shawn, who suddenly understood why he and Bo never felt true kinship. In fact, the two had always been adversarial. In Shawn's eyes, it was hard for Bo to do anything quite right. So it was no shock to him when, several months later, Bo moved in with his newly discovered dad. Hope, however, despised her father-in-law and living in the Kiriakis home and left Bo. She miscarried their baby soon after.

Her marriage was a rollercoaster until Bo explained that his primary motivation in being near Kiriakis was to bring down his crime organization. Then they agreed to play out the separation scenario, which was made complicated by Hope becoming pregnant again. It was also difficult when Bo started to care about his father and agonized about betraying him. Victor admired his son's honesty, but maintained that "business is business."

Marlena tried to help John Black regain his memory through hypnosis, and that led them to the Lafferty farmhouse. John's familiarity with that Stefano outpost made some people speculate that he could actually be Stefano, who had the money and means to create a drastic physical transformation if he wanted one. They tried to locate the doctor who had done the cosmetic surgery. With Kiriakis and the KGB chasing them, John and Marlena headed for West Virginia. When Marlena got a peek at John's tattoo, she was shocked. It was a phoenix, and she thought he could indeed be Stefano as Bo suspected. Later, after seeing before-and-after surgery photos, Marlena realized he could be her presumed dead husband Roman. Although John couldn't remember his past, this man knew he loved Marlena, seemed to have some memories of her, and believed she was his wife. Carrie had a problem dealing with her dad not looking at all as she had known him. After seeing Marlena be affectionate with him, Carrie ran from the house and was hit by a car. She was in a coma for several days before Roman talked her back to consciousness. They shared a new emotional bond after that.

The hospital's young new head of surgery, Robin Jacobs, started out at odds with Dr. Mike Horton, but the two fell in love. Because she was Jewish, religious differences became a problem for them and she started dating Mitch Kaufman. Still, Mike and Robin were brought together in several emotional situations, in a mine tunnel collapse and working side by side after a tornado. By the end of the year, Robin found out she was pregnant and wondered if Mike or Mitch was the father. Meanwhile, Robin's father, Eli, was reunited with his estranged brother Robert LeClair, who was back in Salem and now singing at Blondie's.

Mike's sister Jennifer straightened out her priorities and gave up her runaway lifestyle and moved back in with her grandparents Alice and Tom. She went back to school and during summer vacation she began a nonintimate romance with Glenn Gallagher.

When Jennifer's drug addict friend Matt threatened suicide, Dr. Evans tried to talk him down from the ledge. He was pulled back inside the building, but Marlena fell and lapsed into a nearly month-long coma. When she regained consciousness, her troubles were still not over. She went into cardiac arrest and was not released from hospital care until the middle of August. Not long after she recovered fully, Roman and Marlena Brady renewed their marriage vows.

Shane was arrested on bogus espionage charges. When Bo confessed to the crime, ex-Soviet spy Britta Englund cleared him by testifying that she set up the innocent man. At one time, Bo, Britta, and Steve were like family. Britta was once Bo's lover. They split up when he found her in bed with his best friend Steve. When Britta came to Salem, she and Steve, now known as Patch, rekindled their romance. Britta was a double agent who had information on both Bo's and Roman's pasts. When she heard Victor order a hit on Patch, she ran to warn him and was shot. Victor promised Patch he would be safe on the condition Britta kept her mouth shut and left town. In spite of Patch's expectations that they would live together after Britta was released from the hospital, she left without a word of explanation.

Kayla had left Salem because of Chris's lack of commitment to their relationship. She returned to set up a waterfront emergency clinic and became emotionally attached to Patch.

Britta's brother Lars defected from the U.S.S.R. to the U.S., came to Salem, and started his own dance troupe. He made Melissa his partner and the two carried their heated on-stage chemistry into their personal lives, especially after Melissa learned that Pete was involved in illegal activities with Kiriakis through the club JUMP! Later, Pete suffered a concussion while saving Bo from being crushed by a forklift at Kiriakis's warehouse. He suddenly could not walk. Pete's paralysis was psychosomatic, an unconscious ploy to keep Melissa close and too guilt-ridden to leave him for Lars.

Doug and Julie had gone off on an extended cruise the year before. Unfortunately, they separated. When Doug returned, he bought Howie's detective agency for Bo and Hope as a wedding gift.

Marlena was abducted by Orpheus, a former ISA agent who wanted Roman's help in locating stolen treasury bonds. A corrupt ISA chief, Vaughn, and agent Gillian Forrester were also involved. Clues led to Stockholm and former associates of Bo and Patch. There Roman, Patch, Bo, Hope, Shane, and Kayla all played a part in a dangerous adventure and eventually found Marlena, who had really been saved by the ISA, and brought her back to Salem. Their success only infuriated Orpheus, who planned further revenge.

When Kimberly had accepted Shane's proposal late last year, she told him that she was pregnant. Shane was delighted. However, Kimberly neglected to mention that the father could be Kiriakis. When Shane later overheard that, the couple separated. He did not realize that, for a time, Kimberly was afraid she, like Bo, was Victor's child. That was not the case, but her fears and Victor hoping the child was his, added to the tension between the couple. However, they happened to be together in the West Virginia wilderness when Kimberly went into premature labor. Shane delivered the breech-birth baby, Andrew Shawn. The infant really was Shane's child, but meddling Emma altered the paternity test so everyone believed Victor to be the father. By this time, however, Shane was committed to Kimberly; they stayed together and planned to marry. That only pushed Emma into tricking Kimberly into signing an adoption release, not a hospital discharge sheet, so she could kidnap the baby, and take it to a Cleveland baby broker. Eventually Emma was arrested for her crime, but beat the rap with an insanity plea. However, baby Andrew was not found and the pain of that came between Kimberly and Shane. Even though they realized they loved each other, they broke up, unaware that Andrew was in Salem, the newly adopted child of Paul and Barbara Stewart.

As the year came to an end, Orpheus double-crossed his partner Kiriakis, Vaughn resigned from the ISA, and Orpheus planted a bomb in the Roman Brady house. As Roman watched in horror, it blew up with Marlena inside. She was presumed dead and a memorial service was held shortly before Christmas.

On New Year's Eve, Shane found Emma dead in Neil's study. It first appeared to be a drug overdose, except there were bruises on her body.

1987

Although Shane tried to cover for Kimberly on the night his ex-wife Emma was killed, Kimberly was arrested and charged with the murder. She would have spent life in prison had it not been for Shane's detective work. Shane discovered that Barbara Stewart had visited Emma the night of the murder. He also found a picture of the Stewarts' adopted baby, the Donovans' kidnapped baby boy Andrew. Barbara panicked and tried to leave town but was killed in a car wreck. Fortunately, Andrew survived and was reunited with Kimberly and Shane.

Later, a cab driver told Shane that another woman had been spotted at Emma's murder scene. When the cab driver turned up dead, Shane began to suspect his ISA partner, Gillian Forrester, who had become obsessed with him. After setting Gillian up with the opportunity to kill Kimberly, Gillian made her move, and was caught. After she was arrested, Shane and Kimberly were married. Although the newlyweds enjoyed their honeymoon, they were shadowed by the mysterious Hans.

Soon after Shane and Kimberly arrived home from their honeymoon, Kiriakis petitioned for custody of Andrew, claiming he was the boy's father. He accused Kimberly of being an unfit mother, demanded visitation rights, and took Andrew away. Kiriakis publicly exposed Kimberly as a former hooker. But fate took an unexpected turn. Andrew was hit by a car and rushed to the hospital, where he received an emergency blood transfusion. While typing blood samples, Neil determined that Kiriakis could not possibly be Andrew's father. Further tests ascertained Shane was. Baby Andrew survived, but it was a slow recovery.

Kiriakis wanted Shane off the trail of a mysterious computer disk, even if it meant having him killed. Patch succeeded in pretending to help the mob while secretly helping Shane. Meanwhile, Shane's ex-partner, Gabrielle, posed as a Russian spy and, to get Shane dismissed from the ISA, pretended to have an affair with him. Once Shane was ousted from the ISA in disgrace, Kiriakis turned his focus elsewhere.

Diana Colville and Roman Brady became lovers even though he shot her mother Serena, who had tried to kill him.

While Roman mourned Marlena's death, Orpheus was still alive—and holding Marlena prisoner. Olivia, Orpheus's sister-in-law, sought revenge against Roman for the accidental death of her sister Rebecca. Roman followed her and would have saved Marlena had Orpheus not stayed one step ahead, sending Marlena to the island airport with his henchmen. Roman got to the airport and was horrified as he watched the plane with Marlena aboard explode. No body was found. Roman and Orpheus struggled, and Olivia, who had fallen in love with Roman, took the bullet intended for Brady, who then killed Orpheus.

Kiriakis forged a document that stated he was sterile at the time of Bo's conception and effectively disowned Bo. Soon after, Bo restated his love and loyalty to the Brady family, who were all delighted when Hope gave birth to Shawn-Douglas. The new parents bought a sailboat, packed their belongings, and said good-bye to Salem.

Jennifer inadvertently exposed her boyfriend Glenn Gallagher's plan to uncover his coach's drug dealing. Glenn was lured into a trap, and Jennifer, who had trailed him to the park, found the coach holding a gun to Glen's head. Jennifer enlisted Frankie Brady's help. The coach was arrested and the case was solved. Later, when Jennifer and Frankie were on a class trip, they realized they had strong feelings for each other. Jennifer rejected Glenn's pressure to have sex and turned to Frankie. Together, Jennifer and Frankie foiled a robbery and later helped bust a prostitution ring.

Caroline and Shawn told Frankie and his brother Max, who they'd taken into their home last year, that they would like to adopt them. Max, who had not been able to talk, overcame his emotional problems and began speaking again. Jennifer's father, Bill, returned to Salem and tried to run Jennifer's life. She rebelled by becoming engaged to Frankie. She broke the engagement suddenly when she discovered that both her mother Laura, still institutionalized, and her late grandmother Carrie were schizophrenic. Jennifer feared she would also develop the problem and pass it on to her own children or inflict the pain of dealing with it on a spouse.

Janice Barnes, Mickey and Maggie's now grown foster child, returned to Salem and began an affair with Bill, who was guilt-ridden over his wife Laura's mental illness. He felt partially responsible for Laura's condition because of an affair he had around the time of her breakdown. He broke things off with Janice, who soon dated Mike.

Kayla invited new friend Adrienne Johnson to stay at her home after Adrienne's place was burglarized. Patch and Kayla had grown close, but troubles started between them when Patch started having disquieting memories. He pushed Kayla away and struggled with his nightmares. Later, when Patch recognized personal mementos from his childhood in Adrienne's possession, the young woman admitted she was his sister he had never known. Then Jo Johnson, their mother, was beaten by her husband, Duke, and Patch was reunited with his mother. She admitted giving up Steve and his brother as youngsters to save them from a violent home. Duke came looking for his wife and wanted her to leave the

women's shelter and come home, but Patch helped her get a restraining order. Unfortunately, that infuriated Duke who found virgin Adrienne and raped her. She shot him and passed out. Protecting his sister, Patch took the murder rap. Meanwhile, Adrienne blocked the traumatic incident from her memory. Later, with Kimberly's counsel, Adrienne recalled the traumatic scene of her rape and rushed into the courtroom just as Patch was being sentenced. When the judge learned that Adrienne had acted in self-defense, all charges were dropped. Meanwhile, Kayla was determined to repair her relationship with Patch.

After Melissa suffered a leg injury, she was afraid to tell her dancing partner Lars for fear of losing his love. She was right. Although she managed to avoid Lars until her leg healed, Melissa injured herself again while dancing and Lars realized the damage was permanent. His changed feelings toward her as a dancer effectively ended their relationship.

After Dr. Robin Jacobs's marriage to Mitch was annulled, she was happy when Mike decided to convert to Judaism and they got engaged. Meanwhile, the mysterious Hans, who had tracked the Donovans on their honeymoon, resurfaced in Salem. While trying to approach Kimberly on a pier, Hans was shot by an unseen sniper. He was rushed to the hospital and operated on by Robin but did not survive. After his death, Diana Colville, a college friend of Mike Horton's, found a photo of Hans and her late husband, a medical researcher. Shane and Kimberly learned that Hans was also a scientist. Meanwhile, Robin learned that Hans had a computer disk when he was brought to the ER. While Robin was alone in her office, making a copy of it, she was shot by an intruder who grabbed the disk and fled. Robin barely made it through surgery. While recovering from her gunshot wound, Robin spotted Mike in the chapel praying for her well-being.

Justin, Victor Kiriakis's nephew, married Adrienne Johnson in a lavish ceremony in Greece.

Robin realized he could not fully accept her religion, so she abruptly broke off their engagement. Although Mike was heartbroken, he kept himself busy by helping Diana, who was devastated to learn that her husband had been an impostor and had been working for her estranged father, Philip Colville.

Diana happened to be near Carrie when she was drowning and rescued the girl. Roman was not only extremely grateful to Diana, the two were immediately attracted to each other. But Diana had feigned a relationship with Kiriakis so that she could find out about his involvement with the mysterious computer disk. Diana went to Greece with Kiriakis where Kiriakis's archrival, Serena, got her hands on the disk before he could. Kiriakis vowed revenge against Serena.

Kiriakis's playboy nephew Justin had a fling with Anjelica Devereaux, but dropped her after meeting Adrienne. They dated, but it was not until Adrienne confronted Victor Kiriakis, during her peaceful protest of the Riverfront Renovation Project, that she learned he was related to Justin, who was pretending to be a construction worker. Adrienne felt betrayed by Justin, but Jo convinced her to take advantage of Justin's family connections to help with their search for Billy, her other son. Adrienne was deeply in love with Justin, but was wary of his family. Nevertheless, she happily wed him in Greece. Kiriakis and Diana returned to Greece for the ceremony and Roman soon followed. There Roman and Diana made love and began their romance. Meanwhile, Roman discovered that Serena was mining the rare and valuable mineral that composed the disk. Serena warned Roman away, but when she tried to kill him, he shot her. Unfortunately, when Diana arrived she told him Serena was her mother.

Believing that he was helping Senator Harper Devereaux to fake his death and in order to better investigate the hospital explosion in Mike's lab, where the disk had been hidden, Patch agreed to pose as an assassin. But when Patch fired his gun, the senator was struck by a real bullet that put him into a coma. Patch had been set up by Kai, a Hawaiian working for Victor to find the disk, and the ISA, so he went into hiding. Both he and Kayla were on the run when Kayla discovered that Kai had trailed her to Patch's hiding place. Justin and Adrienne came to their rescue, and they all proceeded to track down a lead concerning ISA head Simon Hopkins, which took them to a university in Los Angeles. Once inside, they discovered that Hopkins was on the board of the Kava Chemical company, located just outside Salem.

When Patch informed her that she was a major stockholder, Diana contacted her father to find out more about Kava. Delighted with Diana's apparent change of heart, Colville welcomed his daughter back into his life. With Diana's help, Patch got on to Kava premises and discovered a connection between Kai and Simon. Diana's father denied any knowledge of their operation, so Diana was able to persuade him to use Kai to trap Simon. Patch lured Simon to the hospital with the information that Senator Devereaux had come out of his coma. When Simon tried to kill Kai, who was posing as the senator, Patch trapped Simon. Desperate, Simon tried to hold Alice Horton hostage, but Roman shot him dead.

Anjelica and Harper's son Jack came to town seeking treatment for Hodgkin's disease. Jack became smitten with Kayla when she was hired as his private nurse. Meanwhile, Jo and Patch discovered that Jack was actually Jo's son Billy but decided to keep the news from Jack. Patch realized Jack needed incentive to pull through his illness and encouraged Kayla to spend time with his brother. Hurt by Patch's rejection, Kayla accepted Jack's wedding proposal and they quickly married, but Jack was unable to consummate the union because of his illness. Soon after, Harper stole Jack's adoption papers from Jo. When they turned up missing again, Harper thought Kayla had them and, to keep his secret safe, he tried to poison her. Patch whisked Kayla away and found the antidote for the poison. While Harper and Jack were searching for Kayla, she became conscious. When Patch told her she had been poisoned by a Devereaux, she refused to believe him and tried to find Roman but collapsed on the pier. When Melissa was arrested on suspicion of trying to kill Kayla, Harper was delighted.

At the sexual abuse clinic, Kimberly befriended a troubled teenager, Eve Baron, who was one of pimp Nick Corelli's girls. Kimberly didn't know Eve, Shane's daughter, believed that she was Emma's daughter. Eve vowed revenge against Kimberly who Eve believed had wrecked her parents' marriage. Kimberly was again pregnant and vulnerable after a rubella scare. Eve was unreasonably jealous of Sarah Horton for her stable home life. Eve stole a car and accidentally hit Sarah. Amid all her emotional turmoil, Eve finally told Shane that she was his daughter. He had his doubts, but admitted it was possible so he took her into the Donovan home where she caused Kimberly lots of stress and aggravation.

1988

To keep her from marrying Kiriakis, Roman abducted Diana. Diana admitted to Roman she was only marrying Victor to help her mother, Serena. Diana escaped from the cabin where she was being held captive and arrived back at the mansion in time to overhear Kiriakis and Serena, who had survived being shot by Roman, plotting together. Diana also learned that her mom had stolen the computer disk. Roman had Diana gather important information from an unwitting Kiriakis and Serena. Meanwhile, Philip Colville was killed by a sniper and Diana inherited the Colville fortune.

Patch believed that Melissa Anderson was innocent of charges of trying to poison Kayla but clearly someone else wanted Kayla dead. Patch and Kayla agreed to meet secretly until after Jack Devereaux's campaign was over. Consequently, they were upset to learn a photographer had been following them.

In an attempt to bring harmony to his family, Shane decided to adopt Eve. However, Nick Corelli forced Eve back into prostitution. When an angry customer tried to assault Eve, she called Kimberly for help. While trying to rescue her, Kimberly was roughed up, landed in the hospital, and lost her baby. When Eve was knifed on the pier, Shane discovered her secret life of prostitution. Soon after, Shane confirmed that his former ISA partner Gabrielle Pascal was Eve's mother, not Emma. Angry and confused, Kimberly left town to sort things out.

Adrienne became concerned over Justin's ties to the mob. Distraught about her pregnancy, she considered an abortion, which enraged Justin. When Adrienne miscarried, Justin mistakenly believed she had deliberately terminated the pregnancy, which added more strain to their tense marriage.

Jack won the election to the state assembly. His victory celebration, however, was cut short when the insinuating photos of Kayla and Patch suddenly surfaced. In a jealous rage, Jack raped Kayla and had Kiriakis's thugs beat up Patch. Kayla and Patch escaped to a mountain hideout, but were trailed by Kiriakis's men, who returned Kayla to Jack. Determined to fight for Kayla's honor, Patch returned to

Salem and confronted Jack on a rooftop. After a struggle, Jack plunged over the ledge and was badly injured. In order to save Jack's life, Patch donated one of his kidneys—their relationship as brothers was no longer a secret. Meanwhile, Kayla pressed rape charges against Jack, but they were reduced. Kayla decided to file for divorce. Jack sought comfort in Melissa's understanding arms. Melissa, however, neglected to tell Jack she'd found the adoption papers and knew his true identity. Harper, meanwhile, framed Melissa for poisoning Kayla.

Diana learned that Serena had been abducted to Peru. Adrienne, Justin, and Roman joined Diana there to find Serena. The kidnappers demanded $10 million for Serena's safe return. When Diana went to make the exchange, she was arrested. Meanwhile, Diana's money was confiscated by thugs posing as the Peruvian police. Roman, who was also arrested, told Diana that her mother and Kiriakis were the masterminds behind the sordid scheme to steal her fortune. Justin and Adrienne helped Roman and Diana escape. Back in Salem, Diana shared living quarters with Roman for protection. To Adrienne's delight, Justin finally broke away from his diabolical uncle.

Frankie had an affair with his Teen Hotline boss, Paula Carson, who was also his teacher. When Jennifer and Frankie eventually reconciled, Eve was devastated. In retaliation, she exposed Paula's affair with Frankie. Meanwhile, Jennifer was shocked to learn the truth.

The serial killer known as the "Riverfront Knifer" claimed a new victim, Janice Barnes. The violent tragedy brought Mike and Bill together. Bill decided to leave town and return to his wife. Meanwhile, Mike turned to Gabrielle for comfort, causing Shane to become jealous. Soon after, Kimberly returned to Salem. Torn between his feelings for Kimberly and Gabrielle, Shane filed for a legal separation.

When Adrienne suffered a second miscarriage, and Kiriakis rushed Adrienne to the hospital, Justin's feelings toward his uncle warmed and they declared a truce. But the tension between uncle and nephew erupted again when Justin confessed his participation in torching the Emergency Center. In Washington, Justin testified against organized crime. When Kiriakis was shot by a member of the Torres crime family, Justin returned to his uncle's mansion to run the Kiriakis business. Adrienne chose not to follow Justin.

Kayla accepted a job when the Emergency Center reopened. Patch became

Kimberly came to the rescue when pimp Nick Corelli lured Eve back into prostitution and a client became abusive. Kimberly suffered a miscarriage.

a liaison between the gangs and the police. Patch and Kayla became involved with Emilio and April Ramirez, street punks who tried to rip off the Center for drugs. April revealed to Mike that she and Emilio were trying to get the drugs for their mother, Rosa, who had cancer. Mike found himself attracted to April and helped her land a job at the hospital. Soon after, Rosa was admitted to the hospital after a serious car accident. Rosa died after her life support system was turned off and April was accused of pulling the plug.

Diana stole a precious Greek icon from a museum after Serena concocted a plan to have the icon sold to Kiriakis so that Diana could get back her fortune. Meanwhile, Roman suspected Diana was involved in the theft of the icon. When Kiriakis was found in possession of it, Roman didn't press charges. Later, Diana confessed that she had swindled Kiriakis. Soon after, she and Roman ended their romance. But their lives became entangled again during Roman's investigation of the Torres family. With Diana's life in danger, Roman persuaded Diana to feign her own death.

Kimberly went undercover to capture the Riverfront Knifer and was arrested for prostitution. When Shane realized she was working undercover, they joined forces. Soon after, their feelings for each other resurfaced; Shane told Gabrielle he was still in love with his wife. Kayla was attacked in her home by the Riverfront Knifer. When Kayla tried to escape, the Knifer tipped over a can of gasoline, which caused an explosion. As a result, Kayla was temporarily unable to hear or speak, and her memory was muddled.

The Torres family targeted Roman when they learned of his deception. With Diana's help, the family was lured into a trap, but Jose Torres was later released on bail. Meanwhile, after Roman and Diana were attacked, she left for Japan. When Roman learned there was a contract on Diana's life, he took her to the Bahamas for safety.

When Adrienne continued to reject Justin, he turned to Anjelica. When Anjelica became pregnant she assumed the baby was Harper's. But an angry Harper told her to get an abortion. Anjelica, however, ignored his order. Meanwhile, Jack stumbled upon his adoption papers at Melissa's house and confronted Harper. Anjelica overheard Harper confess to Jack that he was sterile. Soon after, Anjelica deduced that Harper was the one who was poisoning Kayla, knowing the lengths he'd take to keep Jack's background a secret.

Kayla recalled the identity of her attacker and wrote it down for Kimberly, who rushed to call Shane. But it was too late. The demented Harper had already made his way to Kayla's apartment. Harper took Kayla and Kimberly to the rooftop and confessed that he was the Riverfront Knifer. Just as Harper was about to toss Kayla and Kimberly off the roof, Patch and Shane arrived and Harper was apprehended.

With the danger behind them, Shane once again pursued Kimberly romantically. Meanwhile, Jack denounced Harper and ran against Mickey to fill

Before she became one of Harper's victims, Janice Barnes had an affair with married man Dr. Bill Horton, and then his son Dr. Mike.

Harper's vacant seat in the state senate. Kayla had surgery that helped her recover her hearing. Soon after, she accepted Patch's marriage proposal. Although Anjelica announced that Harper was not the father of her baby, she also told Justin the child wasn't his. Kiriakis, who was desperate for an heir, suspected that the baby was Justin's.

Frankie and Max ran away when Max's real father, Trent, appeared in Salem. Initially, Jennifer covered for the boys, but eventually Trent coaxed Jennifer into revealing their whereabouts. After a car accident, the boys returned to Salem. Frankie, however, remained wary of Trent. Seeing how happy Max was with Shawn and Caroline, Trent left Salem.

After Diana and Roman's return from the Bahamas, Roman was plagued by vague memories. After narrowly escaping a car-bombing by the Torres family, Roman didn't recognize Diana. He finally regained his memory, but was experiencing violent personality shifts. He asked Kimberly to hypnotize him, revealing a killer personality. When Diana ran a missing persons photo in her newspaper for a mysterious man named Orion, Roman recognized first himself, before plastic surgery, then recognized Orion as his Kung Fu master. Roman and Diana tried to find Orion, but couldn't.

Kayla's voice returned during the course of her wedding ceremony with Patch. Jack also planned a second trip down the aisle. Believing that his political chances would be improved if he was married, Jack proposed to Melissa, who then ditched Jack at the altar because she couldn't accept his womanizing ways. Melissa's rejection shattered Jack's election prospects.

Patch and Kayla honeymooned in the Orient, unaware that they were being watched. They encountered a lost deaf boy named Benjy. When they couldn't locate Benjy's parents, Kayla and Patch brought the lad back with them to Salem. It soon became clear that Benjy's life was in danger. A woman posing as Benjy's mother admitted her charade and said it was too dangerous for Benjy's real mother to surface. When Benjy saw a postcard from Bo and Hope, he told Kayla and Patch he had also been to the same country with his mother. Kayla gave the postcard to Roman, hoping the clue would help find Benjy's mother. Instead, it caused Roman to go into a trance. Remembering the place from a flashback, Roman searched Kiriakis's mansion and found a file on himself, a.k.a. John Black. Kimberly deduced that Roman was a victim of post-hypnotic suggestion: certain signals put him into a trance and he became an assassin.

Eve overdosed on pills after harassment by boys who wanted to score with a hooker. She recovered, but vowed revenge on one boy in particular. With Nick's help, she invited the boys to a party, rife with drugs and alcohol, and then tipped off the police. Eve watched gleefully as they were all arrested.

Benjy's mother, Ellen, watched from afar as Kayla and Patch considered adopting the boy. With Orion's help, she contacted the newlyweds and told them she needed to hide Benjy from his evil father. Ellen set a date to retrieve Benjy, but she never arrived. Soon after, Patch discovered her dead on the pier. Roman recognized Ellen and recalled threatening her. In the meantime, Benjy was abducted by his father. Orion revealed himself to be Benjy's grandfather and helped Kayla track the boy down and rescue him. Believing Benjy was on a plane, Orion also boarded it and left the country. Roman was frustrated that this link to his past was gone. His only clue to it now was a mysterious ring.

Adrienne reconciled with Justin, but felt frustrated that she was unable to get pregnant again. She befriended Emilio, who had found work as the Kiriakis

Jack and Harper Devereaux were quite a team. Jack raped Kayla and Harper turned out to be the serial killer, the Riverfront Knifer.

groundskeeper. Seeing Adrienne and Emilio together, Anjelica suspected they were more than friends. Soon after, Emilio ran off, accused of knifing the Kiriakis gardener for the sake of Adrienne's honor, but Emilio's father, Monty, turned him in. With the help of Adrienne, Mike, and April, Emilio was soon released on bail.

After renewing their wedding vows, Kimberly and Shane traveled to England for their second honeymoon. There, Kimberly was shocked to discover that Shane had a twin brother, Drew, who was also an undercover ISA agent. In spite of Shane's warnings about him, Drew returned to Salem with the couple.

Kiriakis devised a scheme to marry Anjelica so that he could claim Justin's unborn son as his own. With Jack's help, Kiriakis engineered a jailbreak for Harper in order to get his hands on Harper's Swiss bank account. Emilio was to take Harper to the airport, but in a police chase, Harper was shot. Jack brought Harper to Kayla at the Emergency Center, where Harper took her hostage. Luckily, Emilio tipped off Patch, who rescued Kayla. Harper was apprehended at the airport and returned to prison.

Shane was alarmed when Roman said Drew, beyond his physical appearance, seemed familiar to him. Following Tarrington, the ISA head, Shane became friendly with Kiriakis to obtain information about his illicit dealings. Shane led Kiriakis to believe he was fed up with the ISA. Meanwhile, Drew phoned someone who would prove to be his real boss to tell him he suspected Shane was up to something.

Roman suspected that Marlena might still be alive and deduced Stefano DiMera was behind all the intrigue. DiMera kidnapped Carrie Brady and held her and Orion hostage on a boat. Meanwhile, Roman and Diana headed back to the Bahamas. Kiriakis agreed to help the ISA bring down Stefano, provided he obtain full immunity from prosecution. Drew, who was actually Stefano's assistant, Iago, invited Kiriakis to the island. Soon after, Drew was joined by Shane and his family. With the entire Brady clan on the island, Stefano began an elaborate game of cat and mouse. DiMera believed Roman was responsible for his son Benjy's loss of hearing. Stefano put Roman into a trance and ordered him to kill everyone. Fortunately, Diana was able to shake Roman out of it, but before Roman could apprehend Stefano, he escaped in a helicopter. Roman got everyone off the island and finally accepted that Marlena was dead.

1989

Finally out of Stefano DiMera's clutches, Roman proposed to Diana. Meanwhile, Patch and Kayla were disappointed when Orion came back for his grandson Benjy. And, to Kiriakis's dismay, Anjelica married Neil Curtis.

Justin, furious because Adrienne had slept with Emilio Ramirez, devised an accident for him in the horse stable. But the scheme backfired, leaving Justin paralyzed. Then, to keep his nephew and Adrienne apart, Kiriakis moved Justin to a private hospital, but kindhearted Emilio brought him to a farmhouse, where Justin was reunited with Adrienne. After Frankie Brady said good-bye, Jennifer became romantically involved with Emilio.

Patch discovered a mysterious, badly burned stranger on the roadside. While the man was healing from his wounds in Patch's home, Patch discovered he was Nick Corelli, who pleaded with him to keep his secret. Nick just wanted to leave Salem to start a new life. Meanwhile, Eve grieved over Nick's death and hid the fact that her schoolmate, Jake, was responsible. That put suspicion on her when she was named beneficiary of Nick's life insurance policy, so she took off. When her car crashed, she was rescued by Eddie Reed, who brought her to the mansion where Nick had relocated.

Anxious to kill an exposé on himself, Jack bought a half-interest in Diana's newspaper, and his interference created problems for Diana. Meanwhile, Diana's wedding to Roman was postponed because there was no death certificate for Marlena, and then Caroline Brady had a heart attack and surgery. After Cal Winters, a former MIA soldier, was admitted to the hospital, Diana postponed the wedding for the third time because Jack stole Cal's file and discovered he was Diana's husband. Jack threatened to tell Roman unless she sold him her half of the newspaper. Diana then rushed the wedding, but Cal crashed the ceremony. After Roman learned the truth, a determined Diana tried to prove that her marriage to Cal had never happened. Artie Doyle, an old friend of Cal's, goaded Cal into shooting Roman. While Roman was in a coma, Diana discovered it was she who had accidentally shot Roman in crossfire. So overwhelmed with guilt, she abruptly left town.

Justin and Adrienne returned to the Kiriakis mansion. Justin regained his ability to walk, but he was impotent and his fiendish uncle slipped him medicine that prolonged the condition. Sensing problems once again in Justin and Adrienne's relationship, Anjelica considered telling Justin he was the father of her child. Meanwhile, Kiriakis schemed to undermine Anjelica's marriage to Neil by encouraging Neil's gambling. When Anjelica gave birth, Neil was unsuccessfully courting Lady Luck as Justin assisted in the delivery of his son, Alexander.

Wearing a mask, Nick talked to Eve, but Eddie told Eve he was searching for money stolen from Harper Devereaux and stashed by Nick. After finding a safe-deposit box key in the mansion, Eddie dragged Eve to the bank but the key was wrong. On the way, Eve was able to drop an unnoticed note for help, and soon Shane arrived. Working behind the scenes, Nick helped Shane navigate the complex tunnels behind the abandoned mansion where he was hiding and triggered a trap door beneath Eddie. Eve was rescued and Eddie was arrested, but later escaped.

Emilio's forgiving attitude turned to revenge and he disabled the brakes on Justin's car. When Jennifer got in the car too, Emilio tried to stop them and was badly injured. Accused of attempted murder, Emilio left town in shame.

Justin helped Anjelica deliver their son Alexander while her husband, Dr. Neil Curtis, spent the night gambling, a situation Victor orchestrated.

Patch had surgery on his eye so he could infiltrate Rev. Saul Taylor's revivalist camp as Daniel Lucas.

Nick, Kayla, and Patch lured the escaped Eddie back to the mansion where he had held Eve. Coincidentally, Eve returned, hoping to find her mystery man in the mask. Eddie stumbled upon them, then escaped again. Then Nick, Kayla, and Patch were charged with conspiring to hide Harper's money.

Robin Jacobs returned to Salem, anxious to revive her romance with Mike, but he had proposed to April Ramirez, a recovering alcoholic. When Robin found out, she told April that Mike was the father of her son, Jeremy.

When Eddie offered to split Harper's money with Jack, Jack preferred to go to Nick and told him he could keep the money for "unspecified future services" and Nick accepted the offer. Meanwhile, anxious to disappear with Nick, Eve agreed to get plastic surgery if Nick would do the same. As Eve was about to have surgery, Eddie burst into the operating room and Eddie told Nick he'd hold Eve hostage until he got Harper's money. Patch and Shane, however, shot Eddie.

When Justin discovered Victor had slipped him pills to prolong his impotency, he moved out of the mansion. Anjelica persuaded Neil to adopt Alexander so that Kiriakis wouldn't take him. Soon after, Kiriakis called in Neil's loan, forcing him to sell Blondie's. Worried for her baby's future, Anjelica made a videotape naming Justin as the real father and slipped it into Adrienne's luggage. Meanwhile, blood tests confirmed that Justin was indeed the father.

Jennifer befriended a homeless pregnant girl, Sally, who got herself arrested in order not to have her baby on the streets, but when the baby was born, officials wouldn't let the girl keep it. In a surprise move, Jack pretended to be Jennifer's husband and they offered the child, Hannah, a foster home. He financially supported both Jennifer and the baby. He fell in love with Jennifer, but Emilio returned to Salem to face attempted murder charges, which Justin managed to have dropped. The two called a truce. Emilio moved into the loft that Jack rented for himself and Jennifer to have a home for Hannah, Jack was consumed with jealousy. Jack's paper, *The Spectator*, published an article about Emilio's alleged ties to a gang. Jack was severely beaten, but Emilio promised to protect Jack; when Jennifer's life was also endangered, Emilio pulled away. Working with Roman, Emilio eventually nailed the gang members. Jennifer found herself torn between Jack and Emilio.

An evangelist preacher, the Rev. Saul Taylor, created problems for Patch at the Emergency Center until Patch rescued Saul's daughter, Faith, from drowning.

Soon after, when Saul's revival tent collapsed in the middle of a benefit, Faith was hit by a falling beam.

Dr. Marcus Hunter was an orphanage friend of Patch. Dr. Hunter investigated the past of a civil rights activist he believed to be his father and began a flirtation with Gail Carson, the new anesthesiologist at University Hospital. Unknown to Patch, Gail was also an undercover ISA agent. Patch and Kayla accompanied Marcus and Gail to South Carolina. Marcus was in search of his roots, while Patch was in pursuit of an arsonist who'd left a matchbook from Charleston behind as a clue. Meanwhile, Marcus's Aunt Lizzie warned Gail that Marcus must never know the truth about his parents.

Nick bought Blondie's and turned it into a nightclub, Wings. Eve took a job there as a singer. April decided to bow out of Mike's life so he could be with his son and Robin. To Mike's surprise, April married Nick. But when Mike and Robin argued over Jeremy's religious upbringing, Eve conspired to get him back with April. Unfortunately, Nick had fallen in love with April.

When Shane disappeared, Kimberly believed he was working undercover for the ISA's Operation Mandolin, but Shane was abducted by Jericho, a former ISA friend. In order to keep Faith away from Marcus, Jericho threatened to expose Saul's past. Back in Salem, Marcus performed an operation on Patch's eye so that he could infiltrate Saul's revivalist camp as Daniel Lucas. There, Patch found Shane's keychain, proving he was alive and likely being held prisoner. He reported the information to the ISA, but the organization continued to treat Shane as terminated.

Despite Anjelica's best efforts, Justin and Adrienne remained together. Justin scored revenge against his uncle by hiring a call girl, Yvette Dupres, to pose as a baroness and seduce him. Meanwhile, Anjelica moved in with Kiriakis because she knew it would infuriate Justin to know his son Alexander was being raised by Victor. Although Anjelica even agreed to marry Kiriakis, Justin eventually stopped the wedding and moved Anjelica into the penthouse. Fed up with Justin, Adrienne left him. Then Kiriakis, trying to take custody of Alexander and Roman, came face-to-face with Yvette.

Anxious to visit Patch, Kayla stowed away in a truck bound for Saul's camp. Patch was on the same truck to investigate cargo and the two were taken to a mountain cave equipped with computers. Kayla escaped and told Gail about the situation. When Marcus tried to enter the camp, he was almost killed. Gail got him back to the hospital where he had a flashback memory of a bombing during his childhood and recognized Saul and Jericho as the culprits who caused his father's death.

Jericho gunned down Saul and returned to the cave, with Patch and Shane on his trail. Jericho triggered a bomb that blew up the mountain. Patch escaped, but Shane was presumed dead. Cal, who had become a private investigator, lent support to a grieving Kimberly. Meanwhile, Eve rebelled when she learned her father had left all his money to Kimberly.

Alice and Tom's great-great-grandson, Scott Banning, returned to Salem and laid claim to the land beneath Wings and became involved in the daily operations of the club. He replaced Eve with Faith as the club's resident singer and became Faith's manager and lover. Nick developed a serious illness but kept the news from April because he was afraid she'd go back to Mike, especially since Robin and

Jeremy returned to New York. Later, at a party, Nick collapsed and was rushed to the hospital. To Eve's frustration, April vowed to stand by her man.

Neil advised Adrienne to get a legal separation from Justin. When Justin also filed for a separation, Adrienne faked a pregnancy to win him back. Fed up with Anjelica's manipulations, Yvette moved out of the mansion and set her sights on Roman, who warmed up to Yvette after she helped him with his daughter Carrie. Meanwhile, Anjelica discovered Adrienne's pregnancy ploy and showed the negative lab report to Justin, and he and Adrienne agreed to divorce.

Marina Toscano, a mysterious woman from Patch's Merchant Marine days showed up in Salem. He was stunned to see her since he believed he was responsible for her death. Meanwhile, she claimed to be married to him. Romance, however, was not on Marina's mind—she needed Patch to obtain the key to her father's estate. Patch had the logbook of the ship from which the key was thrown into the ocean. Marina threatened to blackmail him if Patch didn't help her. Kayla encouraged him to help Marina to get her out of their lives but what they didn't know was that Marina was really working for Kiriakis. Soon after, Jack became involved in the situation, and problems escalated when Kayla found out she was pregnant.

Shane was alive, but the cave explosion had erased his memory. Rebecca, a beautiful woman on the run from her wealthy stockbroker husband, found Shane's wallet but hid his true identity. She created a cover for herself as Shane's wife, but Rebecca's husband, Arthur Downey, tracked her down. A fight ensued and they thought Downey was dead. Meanwhile, Kimberly allowed Cal to get closer but felt guilty. Needing some time alone, Kimberly went to the mountains, but Cal pursued her and they nearly stumbled upon Shane. Shane, when he found his ISA patch on a scrap of shirt, realized that Rebecca had deceived him but the ISA wouldn't believe his tale.

Alone, Patch traveled to Italy while an institutionalized Isabella Toscana tried to warn him of danger. Jack tricked Kayla, who was jealous of Marina, into flying to Italy. When Patch finally found the key he was looking for, Kiriakis was there to snatch it. In a struggle, Patch's eye was grazed, forcing him to wear a patch again. Everyone returned to Salem where Victor realized the key was a fake. Marina hid the real key in Patch and Kayla's home and soon attempts were made on Patch and Kayla's lives.

Kiriakis manipulated Yvette to back away from Roman, and she soon agreed to marry Victor. When Roman discovered Marina dead in her hotel room, he suspected Kiriakis was responsible. In order to protect Kayla from Kiriakis, Patch hid her and told Roman she had been kidnapped.

Jack encountered Isabella at the sanitarium and realized she was quite sane. When Jack told her Marina was murdered, Isabella pleaded for his help.

Back in Salem, Kimberly and Cal made love for the first time, unaware that Shane was standing outside their door. Rebecca and Shane traveled to Chicago to clear her name and discovered that Downey was still alive. Cal's new client was an undercover agent, Renfro, in pursuit of Downey. Gun-toting Downey showed up, so Shane and Rebecca took off back to the mountains.

Kayla had been kidnapped because Kiriakis wanted the key to the Toscano treasure. Kayla was aboard Victor's yacht under the watchful eye of nurse Grace, but she managed to get a message to Patch. After a botched rescue attempt, Kayla was whisked to Miami by helicopter.

Justin remained loyal to the elder Kiriakis. Although Adrienne still harbored strong feelings for Justin, she signed the divorce papers. This pleased Anjelica, who wanted Justin to return to her and their son Alexander.

Nick needed life-saving surgery and admitted to April that he had agreed to the procedure only so he could be with her. April told Nick she would help him through the ordeal, but in her heart April knew that it was over between them—she wanted to be with Dr. Mike Horton. After Nick's operation was a success, he learned of April's feelings for Mike. Feigning disinterest, Nick asked for an annulment. Then Mike flew April to the Caribbean and they returned engaged.

In Salem, Cal set up Kimberly to shoot Shane, whom she mistook for a prowler. In the hospital, Shane learned from daughter Eve that his wife Kimberly had shot him. Not yet having recovered his memory, he couldn't trust Kimberly's prowler story, especially since Cal continued to seek ways of destroying him. Cal enlisted Rebecca's help keeping Shane suspicious of Kimberly.

Jack got Isabella out of the asylum and kept her hidden until Roman found her at Devereaux's loft. Kiriakis was surprised when Isabella showed up at the mansion. She secretly wanted to get clues to Kayla's whereabouts.

Jennifer admitted to Emilio that she was enamored of Jack. Though Jennifer knew Jack considered her a kid, she used her job at *The Spectator* to get closer to him. When Jennifer followed Jack to Patch and Kayla's mansion, she inadvertently found the Toscano key. Patch had already left for Miami, and Isabella, with Roman, went after him. Jack was able to duplicate the key and he headed for Italy in search of the Toscana treasure. Roman, meanwhile, offered Kiriakis the key for Patch's wife.

Shane agreed to go home with Kimberly after she was cleared of criminal intent in the shooting. Kimberly suggested hypnosis to help him regain his memory. Cal, obsessed with Kimberly, murdered Rebecca when she threatened his scheme. Then he took Kimberly to a cave that was decorated just like her home. Shane figured out that they were on the mountain, and after he was able to physically overcome Cal, the nightmare was over.

Isabella was shot while handing over the key to Kiriakis's henchmen. Rushing to the hospital, Roman realized that Kiriakis had genuine feelings for Isabella. Meanwhile, in Italy, Jack located the cave that held the mysterious treasure, the diary of the late Loretta Toscano.

Patch and Kayla made plans to rewed to make their baby legitimate. Patch even reconciled with his brother Jack, asking him to be their best man. But Kayla received a tape from the night Marina Toscano was murdered. On it, Kayla argued with

Isabella turned out to be the one who killed Marina (in self-defense), but she blocked the episode from her memory. Kiriakis had it on videotape.

Arrested for the murder of Marina Toscano, Kayla was in jail when Patch helped her deliver their daughter Stephanie. Separated from her child, Kayla's heartache was compounded when their nanny Sheila kidnapped the baby.

Marina, threatening her. When Roman and Abe received the same tape, courtesy of Kiriakis, they were forced to stop the ceremony and Kayla was arrested for murder.

Justin grew closer to Adrienne as they began to date again. Anjelica became wildly jealous and plotted to sabotage Adrienne's construction company. As part of her underhanded scheme, she bribed Adrienne's associate Hank to bomb a new structure built by Adrienne's company. When Hank had a change of heart, Anjelica forced him at gunpoint to ignite the dynamite. Justin rushed to rescue Adrienne, but she was caught in the explosion. She survived, but Hank was killed. Surprisingly, Justin claimed responsibility for the bombing.

Jack discouraged Jennifer's attraction toward him, but he secretly felt the same for her. He chose not to reveal the contents of Loretta's diary, fearing its contents would hurt Isabella. Instead, he gave Isabella the diary, but with key pages missing. Meanwhile, in Italy, a frustrated Kiriakis discovered that the diary had been removed. Already aware of the damaging contents of the diary, Kiriakis vowed that nothing would happen to Isabella.

Julie Williams returned to Salem, determined to mastermind Kiriakis's downfall. In the meantime, Julie planned a surprise anniversary party for Maggie and Mickey. Unfortunately, workaholic Mickey came late, disappointing Maggie, but the homecoming of daughter Melissa brightened the festivities. When Melissa saw that cousin Jennifer was falling for her ex-beau, Jack, she warned him to stay away from Jennifer. Instead, she pushed Jennifer toward Emilio. But when Melissa and Emilio formed a singing team, she discovered her own attraction to the charismatic entertainer.

Caroline took the fall for daughter Kayla, claiming she was the one who'd murdered Marina. Kiriakis, however, refused to let his former love take the blame and quickly provided an alibi for her. Kayla's trial was halted so that she could give birth to Stephanie Kay. But when the trial resumed, Kayla was eventually found guilty.

Roman knew that if he found Marina's tape recorder, he could exonerate Kayla. The search drew him closer to Isabella. Kiriakis dropped the incriminating recorder in the river, unaware that a homeless man, Fred, was watching. When Fred retrieved the recorder and tried to sell it, Roman stumbled on the evidence he needed. His witness, however, was found drowned.

Anjelica feared that Justin was inching closer toward the truth about her role in the bombing. She fled town with Alexander. When their flight crashed, everyone presumed that Anjelica and Alexander were dead. But unknown to anyone in Salem, Anjelica had caught a different flight. A vengeful Anjelica vowed to return to Salem. Meanwhile, Kiriakis disowned Justin and searched for his estranged son, Bo.

When Kayla opted not to keep the baby with her behind bars, Patch hired Kelly Parker as a nanny. Unbeknownst to him, she was really Sheila, a psychopath who knew Kayla from the hospital. Sheila wanted baby Stephanie because she had lost her own child. When Sheila thought Kayla was returning home, she snapped and abducted Stephanie. When Kayla got the distressing news of her daughter's kidnapping, she escaped from her jail cell. Kayla successfully trailed Sheila to the airport and sent an urgent message to Patch.

Tom Horton told Mike of the dire need for medical volunteers overseas. Mike felt obligated to go and postponed his wedding to April. When Mike's volunteer work continued to keep him in Israel, close to his son Jeremy, April gave up on him. As expected, Nick was there to offer consolation.

Kimberly discovered that she was pregnant. The imprisoned Cal plotted to make Kimberly believe the baby was his. Kimberly, who was frightened and confused, ran away to a seedy motel and took a tumble down a flight of stairs. At the hospital, Shane learned of her pregnancy. A self-satisfied Cal informed Shane of the baby's true paternity. Though forgiving, Shane's relationship with Kimberly was severely strained.

A terrible storm hit Salem. Faith was paralyzed in the aftermath of a near-drowning. Eve conspired to keep Faith and Scott apart by bringing up the specter of Scott's past love, Amy. But as Faith regained her ability to walk, Scott was accepted at a California medical school and the two went off to begin a new life. Having lost Scott, Nick asked April to manage Wings.

Roman urged Isabella to search Kiriakis's attic for anything incriminating. When Kiriakis caught Isabella in the attic, he played the missing portion of the tape. Isabella realized she had blocked out the horrifying memory that she was the murderer of Marina. Roman was forced to arrest Isabella, but eventually she was cleared of murder charges after it was determined she killed Marina in self-defense. Meanwhile, Isabella provided proof that Kiriakis had withheld evidence and Roman took pleasure in finally arresting his longtime nemesis. In the meantime, Guiseppe, Lorenzo Toscano's faithful servant, arrived from Italy to look for the diary.

Desperate to keep Jennifer from marrying Emilio, Jack kidnapped Jennifer on her wedding day. When Jennifer escaped, fell off a cliff, and was knocked unconscious, Jack finally poured out his heart to her. Meanwhile, Emilio was hurt in the rescue. Later, insecure Jack refused to reiterate his love and Jennifer returned to Emilio.

Sheila led Kayla and Patch to Australia, where their paths crossed with Bo and Hope Brady's. Bo told Patch that he was Kiriakis's son. Meanwhile, Kayla and Patch received news that Kayla had been exonerated. Marcus and Grace arrived in Australia to help search for Sheila, who was eventually tracked to the Australian Outback. After a struggle, Kayla was finally reunited with Stephanie. They returned to Salem just in time for Justin and Adrienne's wedding.

As Maggie and Mickey grew more distant, Maggie turned to Neil for solace. When clerical Jo Johnson, who had a crush on Dr. Curtis, found a medical file on surrogate mothers, Neil admitted he was Sarah's father by artificial insemination, although for years, Maggie believed the late Dr. Evan Whyland had been the sperm donor. So when Neil withheld the truth as he grew closer to Maggie and Sarah, they were none the wiser.

Kiriakis's pursuit of Bo forced Bo, Hope, and Shawn-Douglas to flee to Paris. Kiriakis, who was no longer facing charges, surfaced in Paris. Meanwhile, Bo held on to his hatred of Kiriakis. When Hope received a sudden good-bye note from Bo, she returned to Salem with their son. But Bo had not written the note. Loretta's husband, Ernesto, who had been presumed dead, had kidnapped Bo and forged the note. Ernesto was also responsible for sending Johnny Corelli to Salem. In a plot to bring Kiriakis to ruin, Johnny planned to have plastic surgery and assume Bo's identity. Bo, however, convinced Johnny to let him switch roles, and the real Bo went back to Salem. Johnny trailed him there and turned out to be Nick's brother, the renegade ISA agent.

Ernesto arranged for the voyage of the cruise ship *Loretta*, luring his suspected enemies along. Ernesto took Isabella away after he planted a bomb on the ship. Jack and Jennifer revealed that Ernesto had poisoned Loretta because Isabella was Kiriakis's daughter. The explosion shipwrecked everyone, including Victor and Julie, on the very island where Isabella was being held. Jack saved Jennifer's life, and they made love for the first time there. Hope trailed Bo to Ernesto's lair, and taking a wrong turn, ended up in a cage. Ernesto followed her in and the cage erupted in flames over a vat of acid. Meanwhile, Shane and his fellow ISA agent, Johnny, located the group. Shane convinced Bo to accept that Hope had been killed in the explosion and the grieving group returned to Salem.

Shane plunged back into ISA work. Kimberly learned that Cal was seeking visitation rights. She felt estranged from Shane and decided to leave him. Wanting to avoid any contact with Cal, Kimberly left Salem. She was out of town, away from Shane, when their baby was born.

While honeymooning in Tahiti, Justin and Adrienne encountered Carly Manning, a.k.a. Katerina, the heiress to the Von Leuschner fortune, who was on the run. Carly confided to Jennifer that she was running because she was promised in marriage to entrepreneur Lawrence Alamain. Due to a confusion going back to when Carly and Jennifer were teenagers and they had switched dates, Jennifer realized that Lawrence thought she was the missing heiress.

Jack's adoptive father, Harper, escaped from prison and plotted to murder Patch at his wedding. But Harper took a fatal fall from a bell tower when Jack foiled his sniper attack. Suffering from anguishing hallucinations about the violent paternal figures in his life, Harper and Duke, Jack pushed a confused Jennifer away. Feeling rejected, Jennifer switched roles with Carly and traveled to New York to meet Lawrence.

Jencon Oil vied to build a refinery in town. After Shawn-Douglas lost his hearing in an accident on the refinery site, Bo sabotaged Jencon Corporation. Patch uncovered that Bo was the Riverfront Raider and offered to help. Nick tipped off Jencon and Patch was caught in an explosion meant for Bo. At the hospital, Patch came out of his coma only to have his IV poisoned. Patch died in Kayla's arms.

Lawrence Alamain was the mystery man behind Jencon. He flew to his native country, and after a hurried wedding, forced himself on Jennifer, who discovered that long-lost Frankie Brady was being held captive. Jack arrived to rescue Jennifer.

Back in Salem, Kiriakis suffered a stroke and Nick was found murdered.

Roman had a movie production shut down because of arson connected to Nick's murder. Shane and Kayla were convinced that Lawrence was behind Patch's murder. The pursuit of Alamain led them to realize that Carly had engineered to trade Bo for Frankie, a.k.a. Francois von Leuschner. Lawrence wanted revenge against Bo for a long ago slight that had driven him and Carly apart. When Lawrence's diabolical plans went awry, he escaped and triggered an earthquake, trapping the party and killing Leopold Alamain. Once dug out, the group returned to Salem.

At Christmastime, Alice Horton suffered a heart attack, Adrienne suffered through a difficult pregnancy, Roman continued to investigate Nick's murder, and Lawrence Alamain resurfaced in Salem.

Bo and Dr. Carly Manning discovered Emilio's body at Alamain's New Year's Eve gala. The shocking discovery gave Roman two murders to solve and an ample supply of suspects.

After Isabella became concerned that Victor had not responded to therapy, Dr. Tom Horton persuaded Carly to take Kiriakis on as a patient. While a compassionate Carly helped Kiriakis to overcome his stroke, he became enamored of her. When Bo told Carly he couldn't commit to a relationship because of his lingering pain over Hope's untimely death, Carly accepted Victor's marriage proposal. Meanwhile, Bo hid his despair.

Justin remained concerned over Johnny Corelli's influence in his father's business. But Johnny won Justin's grudging approval when he reunited him with his presumed dead son, Alexander. Johnny also provided Justin with an alibi for Nick's murder. This left Justin free to move to Dallas with pregnant Adrienne and their adopted twins, Victor and Joseph. Soon after, Johnny pursued April, against Isabella's wishes. Johnny suspected April had something to do with Nick's death and he wanted to protect her.

In Nick's will he'd left Wings to Julie. Nick also left Eve $10 million, provided Eve marry. Frankie rejected her greed and proposal, so Eve suggested a marriage of convenience to Jack. Although Jack had been engaged to Jennifer, he called off their wedding because he felt alienated from her. Jennifer was still unable to handle intimacy and too ashamed to tell Jack that Lawrence had raped her. Jack accepted Eve's proposal in order to protect *The Spectator* from Lawrence's hostile takeover.

When Peachy contracted the deadly virus, Shane agreed to begin an immunology lab as a cover for the ISA investigation. He suspected Lawrence had something to do with the spread of the virus. In an effort to thwart him, Lawrence lured Shane's ex-wife Kimberly back to Salem. Kimberly was upset to learn that Shane and her sister Kayla had grown close in her absence. ISA chief Tarrington further complicated events when he recruited Kimberly to spy on Lawrence and presented her to Shane as his new contact. Kimberly developed mixed feelings for Lawrence as their contact grew. Kayla was aghast that her sister was spending time with Lawrence. She blamed her relationship with Shane for Kimberly's behavior.

Jack's *Spectator* editor, Vern Scofield, had two sons, Brian and Tanner, and a daughter, Cassie. Tanner was found roughed up in an alley after trying to contact Jennifer about Nick's murder. As Brian continued his investigation, he

1991

found himself attracted to Melissa and broke off his engagement to Madeline Armstrong. Thinking that he was protecting April, Johnny pressured Tanner into implicating Eve in Nick's murder. Eve fled to Miami after her hearing, but Frankie pursued her and convinced Eve to return to Salem—he had discovered new evidence that would exonerate her.

Melissa accepted a singing engagement on the *Old West Express*. When information surfaced that suggested the murder weapon used to kill Nick might have been hidden in the lounge car of that train, Brian, Frankie, Eve, Jack, and Jennifer boarded it and searched for the weapon. The search led them to the storage car. When one of Johnny's thugs uncoupled the car, it crashed, stranding them in the mountains. After leading the group to safety, Eve was hailed a hero. But Eve hid the fact that she gained much-needed assistance from a backwoods recluse named Molly Brinker, who provided her with the vital information needed to expedite their trip back to civilization. When Eve suffered a near-fatal fall from a helicopter that was rescuing them, Frankie vowed his love for her.

Bo lifted April's fingerprints from the murder weapon that Jack found on the train. Then Jo surprised everyone by confessing to Nick's murder. Jo explained she was seeking revenge for her murdered son, Patch. After pleading insanity, Jo admitted herself to a mental institution. Fed up with Johnny's dirty dealings, April broke off their relationship. Soon after, she moved to New York City to join her brother Julio, a talented pianist.

Bo realized how precious life was when Shawn-Douglas, who had regained his hearing, nearly drowned. Bo gave Emmy Borden a love note meant for Carly.

D r. Carly Manning was hired as Victor Kiriakis's personal physician and he quickly became enamored of her. He proposed, and when it seemed Bo had rejected her, Carly accepted. However, Victor's plotting couldn't win her in the long run.

But behind Bo's back, Emmy, who was infatuated with Bo, instead delivered the note to Kiriakis. After reading Bo's proclamation of love for Carly and plea for her to not marry Kiriakis, Kiriakis moved ahead with a new plan to undermine Bo and Carly's romance. Kiriakis masterminded forged notes and had Emmy deliver them to Bo and Carly. Based on Kiriakis's bogus missives, Bo and Carly believed that the other wanted to end their relationship. Although Carly remained in love with Bo, she married Kiriakis. The long-jealous Emmy mistakenly infected Bo with the virus when he drank the champagne intended for Carly. Kiriakis had Emmy kidnapped after she cracked and threatened to expose his evil manipulations. Eventually, Carly discovered that Kiriakis had conspired to keep her and Bo apart. She immediately left Kiriakis.

Sarah discovered that her mom, Maggie, was having an affair with Neil Curtis. Sarah lured Neil into a trap, drugged him, and sent pictures to the tabloid *Chronicle* of the two of them in bed together. Realizing she had to clear Neil's name, Maggie revealed to Sarah that Neil was her father. In the wake of these startling revelations, Mickey and Maggie broke up. Meanwhile, Melissa admitted to Brian that Emilio had fallen from a window during a heated quarrel. Soon after, Brian had Melissa arrested and charged with murder. Although Emilio's death was ruled accidental, it was too late for Brian and Melissa. Instead, Melissa packed her bags and persuaded her sister Sarah to join her in Nashville, where they hoped to begin new lives.

Jennifer pressed rape charges against Lawrence. With Kimberly's help, Lawrence nearly proved that he was the victim of blackouts, induced by traumatic stress dating back to his childhood. He also denied having any memory of forcing

Jennifer finally pressed charges against Lawrence Alamain for raping her after getting his confession on tape. Jack stood by her once he understood the reason for her earlier coolness toward him.

While Carly and Bo exchanged their own vows in Mexico, Kiriakis found himself chained in a cave.

himself on Jennifer. A suspicious Kimberly bugged Lawrence's home and was devastated to learn that he was using her. Lawrence also confessed to her that he raped Jennifer. When Kimberly learned that Bo was sick with the virus, and that only Lawrence could lead her to the cure, she heeded Tarrington's strong warning not to testify against Lawrence. However, Kimberly allowed Jack to obtain the taped confession. Jack played it for Lawrence. After being apprehended by the authorities, Lawrence agreed to a plea bargain. Convicted and sent to prison, Lawrence continued to plot his evil machinations from a small prison cell.

Cal escaped and proceeded to harass Kimberly. She mistakenly thought it was Lawrence's doing, until Cal kidnapped Kayla. Soon after, Kayla was rescued and Cal revealed that Shane was the father of Kimberly's daughter, Jeannie.

Lawrence double-crossed Kiriakis by bribing his henchman, Kurt, who was holding Emmy prisoner. In an attempt to win Kimberly back, Lawrence plotted to lure Bo to Emmy, where he would inject Bo with the cure. When Lawrence's plan backfired, Kurt exacted revenge on Emmy by injecting her with a lethal dose of the virus. Sadly, before Bo could rescue Emmy, she died in his arms. Desperate to win Carly back, Kiriakis contacted Lawrence and offered him the John Black file in exchange for the cure to the virus. But their trade-off was botched when the vial containing the cure was shattered by a gunshot. Fortunately, Carly was able to salvage a small portion and concocted a serum in time to save Bo's life. When Carly welshed on a deal to reconcile with Kiriakis, a vengeful Kiriakis rigged the private elevator to the penthouse Bo had rented at the Salem Inn. The plan misfired and, instead, Carly ended up critically injured.

Eve reluctantly granted Jack a divorce after Julie bought her off. In spite of Eve's unseemly behavior, Frankie forgave her and they went off to Africa. Jack kept Eve's fortune and married Jennifer. After honeymooning in Hollywood, it looked as if Jack and Jennifer finally had found true happiness. But new problems cropped up when Jack allowed a clever grifter named Hawk to swindle the newlyweds out of their money in an elaborate con game, which also left Jack on the run. Jennifer used her trust fund to save Jack's interest in *The Spectator*. Meanwhile, during Jack's absence, Hawk plotted to draw closer to Jennifer.

Tanner grew closer to Molly Brinker as he investigated her mysterious past. Although Tanner didn't know it, Molly's mom, Ginger, was searching for her. Soon after, Ginger arrived in Salem. Howard Hawk Hawkins and his accomplices, Howard Alston Hawkins and Chauncy, worried that Ginger, who knew them from another town, would blow their scam. Realizing that Ginger was Molly's long-lost mom, Genevieve, Tanner pressured her to tell Molly the truth.

But when Ginger told Tanner about the Hawkins gang, Tanner refused to let Ginger reveal her connection to Molly out of concern for Molly's safety.

Isabella denounced Kiriakis and moved out of his mansion. She returned to Roman II and all seemed on the mend until his presumed-dead wife Marlena suddenly appeared after a five-year absence. Roman II learned that Marlena had been kidnapped and held captive on an island, the victim of an induced coma. Meanwhile, Roman I was shown videotapes of Marlena with Roman II, and he escaped his jungle prison. Identical Mexican medallions led Roman II and Marlena to Mexico and the site of Marlena and Roman I's imprisonment, and they ran into Roman I. Isabella, who was in love with Roman II, suspected it was Kiriakis who was responsible for their troubles because he had threatened to take away her happiness in the past. Isabella's Roman II was actually the brainwashed John Black.

In a final attempt to keep Bo and Carly apart, Kiriakis faked his own death. Isabella was the first one to discover the fraud. Bo and Carly trailed Kiriakis to Mexico. Isabella followed, looking for John. Kiriakis was found chained in a cave. After a treasure hunt involving the medallions, Kiriakis was apprehended by the Mexican authorities. Bo and Carly celebrated a Mayan "marriage of the heart." Isabella informed John that she was carrying his child and would stand by him. The group returned to Salem, but John remained tormented because Stefano threw the remaining clues to John's past into a fire before Stefano too seemed to perish.

1992

After Bo discovered Carly's birthmark was identical to one shown in an old photograph of John Black's mystery woman, Rafi Torres's henchmen abducted him to a remote mountain cabin. Roman made a daring deal with Rafi to exchange Bo for drug shipments. The swap turned into a bloody shoot-out that left Rafi wounded and his brother dead. Enraged, Rafi blamed Carly for the double-cross and vowed revenge. Lawrence, meanwhile, saved Carly's life when Rafi set her and Shawn-Douglas adrift on Bo's boat, then nursed her back to health when she suffered a severe fever. But Carly still longed only for Bo.

Roman went undercover, but he and Marlena were threatened when Rafi planted a bomb at the museum party. The bomb exploded just as Shane attempted to disarm it. Both he and Julie were severely wounded. Julie was saved after Chip performed surgery, but Shane refused to have an operation and was left paralyzed from the waist down. Roman couldn't stand his separation from Marlena and finally revealed his disguise to her. She was furious that he was risking his life in this mission but she soon gave in to the passion between them.

Armed with a marriage certificate, Danielle Stevens arrived in Salem claiming to be John's wife. She tried to jog John's memory and rekindle his desires by telling him stories about their supposedly shared past. Naturally, Isabella felt threatened by Danielle's determination but John reassured her of his love and loyalty. Vivian held a masquerade ball, recreating a similar event eight years earlier when a master thief named Romulus had stolen a cache of jewelry, which included a locket Lawrence had given Carly. Carly got a better surprise at this party. Roman had rescued Bo and the lovers were reunited. At the same time, John experienced bizarre flashbacks, which made him begin to believe he was

A holdup at Brady's Fish Market by men impersonating cops left Shawn critically wounded. The attack spurred Bo to join the Salem Police Department.

Romulus. Danielle then tried to convince him that he was actually a private investigator assigned to track Romulus. She told him the truth to his past was locked in a safe deposit box in Switzerland and joined him on the next flight to Geneva. Once there, John was drawn to Danielle as she shared memories at the restaurant where he'd once proposed to her. Later, about to open the safe deposit box, John was arrested for being the jewel thief Romulus and taken to jail. With the help of a fingerprint expert, Danielle convinced police they had the wrong man. Danielle later pointed out to John that Stefano had changed John's fingerprints, so even if he was Romulus, the prints wouldn't match.

Back in Salem, Isabella read Lawrence's file on John and realized he was not Romulus—Danielle was. She notified the authorities and they arrived to arrest Danielle just as she and John were about to make love. However, John made it easy for Danielle to escape.

Vivian recognized the locket from the safe deposit box as the one stolen from her eight years ago. When Lawrence and Vivian opened the crate that should have held the coffin of Forrest, Lawrence's dead brother, the crate was filled with sand. Soon after, John's true identity as Lawrence's long-lost brother was verified through DNA tests. John and Victor Kiriakis discovered that Vivian had swindled Forrest—now John—out of an inheritance from his father Leopold. They made certain John got back his share, but Vivian vowed revenge.

With his life seemingly back on track, John was anxious to marry Isabella. The big day arrived and all their family and friends in Salem gathered at the church. Isabella made a very beautiful and very pregnant bride. Just as the ceremony was to start, she went into labor and gave birth in an adjoining room to Brady Victor. The guests waited excitedly in the church, and the wedding ceremony finally continued without a hitch, and with a new member of the wedding party.

Meanwhile, Roman was still working undercover and thwarted Rafi's planned drug shipment and brought down the entire Torres crime ring. With Rafi finally out of their lives, Roman and Marlena were reunited. The couple now had to deal with Roman's rapidly maturing daughter Carrie, who had returned to Salem a few months earlier. After John ordered her at gunpoint to leave Lawrence's bed before they could make love, Carrie became smitten with Jesse Lombard. He had just been arrested for carrying a gun, and in spite of her dad Roman's disapproval, she moved in with him.

Soon after Bo returned to town, he and Carly left for France where Dr. Goddard told Carly that the baby she'd had was still alive, somewhere. Bo and Carly hired a private investigator named West to find the baby, to no avail. Lisanne, who had become the Alamain corporate attorney and Lawrence's lover, undertook her own investigation. When she returned from Paris she shocked Lawrence with the news that he had fathered Carly's baby. Lawrence confronted Carly, but she denied it. Desperate to know the truth, he too went to Paris to investigate further. He came up empty-handed, but Carly finally admitted he was, in fact, the baby's father. Wanting nothing to do with Lawrence, Carly told him that the baby had died shortly after birth. Meanwhile Vivian's foster son Nikki arrived and became good pals with Shawn-Douglas, Bo's boy.

After Shawn was shot in a holdup attempt at Brady's Fish Market, Bo decided to become a cop. He and Carly became engaged, but her demanding and erratic schedule at the hospital and Bo's unpredictable hours kept them apart. After Carly and Lawrence shared an impulsive kiss, they realized their attraction remained. Still, Carly insisted she would marry Bo.

Hawk was conned into making a full confession of bilking the couple of their money by Jennifer and Jack, who were penniless after Jack's inheritance fell through. Jennifer told Jack she was pregnant, but his joy was tempered by the fear that he was suffering a relapse of Hodgkin's disease. He was unreasonably convinced that he was dying and was determined to find a suitable husband for Jennifer before he passed on. He decided Brian was the man and hired him as Jennifer's bodyguard. To provide financial security, he sold *The Spectator* to Julie. Eventually, doctors convinced the eccentric hypochondriac that he was in perfect health. While Jack became a reporter on the police beat for the newspaper, Jennifer accepted a television job in New York with Calliope. Later in the year, Jack found an old manuscript in the house that Jennifer's dad Bill had given them. Jack arranged to have it published under a pseudonym. And Jennifer gave birth to their baby daughter, Abigail Johanna.

Shane was slowly recuperating from being accidentally shot by Kimberly and was ecstatic when he regained some feeling in his legs, but pulled away from Kayla fearing he still could not make love to her in a completely fulfilling way. So when Kimberly called from Los Angeles and told Kayla about a job opening there, Kayla took Shane's advice and left. Shane then became an instructor at the police academy. When Kimberly returned from Los Angeles only a few months later to announce her engagement, she set into motion a chain of dramatic events. As soon as she got to Salem, she was run over by drunk driver Roger Lombard. Stunned to witness the accident happening, Shane leapt out of his wheelchair and took a few steps as he tried to save her. Kimberly was rushed to the hospital where she remained in a coma for several days. When she came around, her behavior seemed a little strange, but the extent of her problem was deviously well hidden. Kimberly suffered from multiple personality disorder. Kimberly sometimes became the streetwise tart Lacey, who wore a red wig and danced up a storm many nights at Casey's Roadhouse. One patron there, Randy Huston, found her very attractive and they left Casey's together, but when he came on to her, Lacey backed off. Angered that she was a tease, Randy threatened her with a knife. They struggled and Lacey stabbed him to death in self-defense. Kimberly suffered flashbacks of sexual abuse by her knife-wielding uncle. When incriminating evidence tied her to the murder of Randy, Kimberly's fiancé Phillip Collier postponed their wedding and tried to help Kimberly through hypnosis. Kimberly's third personality, Clare, threatened to harm Kimberly if Phillip interfered. As Clare, Kimberly shot her brother Roman, but after brain surgery to remove the bullet, he survived. Shane, meanwhile, clearing the way for Kimberly and Phillip and avoiding past memories with her, left for Europe on a daring ISA mission.

Roger Lombard, the drunk driver who hit Kimberly, was out on bail and was being counseled by Marlena. In fact, Roger's entire family was invited to therapy sessions, but his son Jesse and wife Stella refused to return after the first session. Worse, average-looking Stella became insanely jealous of Marlena's beauty and intelligence. At first, Stella tried to imitate Dr. Evans, but when Roger painted Marlena's portrait, Stella slashed the canvas. Stella was wrongly convinced that Roger was having an affair with Marlena. At a dinner party, Stella slipped Marlena a mickey, which made the usually refined Marlena appear drunk and somewhat foolish.

John and Isabella enjoyed a grand and gloriously romantic honeymoon in Italy. The happy couple then returned to the heartbreaking news that Isabella had inoperable pancreatic cancer. Totally devastated, John went into denial and insisted Isabella would recover, and their beautiful love story would continue. Isabella made him accept the truth and, after making a list of things she wanted to do before she died, they returned to Italy in the fall. There, she died peacefully in the loving arms of her husband.

After Molly Brinker fought off Prof. Gavin Stone's sexual assault at the cabin, she told Tanner what happened. Tanner, who had figured out that Gavin was the mystery man behind his mother's rape and suicide, could no longer hold his anger in check. Tanner and Molly's mother, Ginger, kidnapped Gavin and took him to a cabin where Ginger terrorized him with a hot poker. After the police took care of Gavin, Tanner wanted to move in with Molly, but her episode with Gavin had left her badly shaken. She decided to live in the dorm and sought counseling from Marlena. Eventually, they became lovers. Brian Scofield and Ginger went to Chicago.

By late October, Lisanne planned to blackmail Vivian over Nikki's true identity. During their confrontation, Nikki shoved Lisanne and she stumbled, hit her head on a stone cat, and died. Lawrence and Vivian hid the body in a car, Vivian's servant, Ivan Marais, faked a car crash, and the body was cremated. When Lawrence turned on Vivian, she had a heart attack. DNA tests proved Lawrence's claim that Nikki was his son with Carly, but because of Nikki's involvement in Lisanne's death, he convinced Carly not to tell Bo until the investigation was over. In early December, Vivian kidnapped Nikki. Lawrence interrupted Bo and Carly's wedding with the news and also announced that he and Carly were Nikki's parents. Before Bo could react, Lawrence grabbed Carly and they rushed to find Vivian and Nikki. Bo refused to get involved and left on an impulsive trip with Shawn-Douglas. However, he found information that led him to Vivian and Nikki. By the time the four returned, Carly and Lawrence were reminiscing about their past, although everyone kept the identity of his mom from Nikki.

Deranged Stella kidnapped Marlena as she left on a business trip and threw her into the boiler pit of an old warehouse and kept her there over a month. Knowing the warehouse was going to be demolished, Stella booked a flight to Arizona. However, on the way to the airport, she changed her mind and called the police from a phone booth. Before she could complete the call, a skid-

ABOVE: Carly, Bo, and Bo's son Shawn-Douglas.

BELOW: Lawrence stopped the wedding by announcing that he had fathered Carly's son Nikki who was still alive.

ding truck crashed into the booth and killed her. Following clues, John arrived at the warehouse just as it exploded and became trapped with her until Abe brought them to safety. The ordeal rekindled Marlena's feelings for John, but she managed to control her passion.

When Salem newcomer Billie Reed's cocaine habit cost her job, Carrie took her in and Bo got her work at Casey's Roadhouse. Billie almost fell into prostitution, but changed her mind at the last minute. An old crime pal, Tony Becker, popped into town with $100,000 he needed stashed while he was carted off to jail. Billie's brother Austin had a hard time getting free of his old ways too. Carrie knew Austin was supposed to throw his prizefight and managed to get him stranded in a mountain cabin. Her scheme enraged him, and by year's end, it appeared their new relationship was already over.

1993

As Austin stepped into the boxing ring, he was faced with a moral bout. He had every intention of going for a win until Gus, a shady character involved with the gambling ring, demanded he throw the fight. His sister Billie told him he would be crazy to defy Gus—the consequences would be unbearable. So Austin was on the mat at the end of the third round, but Carrie, at ringside, roused him to victory. Although it seemed that should be a victory for Austin as an athlete and for the couple, there were tragic consequences. After becoming a Face of the '90s finalist, Carrie was hit in the face with a vial of acid intended for Austin. When Austin arrived at the hospital with an engagement ring, Carrie sent him away. She feared her father would arrest him for his involvement in the gambling ring if she continued to see him. Meanwhile, Gus was found dead in his motel room.

Jack, who was obsessed with buying back *The Spectator*, found money that Billie had hidden for Tony Becker in an abandoned barn. Not long after Jack used the money as a down payment on the newspaper, Tony returned. When Billie realized Jack was responsible for the cash disappearing, they tried a variety of odd ways to raise the money.

When Marlena vowed to stay with Roman, John tried to push aside his feelings for her by dating assistant DA Rebecca Morrison. Marlena made a focused effort to pay more attention to Roman, but her sensual dreams about John quite often got in the way. John was not doing much better and planned to leave town. He got as far as his private jet, then Marlena came to say one last good-bye. The two fell into a passionate embrace and an uncontrollable flood of desire. After they made love, Marlena went home to discover a wedding anniversary surprise party. In a short while, John came through the door. He had decided to stay in Salem.

While Carly and Lawrence tried to hide Nikki's part in Lisanne's accidental death, Carly's half-truths and secrecy drove a wedge between her and Bo. Although Lawrence was arrested for Lisanne's death, the judge dropped the charges after Nikki admitted pushing Lisanne to protect his Aunt Vivian.

After Nikki learned the truth about his parents, Vivian, who was diagnosed with a fatal heart illness, became determined to kill Carly in order to keep the boy. Lawrence, who already had Bo's police partner Taylor under his control, framed Bo by hiring a Bo lookalike to beat up petty thug Cash. As Lawrence had orchestrated it, a highly publicized police brutality investigation ensued.

Win or lose, Austin Reed's boxing match was destined to change the course of his romance with Carrie.

Kate Roberts, a successful and self-assured career woman, came to Salem and became the head of Titan Publishing. She had a fascination for a seventeen-year-old newspaper headline that read: PREGNANT WOMAN FOUND BATTERED ON HIGHWAY. Marlena seemed to know some of Kate's secrets, and Alice vaguely remembered that Kate, with a different name, once lived in the house that Jack and Jennifer presently owned. Jack had found a manuscript in the house and, under a pseudonym, rewrote it as a novel never realizing it was Kate's own story. When it was submitted to her publishing company, she kept it under lock and key. Within a short time, Kate moved into Victor Kiriakis's huge mansion and they soon became lovers.

Carrie celebrated being named the Face of the '90s title by *Bella* magazine, but by the end of the evening acid had been thrown at her and she was disfigured. Her emotional scars lasted longer than the physical ones, however.

Julie Williams left town to join her ex-husband Doug in Switzerland. And Sami Brady, Roman and Marlena's teen daughter, returned to Salem and immediately became infatuated with a good-looking guy she kept running into. She had no idea it was her sister Carrie's boyfriend Austin until weeks later, and by then she was totally smitten.

Kristen Blake was new in town too. One of her first misadventures was being attacked by thugs. John saved her and became intrigued with this feisty, independent social worker. While John tried to help Kristen finance a community center, she made calls to a wheelchair-bound man wearing a ring that bore a phoenix. In spite of their attraction, John and Kristen stayed apart until Alice played matchmaker and encouraged each, individually, to visit the Hortons' island cabin for a few days.

Bo realized he was being framed, but before he could find the impostor, Lawrence ordered Taylor to kill her lover Mitch, who had played Bo's part in the frame-up. Taylor shot Bo by mistake. When Bo and Billie stalked the hired killer, a disguised Taylor panicked and ran in front of a car. Although she died, she left behind a taped confession that cleared Bo of all charges. While Carly and Bo's relationship showed strain, Billie continued to fall more in love with Bo.

Devious Vivian, diagnosed with a deteriorating heart condition, intended to frame Carly for her own murder. At Shawn-Douglas's birthday party, Vivian goaded Carly into an argument on the terrace. Ironically, Vivian accidentally fell. After Carly saved her life in surgery, Vivian disguised herself as a nurse, took mysterious herbs she believed cured her heart condition, and began killing Carly's patients by injecting them with cleaning fluid.

Marlena learned she was pregnant, but didn't know if John or Roman was the father. Although she considered an abortion, she was mugged and landed in the hospital where her pregnancy was announced. Roman asked John to be the delighted godfather.

Sami became friends with Kate Roberts' son Lucas who came to Salem right out of military academy. In exchange for taking her to the Spring Fling wearing his uniform—to make Austin notice her and possible make him jealous—Sami helped Lucas investigate his deceased dad. Lucas had already found out Kate had lied about his dad being a West Point graduate. With Sami, he learned that the photo supposedly of his father was bogus. To keep Carrie and Austin apart, Lucas encouraged Sami to go on a crash diet and be more aggressive about going after Austin. Lucas pointed out that Sami had a good chance now, and if he played his cards right, Lucas might land Carrie for himself. Lucas also convinced Carrie to have some plastic surgery and accept the Face of the '90s title for *Bella* magazine. There was an added bonus for that: a new car from his mom.

Kate, trying to mend the rift between her and Lucas, told him that she had been married before and had two children. Those first babies were taken by her abusive husband who later told her they were dead. Kate also paid secret visits to Laura Horton in the sanitarium to warn her never to reveal who Lucas's dad really was.

Abe Carver's brother Jonah, a med student, delivered his first baby, in a taxicab. Abe's wife, Lexie, wanted to have a child too, but voiced serious concerns that the world was too troubled to raise children. As if in answer to her call for a crime cleanup, a vigilante, dubbed "The Pacifier," went to work in Salem. Lexie soon found out Jonah was the Pacifier, and when she was unable to dissuade him, tried to protect him. When they were found out, Lexie was thrown off the police force and Jonah had to leave the hospital. The whole situation was heartbreaking for Abe.

Vivian, going a bit more insane each day, continued to make it look as if Carly was killing her own patients. When Carly caught Vivian about to give Caroline Brady a lethal injection, they struggled and Carly got the heavy dose of morphine she had been about to administer. Once Carly was unconscious, Vivian took the opportunity to drug Carly with herbs that induced deathlike paralysis, and Carly was pronounced dead. Vivian was not satisfied. She knew Carly was still alive, for the moment. Vivian manipulated circumstances that allowed Carly not only to be buried alive, but able to hear Vivian taunting her via a walkie-talkie from aboveground. As the herbs wore off, Carly begged for release. When Vivian's head cleared, she confessed her macabre mayhem to Lawrence, who dug up Carly just in time. Because of amnesia, Carly related to Lawrence as his former persona, James, whom she had loved. With no memory of Salem, Nikki, or Bo, Lawrence took advantage of her state and kept her hidden at the Alamain mansion.

After a mystery man warned Kristen to keep her true identity a secret, a gunshot exploded near her, John, and DA Rebecca Morrison, wounding Rebecca. As soon as she was well enough, she left town. While Billie was becoming more attracted to Bo, she recognized the sniper as her own supposedly dead

ABOVE & OPPOSITE: **K**risten Blake and John Black shared some of their first most powerful emotions on Smith Island where he saved her from harm on more than one occasion.

father Curtis. Later, when Bo brought them face-to-face, Curtis convinced his daughter to lie for him. Meanwhile, even though Kristen tried to fight her feelings for John, the two made love at the Horton cabin where they were trapped by a storm. Soon after, Kristen and her brother Peter's adoptive father Stefano DiMera returned to Salem in a wheelchair but was unable to talk due to a debilitating stroke. He remained unseen at the DiMera mansion for many weeks.

Jack and Jennifer's daughter Abigail had been having bouts with a recurrent fever and was diagnosed with aplastic anemia. Austin came to the rescue, able to provide a bone marrow transplant. Jack began snooping in Kiriakis's secret files. After Victor, the new owner of *The Spectator*, married Kate and fired him, Jack became determined to destroy Victor. Meanwhile, Jennifer and Austin grew closer and dug deeper to find the environmental cause of Abigail's illness. In Victor's files Jack found out that while working for his father, Harper Devereaux, he had blindly signed some papers that allowed illegal toxic waste dumping. He felt overwhelming guilt for Abigail's illness and left town.

Sami, who had become bulimic and emotionally mercurial, finally confronted Marlena about John after having spotted the two of them nearly make love. Shortly later at the Horton cabin, John and Kristen delivered Marlena's premature baby girl. Suspicious, Sami pried in hospital computer records and confided to best friend Jamie Caldwell that the baby had been fathered by John, not Roman. After altering blood test results to keep the paternity a secret, Sami planned to steal Isabella and put her up for adoption. She felt the baby's presence in Salem would be a constant threat to her dad Roman's happiness, a reminder of her mom's disloyalty.

Carly's health was improving and when she ventured out for a walk alone, Bo and Billie saw her, but she didn't recognize them. After Lawrence told Bo and Roman of Vivian's crazed plot, she escaped. To keep a still-amnesiac Carly from leaving the country with Lawrence, Bo had her arrested for the murder of her patients. When Vivian confessed to those murders, Bo had to release Carly. Although she eventually regained her memory, she still chose to leave with Lawrence and Nikki. Vivian was institutionalized and soon grew curious about Kate's visits to Laura. Finding out about them became Vivian's next project.

When Kristen arranged an exchange of ransom for Stefano, who had been kidnapped by lowlife Curtis Reed, John followed and learned that Stefano DiMera was Kristen's adoptive father. Although Stefano's fatal illness made Kristen's wedding to Tony more urgent, John tried to dissuade Kristen from marrying his archenemy's son. At the same time, Stefano and Peter plotted to kill John. Then, on the day of their wedding, Sami kidnapped her sister Belle, who she knew was her half-sister fathered by John, not Roman, and Kristen left Tony at the altar, saying she wanted to help John find the stolen child first.

RIGHT: **K**ate Roberts became Mrs. Victor Kiriakis, or so she thought. She found that marriage and pregnancy were especially difficult in the Kiriakis mansion.

BELOW: **M**arlena and Roman were happy beyond words when baby Belle was retrieved from a kidnapper. The complete joy of the moment was tarnished by the realization that their older daughter, Sami, was the culprit who stole the baby in the first place.

While Bo and Billie grew closer, he uncovered Curtis's link to the DiMeras. Curtis knew Kate and blackmailed her about her past. He also stole Billie's necklace, hid in her basement, and continued to taunt her about their incestuous sexual past. He also drugged her and nearly raped her again. When Curtis was found shot to death, there were many suspects—including Peter, Lucas, Victor, Kate, and Austin. But Billie was arrested for the crime after her gun proved to be the murder weapon. Since her father had injected her with drugs, Billie couldn't remember what had happened on the night he was shot. Although Billie refused to tell Bo anything about her past, he mortgaged his boat to post her bail.

Much loved and respected Dr. Tom Horton collapsed and was hospitalized as the year came to a close. As a special gift to the Hortons and to show Kristen he was unlike his father Stefano, Tony flew an internationally renowned surgeon from Europe to operate on Tom.

John and Kristen's efforts to find Belle reached a bittersweet conclusion when they discovered Sami was the kidnapper. But for the moment, the holiday season became all the more joyous when John walked down the aisle during the Christmas Eve service and placed the baby in Marlena's arms.

1994

Kate discovered Vivian had been sneaking out of the asylum and had actually come to Salem disguised as a man when Jennifer brought non-speaking Laura back for a New Year's gala. Certain Vivian was a threat, Kate informed the hospital of the outings and Vivian was quickly scheduled for a lobotomy. As surgery was about to begin, a fire broke out at the hospital. Vivian's ever-faithful servant and confidant Ivan rescued Laura and Vivian. While hiding out and recuperating at the Alamain mansion, Laura realized the link between Curtis and Kate. Vivian now felt she could win Victor back from Kate.

At Billie's trial for the murder of Curtis Reed, Laura made a dramatic entrance and revealed Kate's marriage to Curtis while Kate was on the stand. Kate admitted Curtis had fathered her two children, then took them away from her. After Kate was implicated in the murder, Lucas confessed to the crime to save her. Billie was released after Bo found DiMera henchman Fred, who testified that Stefano had killed Curtis in self-defense and framed Billie. The trial revealed Billie's incestuous abuse, making her fear Bo would never care for her. He proved her wrong. Austin and Billie were also revealed as Kate's children. Curtis had lied about their deaths. Billie could not accept Kate as her mother; Austin, after some hesitation, did. Lucas did not want to give up only-child status and distrusted both his half-siblings. He particularly hated Austin for his relationship with Carrie. Sadly, because Kate had still been legally married when she wed Victor, her marriage was invalid, to Vivian's delight. Several months later, at a major Titan Publishing press party, Vivian goaded Laura into revealing that Kate's son Lucas was fathered by Bill Horton.

Meanwhile, Stefano got Belle's blood sample for DNA testing to prove paternity. Marlena wanted to confess her affair with John to Roman, but John and Sami stopped her. During Belle's baptism ceremony, however, Stefano intimidated Marlena into confessing in front of the entire congregation that she had slept with another man. Roman realized that the secret was the root of Sami's emotional problems and that John was the other man.

ABOVE: **S**ami thought she had found a friend in Alan, but he raped her when he was unable to rape her sister Carrie.

OPPOSITE: **B**o and Billie had their pain, but lots of passion too.

Tony and his father clashed after he learned Stefano was responsible for John's imprisonment and brainwashing years earlier. Stefano would have told Kristen, but was afraid she'd call off the wedding. Stefano still feared she'd balk, so he revealed that John was Belle's father to shed a tainted light on Kristen's image of John. Sami confessed to switching blood-test results in the hospital computer. Marlena was publicly humiliated and, with Belle, moved into Alice's house while Roman filed for divorce.

At church, before Kristen and Tony's wedding ceremony, John told her the police had evidence linking Stefano to Curtis's murder. Stefano and John argued and when John pursued Stefano and shot at his car, it exploded into a fireball. Kristen blamed John for her adoptive father's death and went ahead with the wedding, not realizing Stefano had yet again faked his own death. Tony, meanwhile, learned the truth but kept it from Kristen, even though they had pledged not to keep secrets from each other.

During a ski weekend, Carrie was almost raped by an intruder she didn't recognize as Lucas's pal Alan, who dated Sami to get close to her sister. After Austin and Carrie made love for the first time, Alan vowed instead to have Sami. When Sami went to his apartment to cook dinner, Alan tricked her into posing for some playfully suggestive photos and then raped her.

In a desperate move to win Victor back and have another child, Kate agreed to in-vitro fertilization. If she could bear a son for Kiriakis, she knew he would marry her again. Likewise, Vivian realized having Victor's son was her best chance at becoming Mrs. Kiriakis. Through incredibly masterful trickery, Vivian had Victor and Kate's fertilized egg implanted in herself.

John, receiving puzzle pieces from supposedly dead Stefano, remembered the puzzle picture as Maison Blanche, the DiMera family house in Louisiana. Stefano, hiding there, was stunned when Kristen arrived without warning. He had his ex-mistress Celeste drug her. When John arrived soon afterward, he saw Kristen but was captured by Stefano and imprisoned in the dungeon, where Stefano began brainwashing him again. Stefano tricked Marlena into coming to Maison Blanche, then forced her to call Roman and tell him she was with John, giving that marriage's faint hope of reconciliation its final blow.

The mystery at Maison Blanche deepened with the presence of a woman who looked like the late Hope Brady, who was fascinated by the newly arrived guests. Tony, Jennifer, Peter, Bo and Billie, arrived in New Orleans for the charity cotillion Kristen sponsored. That weekend, Peter and Jennifer made love for the first time. Roman, on the trail of Peter's lowlife cohort Leo, was led to Maison

RIGHT & BELOW RIGHT: Dr. Tom Horton died a happy man surrounded by loving family and friends who still pause a moment in fond remembrance when his name comes up. Tom was generous with his time, money—and love. He often cared more deeply for others than himself. Tom learned a lot from life and love, and from his best friend of all, Macdonald Carey (1913–1994).

Macdonald accumulated outstanding radio, stage, television, and fifty-plus film credits during his career prior to his twenty-nine years in Salem. He won several Emmy awards for his work on *Days*. Macdonald used the public spotlight to affect personal growth for many through his writing (his autobiography, *The Days of My Life*, and several volumes of prizewinning poetry) and involvement with mental health issues on the local, state, and national levels. A devout Catholic, he was active with secular groups within the Church.

Macdonald was married for twenty-six years to Betty Hecksher, with whom he had six children. Sober since 1982, Macdonald understood the painful and debilitating addiction of alcoholism. He rose above his troubles to bring an example of strength and courage to millions. His life was a testimony to fortitude and spiritual growth that manifested practical goodness and genuine kindness toward family, friends, and strangers.

Blanche. He had a warrant for Peter's arrest for drug trafficking. After a hurricane hit, Celeste released poison gas into the dungeon and set fire to the mansion. Roman rescued John and Marlena. John convinced Kristen that Stefano was still alive. Tony was blinded by an explosion during the fire.

Stefano took the mystery woman to his boat, but John followed and they fought. Stefano disappeared into the water and John took "Hope," Bo's presumed dead wife, to the lodge where Bo had just proposed marriage to Billie. The woman believed her name was Gina but, once back in Salem, no match could be found for her fingerprints, and DNA testing was inconclusive. Over several months, Gina became more convinced she was Hope. Bo was attracted to her, and eventually admitted he believed Gina was Hope. Meanwhile, Celeste, in disguise, successfully fed Gina hypnotic suggestions and planted memories only Hope would have.

John pushed Kristen to tell Tony the truth about them. But Tony was not only blind, he also had a brain aneurysm that could be fatal. After the latter crisis passed, Kristen overheard Tony tell Peter he lied to her about knowing Stefano was alive. That pushed Kristen back into John's arms, but she didn't leave Tony. After she broke the code for Stefano's computer, Kristen learned John was once a priest and broke off their romantic relationship. John balked at being a priest until, at a parish in which he had served, a parishioner's greeting and a matching handprint in cement finally made John accept that piece of his past. Meanwhile, Tony overheard gossip about Kristen and John's affair. He got a gun and, although blind from injuries during the Maison Blanche fire, learned to use it. Tony would have killed John if Kristen hadn't told him John was a priest. Tony then trusted John with Kristen until he regained his sight and saw them together. But Tony pretended he was still blind, hoping to catch Kristen being unfaithful to him.

Vivian faked a fall down the stairs so she could stay in the Kiriakis mansion and manipulate the lives of Victor and Kate during Kate's pregnancy. During a power blackout in Salem, Vivian and Kate were trapped in a stalled elevator until Lucas and Austin, in a joint effort, saved them.

Laura stole prescription pads to medicate herself. When Bill threatened to have her recommitted, their son Dr. Mike Horton took responsibility for her. He was recently back in Salem from the Middle East. He bore a heavy emotional burden—he was duped into running weapons for a woman he loved, he told Bill. He was betrayed and innocent people were killed.

After Laura spotted Peter with lowlife Leo, Peter worried that Laura could be an obstacle to his relationship with Jennifer. When Jennifer told him Laura had hired a private investigator to find Jack, Peter schemed to make it appear Laura was having a mental relapse. Jack did, in fact, return to Salem and spied on Peter romancing Jennifer. Peter decided to use his partner in deception, Daniel, to gaslight Laura. Because of a toxic agent he and Daniel put in the paint on her newly redecorated office walls, Laura hallucinated. She also heard voices, which were actually coming from a hidden transmitter. Laura's family decided to send her back to the hospital. But Laura fled, again with Vivian's help. When Jennifer got sick from the fumes in Laura's office and was hospitalized, Laura returned. Mom and daughter fell off the hospital roof and were in grave danger until Peter rescued them, looking like a complete hero. Mike figured out the fume problems, but not the connection to Peter and Daniel, and Laura was proven sane. Laura checked into The Meadows, a healing center, unaware that her former son-in-law

Caroline and Sami rallied to help Jamie, once she admitted her father had been sexually abusing her.

was also there. Like all patients, they used pseudonyms. They were paired as partners to work out their emotional problems and eventually became lovers.

Sami tested negative for both AIDS and pregnancy. After Lucas found suggestive photos of Sami in Alan's wallet, she admitted Alan had raped her. Lucas then told Carrie and they hatched a plan to trap Alan. But the blackout ruined the plan and Alan trapped Carrie. When Sami entered the scene, he held them both hostage. They were rescued, but rape charges against Alan could not be filed until Sami agreed to testify. When Sami did testify, she looked like a liar. The charges against Alan were dropped. When a tabloid published Sami's seductive photos, she decided as revenge to break up Austin and Carrie so her sister would understand what it was like to be alone. Alan tried to attack Sami at the Titan costume party, but Austin rescued her. The incident made Carrie believe that kind of ploy would help keep Austin close to her and she repeatedly cried wolf to bring Austin running to her and win his sympathy, if not his love.

Gina and Billie continued to compete for Bo's love. Gina's mind was filled with memories that only Hope could have, but she had no idea that Celeste was planting them. When Bo was certain Gina was Hope, he felt obligated to give his marriage a chance and reluctantly turned away from Billie. Meanwhile, Billie discovered Celeste's influence over Gina but couldn't convince Bo. After Celeste mistook Billie for Gina and dropped the book of memories during her exit, Billie had tangible proof. But Bo and Gina were off on their second honeymoon. Billie raced to find them, and when Bo still refused to believe her, Billie realized he was falling in love with Gina. Meanwhile, Gina found the book Billie had left behind during her hasty retreat and threw it into the fire, but her conscience made her retrieve it. Bo realized the truth and took off after Billie, who was leaving Salem by train. They reunited and planned a New Year's Day wedding, with Gina as a bridesmaid. Meanwhile, Hope's Grandmother Alice had not given up her suspicions that Gina was truly Hope.

Celeste got Mike to cozy up to his professional associate and friend, Dr Marlena Evans. Blackmailed by a voice on the phone that knew about his connection to the Middle East and innocent deaths there, Mike got access to Marlena's townhouse security code. That enabled Stefano, who had become truly enamored of her at Maison Blanche, to rig her armoire for entry from an adjacent unit. With the help of mind-altering drugs, Stefano led her on nightly outings that may have been fact or fantasy. Marlena's physical health deteriorated, and she did not seem her old self anymore. Marlena saw a beast in her bedroom, and sometimes felt an eerie evil near her. The town's Christmas tree went up in flames as a mysterious "Desecrator" caused destruction. In private moments, Marlena's eyes glowed a fiendish yellow. A presence more powerful and evil than Stefano DiMera had come to Salem.

A s the year began, Salem was already in Satan's evil grip.

Bo and Billie had made it to the church in a glow of happiness—until the chandelier came crashing down. As if that were a signal, things went from bad to worse. Alice, still convinced that Gina was Hope, stopped the ceremony. No amount of arguing could convince the clergy to continue if there was the least shred of doubt that Hope was alive and therefore still wed to Bo. After much soul searching, Gina signed papers to have Hope declared legally dead, and the star-crossed Bo and Billie were finally married. At the reception, Satan brought Marlena into the crowded celebration totally naked. Marlena, arrested, shot her police guard and nearly shot John as well.

From Marlena's hospital bed, Satan manipulated Sami, Carrie, and Austin into further estrangement and seduced Stefano into helping Marlena leave the hospital. Meanwhile, trying to soothe her conscience, Kristen confessed her affair with John to Tony and they renewed their wedding vows. By chance, John was the officiating priest. Satan took the occasion to have Marlena set fire to the church. Later, John found Kristen chloroformed, naked, painted with a pentagram, and chained to the church altar rail. Continuing after John, Satan transformed Marlena's body into Kristen's. In a sexy teddy, "Kristen" showed up at John's apartment and tried to seduce him but Tony burst in and vowed to destroy John's reputation as a man and priest.

When Alan attacked Sami at gunpoint, she got hold of the weapon and shot him in the groin, castrating him. When Sami caught heat from local guys who taunted her for what she did to Alan, she turned to Lucas for comfort and they made love. When Austin walked in on them, he thought Lucas was making love to Carrie and left. Sami and Lucas let Austin believe that. Then Sami drugged Austin so he would make love to her thinking she was Carrie. When he realized what he had done and refused to continue an affair, Sami left town. Meanwhile Carrie figured out that Austin had slept with someone else, but she did not know who. Although emotionally estranged, Carrie and Austin took off together to find Sami. Their attempts to find her failed, but they did renew their romance.

When Jennifer tried to find Clark, the man her mom Laura met at an emotional development center, she and Jack were caught in a blizzard while driving back from Chicago to Salem. They crashed into a snowbank and became lost. Jennifer, wet and feverish, was delirious so Jack tended to her in a cave. Once back in Salem, she thanked him for saving her life, but insisted their closeness was momentary. She loved Peter. No matter how Jack tried to convince Jennifer that Peter was still linked to the DiMeras' shady businesses, she refused to believe him. With legal right to do so, Jack moved into the house he owned with Jennifer. Laura learned her ex-lover Clark was really her former son-in-law Jack. They agreed to respect their present relationship, but Laura continued to yearn for what they once had and was convinced she could have Jack to herself once Jennifer was married to Peter.

1995

In an elaborately planned wedding rehearsal Vivian managed to marry Victor without his realizing it. Weeks later at Kate and Victor's wedding, Vivian went into labor, stopped the ceremony, and gave birth to a baby boy. Later, Kate disappeared after a plane crash over the ocean, and Vivian had Victor to herself. Unfortunately, Victor's emotional loss did not leave him receptive to Vivian's romantic plots and ploys to make him her lover. Lucas, who knew Vivian's manipulations of marriage and suspected her part in Kate's presumed demise, blackmailed her into helping him get Sami back to Salem to stop Austin and Carrie's wedding. Lucas wanted the bride for himself. He knew Sami was committed to landing Austin and would stop the wedding for certain. Sami did. At the ceremony, she announced that she was pregnant and the groom-to-be was the father. Carrie walked out of the church. Sami did not have Austin's love, but she had manipulated his sense of guilt and responsibility into a loyalty to her she expects will some day grow to be real love.

Earlier, when Marlena was revealed as the Desecrator, John blamed physical and emotional problems for her behavior. Although still unconvinced about devils, John finally accepted the homeless man Gabe as an angel when Gabe miraculously brought a child back to life. After many plagues upon Salem, including a heat wave and drought, a swarm of bees attacking guests at Austin and Carrie's engagement party, a snake threatening Kristen and a panther attacking a religious scholar, Fr. Francis finally convinced Fr. John Black that they needed to perform an exorcism to save Marlena's soul. Months of dramatic ritual, attacks by

OPPOSITE & ABOVE: Another Salem had its witches; this Salem had Satan wreaking harm and havoc.

demons, deception in the form of John's late wife Isabella, and demon tricks in Tony's mind seemed, at first, only to bring Marlena's death. Eventually, the demonic ploy culminated in a battle between Satan and John Black. God and John won. Marlena was really alive. Salem was freed of Satan's grip.

Gina entered the Salem Police Academy with personality test results hauntingly similar to Hope's profile. More and more evidence mounted. Bobby Lee admitted that the woman brought to the hospital many years ago, the one known as Gina, was wearing a bracelet engraved with: "To Hope with love from Bo." By midsummer Gina found the puzzle box. Only Hope and the late Tom Horton could successfully complete its configuration. Gina was able to unpuzzle the box. Later, hypnosis sessions with Dr. Laura Horton and a flashback at the police firing range brought her memory back completely.

At the time John was released from his priestly vows, Kristen was convinced that her marriage to Tony was over. There had been too many lies, too much deception. Although she pressured John into renewing their romance, he would not make love to Kristen while she was still a married woman. She put the wheels in motion for an annulment of her wedding vows to Tony. John felt he might have been a contributing factor in Marlena's possession, leading her astray by having sex with her while she was married to Roman. Kristen realized that she had a fertility problem that could stop her from ever having children if she didn't take the small window of opportunity she had to get pregnant. She wanted to have John's child. Tony's attempt to kill John failed, and shortly afterwards Tony was diagnosed with leukemia. Still, he continued to conjur a way to eliminate John from Kristen's life.

Like John, who turned a deaf ear to Kristen's early warnings about the Devil, Stefano found it hard to heed Celeste's insight into faith and spirit.

John, however, realized he still had deep emotional attachment to Marlena. That became another obstacle to his relationship with Kristen. Marlena, out of guilt and seeking to make amends for the things she did while possessed, helped Stefano in his recovery—physically, mentally, and emotionally. He had been injured and lost his memory when thrown from the penthouse balcony by an incarnate demon during Marlena's possession. Marlena actually moved into the DiMera penthouse but kept her relationship with Stefano on a professional level. Marlena was also busy with her pregnant daughter Sami. And Marlena continued to help Carrie, her stepdaughter, through the emotional fallout of the betrayal by Sami and Austin. Austin remained totally in love with Carrie, but because of the baby, Austin felt a heavy responsibility to Sami and helped her with Lamaze classes and emotional and financial support.

Gina regained her memory and realized she truly was Hope. Bo realized that he was, therefore, still married to Hope. Shawn-Douglas's mother was alive. Even though Bo decided to stay with Billie and remarry her, it became clear that the love triangle would only cause everyone, including Shawn-Douglas, too much pain. Billie nobly decided to leave town to let Bo explore his emotions without torn loyalties. She was a much stronger woman than when she came to Salem, and she could make a life of her own. While still harboring hope that one day Bo would come for her, Billie left Salem. Although Bo and

Hope still have a deep and undying love, so much has happened to them both that their relationship will take a lot of time to rebuild. Hope was rejected too often by Bo during the time she was trying to prove her identity that, in spite of Billie's absence, she backed off emotionally. Hope hid behind a wall of pride and hurt.

Jennifer and Peter visited the mysterious place called Aremid and learned more about the Blake family. Jack followed them there and did his own investigation. Since he could not have Jennifer back, he at least wanted to know about the man who would become her husband and stepfather to Abigail. The beautiful wedding went off without a hitch, but tragedy struck shortly afterward when Tony, who had been stalking John for months, met his own demise. In a surprising twist, Kristen turned against John.

As the year comes into its final month, things in Aremid are heating up. There's a mystery woman in white who holds secrets to John's past. Celeste holds secrets of her own that will affect Lexie and Abe Carver. In Salem, Sami and Austin are married but far from happy. Stefano's memory is clearing and his old personality starts to emerge. Bo and Hope are finding sparks of their old love growing hotter.

The people of Salem continue to find adventure, mystery, trial and triumphs, and enduring love. No matter the odds.

John Black returned to his past as a priest to save the soul of Marlena, the mother of his child. His former lover Kristen also joined the battle against darkness.

Families

T here are no granite walls around the families of Salem. To the contrary, each has gossamer tendrils that reach out and become entwined with others, nearby and far away. The relationships created in the process are exciting, surprising, dangerous, and delightful. Social status and economic differences pale as personal destiny and desire bring unlikely individuals together to share adventure, tragedy, gaiety, and love.

In 1965, the Horton household was the Salem stage. There were Merritts and Martins in transition. In the early seventies, the Anderson and Peters families were introduced as solid Salem citizens with their accompanying problems and gifts. Fascinating, trouble-making, and mysterious out-of-towners came and went.

While Salem would always see an ebb and flow of newcomers, by the early eighties several key families had become actively involved with the Hortons. The Bradys, Carvers, Johnsons, and DiMeras, each family with a distinctive personality, broadened the social spectrum. Together, these families would reflect the main history of the town and its people. The Horton family had been enticed and pulled into a larger, far-reaching community that eventually encompassed the world on a regular basis. It was a time of international adventure.

In the nineties, the adventures are on a grand scale, and family tales go deeper into personal psyches. The mind, the heart, and the soul are explored and extolled more deeply, more completely, than ever before. The family is still—and always—the bond that balances, nurtures, and loves.

THE HORTON FAMILY

Three decades after Tom Horton married Alice Grayson, the Horton family remains the very heart of Salem.

Their love spawned five children: twins Tommy and Addie, Mickey, Bill, and Marie. Their lives took wonderful and sometimes dangerous dips and curves. But they've survived and continue to flourish.

Tommy married Kitty and, while he was off to war, she gave birth to their daughter Sandy, who became a doctor. When he first returned to Salem, he was unrecognizable due to war injuries, surgery, and amnesia. He and his sister Marie fell in love, but the truth of his identity was discovered before they consummated their relationship.

Addie married Ben Olson and they had a daughter, Julie, and a son, Steve. After Ben died, Addie married Doug Williams and they had Hope, who eventually married Bo Brady and they had a son, Shawn-Douglas. Today Bo and Hope are one of Salem's most romantic, enduring couples.

Julie had a son, David, by David Martin, who was killed by his wife, Susan. Julie gave up baby David for adoption and then married Scott Banning, the adoptive father, after his wife died. Later, she married Doug (twice!), so she became her half-sister Hope's stepmother. Julie and Doug shared one of the greatest love stories Salem has ever known, so it must be a family tradition that Hope and Bo then spanned more than a decade in romantic and sometimes tragic adventure.

Julie's son David Banning married Trish Clayton after she became pregnant with his son Scotty.

Steve, Addie's other child by Ben Olson, stayed in Europe until he was a young adult. Then he came to Salem and left again when Mary Anderson refused to marry him. As far as we know, he never married and has no children.

Marie, before she entered the convent, had an affair with worldly Alex Marshall. They had a daughter, Jessica Blake, who became a nursing student in Salem and was legally adopted by Alex before she married Joshua Fallon and left town.

Mickey was sterile and never had any biological children. However, he raised Michael as his own, unaware that Laura had been raped by Bill and had

Christmas has always been a special time for the Hortons. Each year their tree is decorated with ornaments that bear the hand-painted name of a family member. Alice in particular was always delighted when a new addition was hung. At the hospital, where Alice is head of the volunteers and Tom was chief-of-staff, the Hortons would make the holiday rounds visiting patients, and Tom often read the Christmas story to the children.

borne his child. Mickey's son was really his nephew. Mickey also had an extramarital affair while with Laura: Linda Patterson bore a daughter, Melissa, who was actually fathered by another of her lovers. Mickey and his second wife, farm girl Maggie Simmons, eventually adopted Melissa when she was a teen. Prior to Melissa's return, Mickey and Maggie took in a foster child, Janice Barnes, but her biological mother returned and took her back. Maggie also had a surrogate child, Sarah. She was supposedly the progeny of Dr. Evan Whyland, but years after his death, it turned out that Dr. Neil Curtis was the sperm donor.

Bill, the biological father of Michael, raised by Mickey and Laura, later married Laura, and the couple had a daughter, Jennifer Rose. Michael had a son, Jeremy, after an affair with Robin Jacobs who left town with the boy. Jennifer married Jack Devereaux and they had a daughter, Abigail.

Although he was not aware of it until 1994, Bill also fathered another son, Lucas Roberts, during an extramarital affair with his mother, Kate.

THE BRADY FAMILY

Rough-and-tumble Shawn Brady married more refined Caroline and raised their family with plenty of love, through thick and thin times in Salem.

They nurtured four children: sons Roman and Bo; and daughters Kimberly and Kayla. Later, they took in two youngsters, Frankie and his little brother Max.

Roman married Anna and they had a daughter, Carrie. After their divorce, Anna married Tony DiMera. Later, Roman married Dr. Marlena Evans and they had twins, Eric and Samantha.

Kimberly married Shane Donovan and they had a son, Andrew Shawn, and a daughter, Jeannie.

Kayla married Jack Devereaux, but that mistake was quickly righted. She then married true love Steve "Patch" Johnson and they had a daughter, Stephanie Kay.

Caroline Brady could have married a millionaire but chose to remain with down-to-earth Shawn and their family. She manages the Brady Pub and put herself in real danger when she participated in former daughter-in-law Marlena's exorcism. Caroline is fearless under any circumstance, especially so for her family and loved ones.

Bo, actually fathered by Victor Kiriakis, married Hope Williams and they had a son, Shawn-Douglas.

As Caroline (Peggy McCay) points out, "The Brady family is not upper class, not as genteel as the Hortons who are doctors and lawyers. Shawn was a fisherman who became a pub owner. The boys became cops. Kayla was a nurse and Kimberly counseled children. But the Bradys are more emotionally expressive and explosive. They show their passions more readily in their outspoken, down-to-earth way."

THE DiMERA FAMILY

Mysterious and powerful Stefano DiMera (Joseph Mascolo) claims to have "sowed his seed all over the world." But few offspring seem inclined to stay in close touch with their dad.

Stefano has always been proud of his son, Count Antony DiMera. More dashing than devious, Tony inherited the DiMera wealth and power but worked hard to keep his darker side in control. Yet he was a DiMera through and through. Tony arrived in Salem saying his divorce from Liz Chandler was never finalized and terrorized Liz into living with him so he could have an heir, but Liz was pregnant by Neil Curtis. Then he fell in love with Renee Dumonde, but her mother Lee succeeded, for a time, in making Tony believe Renee was his half-sister by Stefano and they never wed. Tony did marry Anna Brady, Roman's ex-wife, and they had a passionate marriage but had no children before they divorced.

In the mid-eighties, Stefano's devious daughter, Megan Hathaway, was accidentally killed by Larry Welch, whose father had invented the three powerful prisms Stefano was after. There is only one other known DiMera offspring, Benjy, whom Patch and Kayla came across during their honeymoon in the Orient.

Stefano DiMera loves his family but rules them with an iron hand. He faked his own death to push an ambivalent Kristen, his foster daughter, into going through with her wedding to his son Tony. And while her brother Peter wants to break from shady DiMera business ventures, Stefano has him on a tight rein, too.

Although the deaf boy came to Salem for a short time, he was taken to live with his maternal grandfather in the east. He would be a teenager now.

Stefano's foster son and daughter, Peter and Kristen Blake, came to Salem. Although Kristen fell in love with John Black, she honored her long-standing betrothal to Tony and married him. After several years of turmoil, she sought an annulment. Jealous Tony, no longer in control of his darkest DiMera side, plotted to kill John, but Tony died instead.

THE CARVER FAMILY

Abe Carver, Salem's level-headed chief of police, has been Roman Brady's best friend for over a decade. Even he believed John Black was Roman, and when it proved untrue, helped both the real Roman and John through a tough transition.

His younger brothers Theo and Jonah were always close. That made Theo's death all the more tragic. He died in Abe's arms after being shot by corrupt chief of police Richard Cates, who was a kingpin in Savannah Wilder's drug ring. Theo was trying to find out who murdered his friend Danny Grant, but his involvement in crime fighting led to a tragic end.

Jonah left Salem for a while and returned as a medical student, but his own unofficial crime fighting as "The Pacifier" got him bounced out of school. Lexie, a police officer who tried to protect Jonah on his vigilante outings, lost her job as well. She's now pursuing a medical career.

Lexie's Aunt Frankie, now calling herself Celeste, is Stefano DiMera's long-time confidante, privy to several secrets that threaten to shake up the Carver family.

Salem police chief Abe Carver's wife, Lexie, was infatuated with Abe's younger brother Jonah, but let sexy fantasies placate her desire rather than destroy a good marriage.

Jack Devereaux and Steve "Patch" Johnson came to Salem separately and discovered they were long-lost brothers. The two came to blows over Kayla Brady and afterward, Jack needed a kidney. Steve obliged. A bit of a bumbler, the smartest thing Jack ever did was marry Jennifer Horton. Unfortunately, he later divorced her.

THE JOHNSON FAMILY

Raised in an orphanage, alone after his infant brother was adopted, Steve "Patch" Johnson lived a life of gypsy adventure. In Salem, working as a Kiriakis henchman, he discovered his former best friend Bo Brady and long-lost family.

Adrienne, a sister he'd never known he had, found him and reunited him with his mother, Jo. The two were on the run from the abusive Duke Johnson. Duke raped his virgin daughter Adrienne, and until she unblocked her traumatic amnesia, Steve took the rap.

Family matters got even more complicated when Jack Devereaux turned out to be the little brother Steve had loved and lost. Jack had been adopted by a wealthy but corrupt politician and was unaware of his true background. The secret would have stayed under wraps, except that Steve and Jack fell in love with the same woman—Kayla. After a confrontation over her, Steve accidentally pushed Jack over the edge of a building causing Jack to need a kidney transplant. That's when their relationship became known to everyone.

After a one-night marriage to Jack, Kayla and Steve were reunited until, only a few years later, Steve died in her arms poisoned by a drug intended for someone else.

Presently, Jack is back in Salem trying to win his ex-wife Jennifer Horton Devereaux back. She, however, is engaged to Peter Blake, Stefano's foster son.

THE REED FAMILY

When Kate Roberts came to Salem she was stunned to discover Austin and Billie Reed were her children. She thought they had died as youngsters. They were dating Carrie and Bo Brady.

When streetwise Austin and Billie Reed wandered into Salem they had no idea of how new relationships, and surprising old ties, would change their lives.

Before long, Austin and innocent Carrie Brady met and fell in love—to the dismay of her police officer dad, Roman. Billie was attracted to tough and tender Bo Brady. Since Bo was involved romantically with Dr. Carly Manning, Billie and Bo grew close as friends while their desire slowly smoldered.

By the time Bo was free to love again, Billie's incestuous father, Curtis, had come to town, threatening to shatter his children's hopes for a new life of respectability. When he was found dead, Billie was the prime suspect. During the murder trial secrets exploded like heat-seeking missiles:

Lowlife Curtis had been the first, and never officially divorced, husband of Kate Roberts who had married wealthy businessman Victor Kiriakis. Laura Horton, released after eighteen years in an asylum, made that shattering announcement in a courtroom full of Salem residents. Kate's new marriage was therefore invalid, since Curtis was alive at the time of the wedding.

Austin and Billie were Kate's children by Curtis. The abusive Curtis Reed had stolen the young children from her when they split and then later told her they had both been killed.

Kate's son Lucas, a military academy graduate and spoiled only child—until now—turned out to be the illegitimate son of Bill Horton. Laura, embittered because Kate had been the other woman who destroyed her marriage and drove her to madness, made that juicy announcement during the press conference that should have been Victor and Kate's shining hour.

Presently, Kate is presumed dead after a plane crash. However, she's alive, aboard a fishing vessel long at sea. Billie married Bo, but his wife Hope has returned from the dead and drug-induced amnesia. Austin was just about to marry Carrie when her sister, Sami, announced she was carrying his child.

The Reeds have learned that Salem is not a simple, quiet town.

Lovers

L

overs follow their hearts wherever the road to romance may lead. In Salem, that may mean straight to mystery, mayhem, and adventure.

Tom and Alice's rock-solid relationship was an example of loyalty and dedication over more than six decades. Their kind of old-fashioned, enduring, and nurturing love is a goal few attain. But knowing it is possible gives hope as modern romantics face new challenges.

Love, even in fleeting glory, warms the soul and gives the spirit wings to fly. Just ask Julie, Addie, Doug, Billie, Bo, Hope, Kimberly, Shane, Kristen, Jennifer, Roman, Isabella, John, Marlena, Carrie. . . . Anyone touched by deep love admits that the joy is always worth the sorrow that too often comes in tow.

Master manipulator Stefano knows love too. With world-moving power at his disposal, he has always been ready, and oh so willing, to crush any threat to those near and dear to him. He doesn't forgive; he doesn't forget. He loves deeply enough to try to fight the forces of hell. And John proved that with God and love those forces can be beat.

Grand or sweet and simple, romance rarely runs smoothly in Salem. Stumbling blocks are tossed in the paths of lovers. Lost lovers come back or past secrets surface when least expected and devoted duos split up. Other times, new faces tempt a fickle heart.

True love may not always conquer, but it never gives up!

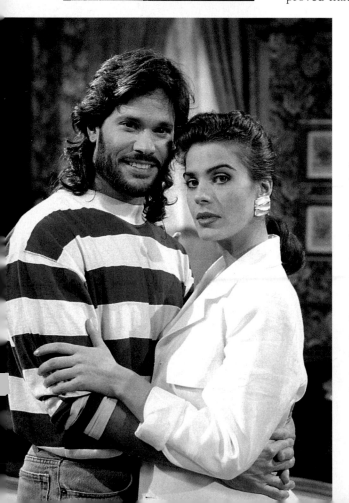

ABOVE LEFT: Pete was a juvenile delinquent. Melissa was a model teen. These opposites attracted in a big way, but their differences, and fate, always came between them.

LEFT: Rough rebel Bo Brady met his match in sassy teenager Hope Williams. His protective attitude toward her eventually became desire but the would-be lovers were kept apart by her dad and then a forced marriage to a corrupt politician. Eventually, Bo and Hope consummated their love and shared a rich marriage.

OPPOSITE: Kayla was the woman in the middle of the Johnson brothers, Steve and Jack. Although Steve loved her with all his heart, he shunned her, clearing the way for her to wed ailing Jack, who needed a reason to live. But the marriage ended when the new bride ran to Steve's arms on the wedding night.

OPPOSITE: **B**est friends Frankie and Jennifer stuck together through thick and thin during their high school years. While she dated another guy, Frankie stood on the sidelines gathering the courage to confess his real feelings for her. When he finally did, they enjoyed a romantic—and very innocent— courtship.

LEFT: **W**hen it came to romance it never went smoothly for Tony and Renee. Thinking Tony was her brother, she married David. By the time they split, Tony had already been manipulated into marriage by Anna.

ABOVE: **D**r. Mike Horton fell in love with April Ramirez, a girl from the wrong side of the tracks with a thirst for alcohol. She had straightened out her life, but his took a curve when his ex-girlfriend Robin Jacobs returned to Salem with startling news: he was the father of their son, Jeremy.

ABOVE: Salem's wackiest duo was, without a doubt, eccentric Eugene Bradford and flamboyant fashion designer Calliope Jones. Their unconventional romance led to a bizarre New Year's Eve outdoor wedding. The honeymooners jetted off to Hollywood, where the highlight of the trip was their appearance on *The Newlywed Game*.

OPPOSITE: Shane and Gabrielle were secret agent partners, but she kept a secret of her own. She was really the mother of his love child Eve. When that revelation came to light, Shane's marriage to Kimberly hit another major snag in this constantly troubled love story.

ABOVE LEFT: After the death of his one true love, Hope, Bo believed he was destined to a life of solitude. That is, until Dr. Carly Manning arrived in Salem. Their sparring banter turned to attraction, but in the long run, their different lifestyles separated them.

ABOVE RIGHT: Playboy Justin Kiriakis became a one-woman man after he met Adrienne Johnson. Her dark past (she was raped by her father) shattered her faith in men. Slowly, Justin helped her pick up the pieces of her life, move on, and in the process they fell deeply in love.

LEFT: It didn't exactly begin as a storybook romance. He was a slick, shady pimp, and she was his young prostitute. But, in time, Nick Corelli and Eve Donovan discovered they had deep feelings for one another. Their affair shocked Salem.

OPPOSITE: Of all the women in John Black's life, few compared to the fair Isabella. The epitome of goodness and light, John couldn't help but lose his heart to her. But destiny was to shatter their marital bliss and happy family when Isabella was diagnosed with cancer. She died in John's arms.

LEFT: First love has proved to be real love for young Carrie Brady. From the moment she laid eyes on handsome Austin Reed, Carrie knew he was the man of her dreams, despite her dad's adamant opposition to their union. Austin ditched his illegal dealings for the love of his life, but these star-crossed lovers are still finding the course of love filled with land mines.

BELOW: When John still believed he was Roman Brady, he found romance and adventure with Diana Colville. Their stormy courtship took them to Greece, the Bahamas, and Peru as they battled the evil Orion and Victor Kiriakis. Unfortunately, their escapades proved more successful than their attempts to join each other in marriage. After three wedding postponements, they called it quits and Diana left town.

OPPOSITE: Three definitely wasn't company for Billie, Bo, and Gina. At the very moment Bo proposed marriage to Billie, this dead ringer for his late wife Hope surfaced. After months of investigating Gina's identity in vain, Bo and Billie wed. When it turned out Gina was indeed Hope, Bo was caught in the middle again.

ABOVE: The romance of Jack and Jennifer began as strictly a business affair. He was her editor, and she was his rookie reporter. They fell in love and had a baby, but when little Abigail became ill, Jack realized his antiecological business dealings were to blame. Out of guilt he left town and divorced Jennifer. Now he's back and wants to be husband and father again. But he has competition.

LEFT: Bad boy Tanner Scofield gave backwoods beauty Molly Brinker a crash course in love. After they found one another in Salem, he unlocked the mystery of his mother's death and helped Molly find her mom. They left town together to start anew.

Weddings

Days of Our Lives celebrates love in its fullest splendor amid silk, satin, and lace. With breathtaking gowns, heart-tugging vows, and music that touches the soul, Salem's favorite couples become husband and wife.

Most wedding ceremonies, no matter the size, are grand and glorious celebrations of love that has often surmounted sizable obstacles. A few marriages are manifestations of mayhem and manipulation. They are always memorable.

Weddings, with their rituals and declarations, are an affirmation of hope that the days of our lives together will be shared in love.

1981

Doug & Julie

The second time around was twice as sweet. Doug finally stood up to ex-wife Lee and locked her away before marching down the aisle with Julie. He sang to his bride and recited poetry. It was the romantic remarriage of two people meant always to be together.

1982
JESSICA & JOSH

Marie Horton's troubled daughter by Alex Marshall, Jessica, married Joshua Fallon in a spring wedding and left Salem behind.

1981
LIZ & DON

It was a simple ceremony but complicated union. Soon after Liz married lawyer Don Craig, she realized she was in love with Dr. Neil Curtis and still married to Antony DiMera, who came to Salem and kept her a virtual hostage. Tony wanted an heir. Liz was already pregnant by Neil.

1983
MARLENA & ROMAN

Doc married the cop. Marlena and Roman had a courtship built on danger, a wedding day bedeviled by assassins, and a married life filled with incredible adventure and lots of love.

1983
RENEE & ALEX

Unlucky at love, Renee Dumonde wed Alex Marshall but learned he wanted her money. Soon after, Renee was mysteriously murdered.

1984
HOPE & LARRY

The wedding of corrupt politician Larry Welch and Hope Williams was interrupted when Bo Brady stole her away right out of the church. When Welch's thugs got her back, threats to Bo and her family convinced her to go through with the ceremony. The marriage by manipulation was doomed.

1985
MELISSA & PETE AND MAGGIE & MICKEY

On Valentine's Day, Melissa married Pete Jannings in a double ceremony with Mickey and Maggie, who exchanged vows for their third time since 1974.

1985
BO & HOPE

Truly a match made in heaven, working-class Bo and Hope had a fairy tale ceremony in springtime England surrounded by family and friends. Beautiful Hope wore an appropriately exquisite $25,000 gown and British royalty picked up the entire wedding tab.

1985
TONY & ANNA

After two bogus marriage ceremonies, Tony and Anna finally became legitimate husband and wife. Married or not, their fire and passion made them a perfect pair.

1986
MARLENA & ROMAN

After being held captive, brainwashed, and transformed in appearance by Stefano DiMera, Roman was back in Salem and Marlena helped him remember his past. The magnetic couple renewed their wedding vows, pledged their love, and joyously started over.

1987
KIMBERLY & SHANE

OPPOSITE TOP: Their love conquered the baby-stealing schemes of Shane's ex-wife Emma and his ISA partner Gillian, who was so obsessed with him she murdered Emma and tried to kill Kimberly. Their wedding day was the high point of their roller-coaster romance.

1988
PATCH & KAYLA

OPPOSITE BOTTOM: After a romantic summer wedding aboard a yacht, Patch and Kayla took off for a honeymoon in the Orient that led to mystery, adventure, and danger.

1990
ADRIENNE & JUSTIN

Torn apart by Anjelica's scheming ways and Victor's control over his nephew, Adrienne and Justin divorced but finally found happiness after their second marriage.

1990
PATCH & KAYLA

When Patch's presumed-dead wife Marina returned, his marriage to Kayla was deemed invalid. After Marina was found dead the couple was about to exchange vows for a second time when pregnant Kayla was arrested on suspicion of Marina's murder. Eventually, they did marry but, by the end of a year filled with heartbreak, Patch died in Kayla's arms.

1991
JACK & JENNIFER

After divorcing Eve and keeping her money, Jack married Jennifer. They honeymooned in Hollywood, where Hawk, a clever con man, swindled the newlyweds out of their fortune. Jennifer quickly found out life with Jack would be one misadventure after another.

1991
CARLY & VICTOR

Bo and Carly were in love, but Victor became enamored of Dr. Carly Manning when she treated him after his stroke. With the help of Emmy Borden, who had her sights on Bo, Kiriakis managed to marry Carly. However, when Victor's machinations came to light, the unconsummated union was declared invalid.

1992
JOHN & ISABELLA

OPPOSITE: Nuptials were delayed after scheming Danielle claimed she was John's wife. When Isabella and John made it to the altar, the very beautiful, very pregnant, bride delivered their son, Brady Victor, in the church office minutes before becoming Mrs. Black.

1994
TONY & KRISTEN

Up to the very last minute, Kristen was torn between Tony, her betrothed, and John, her lover. When Stefano made it look as if John had killed him right outside the church, Kristen and Tony wed in a tribute to the senior DiMera as well as to celebrate their love.

1995
BO & BILLIE

A crashing chandelier interrupted their first ceremony, but when Alice voiced her concern that Gina was likely Hope, and Bo's living wife, the wedding came to a halt. Much paperwork later, Bo and Billie finally became husband and wife in late February. But by midsummer, Hope's identity was confirmed.

1995
CARRIE & AUSTIN

The glowing couple's dream-come-true wedding day became a nightmare when the bride's sister fainted during the ceremony. Pregnant Sami claimed that the would-be groom was the father of her child.

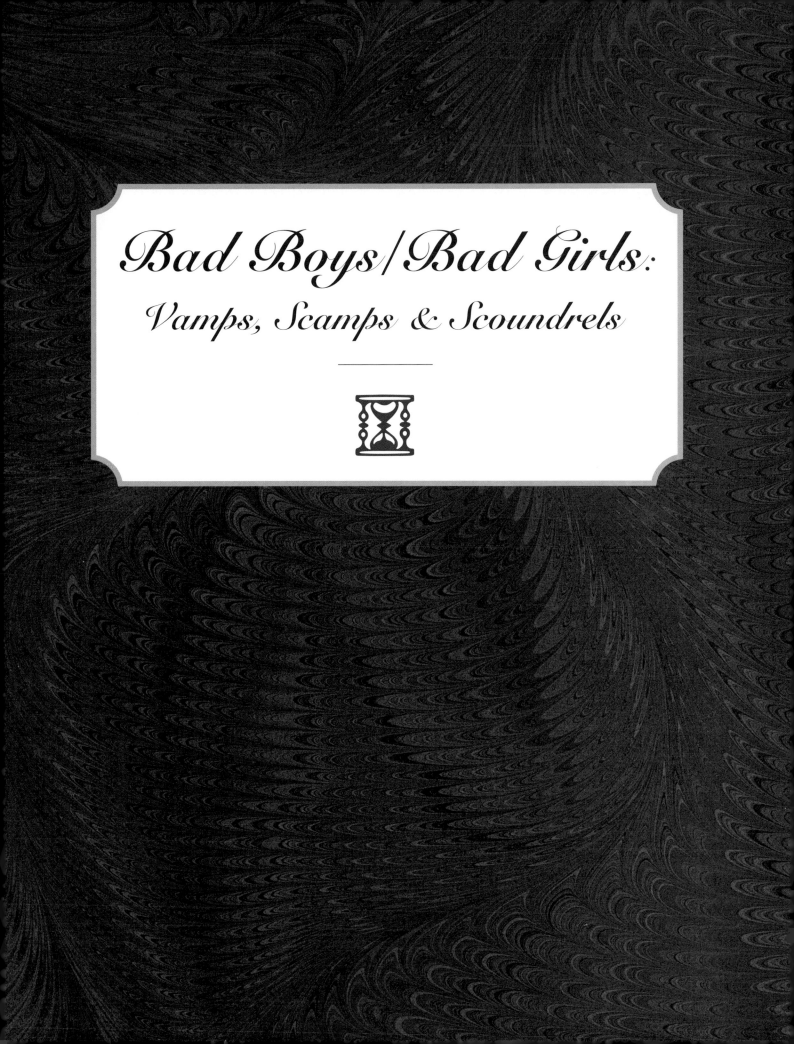

Bad Boys/Bad Girls:
Vamps, Scamps & Scoundrels

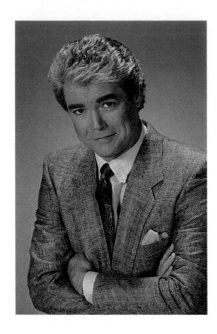

Their pretty faces and handsome smiles seduce and cajole, but watch out—these naughty vixens and unscrupulous bad boys can wreak havoc galore. Be it blackmail, embezzlement, kidnapping, murder, or the more legal but deadly emotional manipulation, their wicked antics keep viewers glued to their sets, booing and hissing, yet always watching. After all, the daytime world would be duller than dishwater without these troublemakers serving up their daily doses of torment and tribulation, adding excitement to every scene.

Among Salem's most memorable scoundrels: the demented Jake Kositchek, Kellam Chandler, and Ian Griffith; crooked politicos Larry Welch and Harper Deveraux; and spider women Savannah Wilder and Brooke Hamilton. While some eventually turn over a new leaf and reform—à la Steve "Patch" Johnson and his brother Jack—others never learn that crime doesn't pay—Stuart Whyland, Larry Atwood, and Alex Marshall, to name a few.

The list of degenerates who have passed through *Days of Our Lives* is too numerous to mention. Here are just a sampling of the scamps.

More misguided than malevolent, Dr. Neil Curtis had a winning way with women but Lady Luck always had him beat. His roguish charm and good looks helped him maneuver into many a rich society matron's bed.

When clever Lee Dumonde came to Salem she was a gold digger after Doug Williams's inheritance. Only later did the truth come out that she had been Stefano DiMera's mistress. The troublemaker claimed that her sister Renee was really their daughter to keep Renee and Stefano's son Tony apart. Salem would not have been the same without Lee.

Since they were already partners in crime, Victor Kiriakis and "The Phoenix," Stefano DiMera, had more in common than most people could have guessed. When Victor's crime syndicate was exposed, he managed to escape imprisonment by blackmailing Larry Welch into taking the fall. Then he hired Alex Marshall and bought up riverfront real estate for future shady dealings in Salem.

When Marina Toscano Johnson came to town, it was a dark day for Patch and Kayla. Their marriage was declared invalid, and Marina blackmailed Patch into helping her retrieve the key to her father's hidden fortune. She was really working for Victor Kiriakis, plotting a double-cross, but turned up murdered. Even in death Marina caused nightmares for the couple, when Kayla was arrested for the murder and imprisoned while pregnant.

ABOVE: Orpheus was Roman Brady's former ISA partner, but he blamed Brady for his wife's accidental death. Crazed over her loss, vengeful Orpheus kidnapped Marlena but the ISA rescued her in Sweden. Later, he made it look as though she had been blown up in the Brady house even while he kept her prisoner on an island, tending to his children.

TOP RIGHT: Maxwell Hathaway appeared to be a wealthy New Orleans banker, but he was really the man controlling corrupt politician Larry Welch and in search of the three prisms for his boss, Stefano DiMera. When Bo went to work for him, Maxwell had him prove his loyalty by ordering him to kill Diane Parker.

BOTTOM RIGHT: Shady Carlo Forenza knew Neil Curtis was really Allen Jackson who, with Carlo's father, had turned state's evidence against a crime syndicate. He was going to blow Neil's cover so he could have Liz, but Neil faked Allen's death. Carlo interupted Neil and Liz's plans to leave town and, after a vicious fight, died of injuries.

OPPOSITE: Pretty but dangerously devious Megan Hathaway was Bo Brady's high school girlfriend, and she was determined to get him back. Unknown to most people, she was also Stefano DiMera's daughter. She too planned to kill Hope—by electrocuting her in a hot tub—but accidentally met her own death instead. Hope still suffered, though, as the prime suspect in the murder.

LEFT: Sociopath Alan Harris wanted Carrie Brady, but when he was rejected, tried to rape her. When that failed, he date-raped her already troubled sister Sami, unleashing the worst in her: Sami blew away Alan's manhood with a gun and then set her sights on Carrie's beau, Austin, tricking him into bed.

BELOW: Eve Baron turned out to be Shane Donovan's troubled daughter by his former ISA partner, Gabrielle. Before she learned who her mother really was, Eve caused plenty of problems for Kimberly Brady, who befriended her and helped her avoid falling back into prostitution. Unfortunately, Eve wrongly believed Kimberly had caused the breakup of her dad's marriage to Emma, who she thought was her mom. Scott had her number and only wanted to promote her singing career. Meanwhile, Eve fell in love with her ex-pimp, Nick, but married Jack for money.

NEAR RIGHT: Vivian Alamain's repertoire of crime has included killing Dr. Carly Manning's patients, burying Carly alive (and tormenting her from aboveground by walkie-talkie), and stealing Victor and Kate's in-vitro fertilized egg so she could bear his only son.

FAR RIGHT: After Dr. Marlena Evans became her husband's therapist, Stella Lombard became Marlena's worst nightmare. Certain Marlena was after her man, Stella dumped her in a pit and terrorized her for weeks in an abandoned warehouse.

BOTTOM RIGHT: Manipulative Lisanne Gardner had set her sights on Lawrence Alamain and his millions. She became his lover and cohort, but got in over her head when she tried to blackmail Vivian with her knowledge that Nikki was really Lawrence and Carly's son.

LEFT: Man-in-the-middle Peter Blake was raised by crime lord Stefano and was following in his footsteps until he met good-girl Jennifer Devereaux. He wants to clean up his act but Stefano won't allow it. Stefano knows Peter gaslighted Jennifer's mom and keeps a tight rein on him.

ABOVE: Whether alive or dead, Curtis Reed did the devil's work. He was Billie's incestuous father, Kate's abusive husband, and all-around sleaze.

Behind the Scenes

Joseph Mascolo (Stefano) had little choice but to rest with his "cast" between scenes. Even though his character had amnesia, he was just fine in his dressing room.

To make up for the lack of a window in her quarters, Eileen Davidson (Kristen) painted one of her own, complete with curtains and trouble-free plants.

Thyme Lewis (Jonah) brought the great outdoors into his dressing room by painting a Caribbean island theme on his walls.

Days of Our Lives airs for one hour, five days a week, 52 weeks a year, with generally few preemptions. In its 30-year history, over 7,600 episodes have been produced. The telecast presently originates from Studios 2 and 4 on the sprawling NBC lot in Burbank, California. These huge, hangar-like structures include not only the actual shooting sets, but floors of dressing rooms, writing and production offices; the control booth; audio and editing chambers; cavernous set storage and construction spaces; and the adjacent outdoor Salem Place set.

Like a beehive, the studios swarm with hundreds of people nearly twenty-four hours a day. Through passages, stairways, workrooms, and studios, actors move from dressing rooms to makeup to commissary to sets, up and down stairs, through halls and across parking lots, some still in T-shirts or robes, white napkins protecting their collars from makeup. There are about 30 contract actors, nearly twenty day players, and sometimes even more atmosphere people—or extras—in addition to production staff, writers, creative crew (props, makeup/hair, wardrobe, set design), and technical crew (control booth, stagehands, and electricians). Add to this messengers, journalists, photographers, personal managers, publicists, and friends. Large groups in NBC tours pass along the edges of the inner sanctum, too.

Two sets of double doors face each other across a hallway intersection where a security guard keeps an eye on visitors and traffic flow. An illuminated ON AIR sign over one stage door warns against noise and unauthorized entry. On this day the other stage door is open, and beyond, a swarm of stagehands pick sets apart and a wall from the Kiriakis mansion is rolled past on a cart on its way to storage. A visitor is nudged aside by a wardrobe person rushing by with two armloads of taffeta evening gowns, two tiaras balanced on her head.

A runner dashes up the stairs with bundles under his arm marked PRODUC-ERS. He quickly and carefully avoids two actors sitting on the steps going over their lines as they wait their turn in makeup. At the top of the stairs, open doors reveal an assistant cursing a stalled copy machine; a publicist with phones in both hands and a third ringing; atmosphere players lined up to sign their contracts. The producers' office doors are all closed, with meetings in progress.

On the lower floor, the control booth is humming in its dim-lit glow and wall of monitors. A production associate stares at a stopwatch; an associate director whispers into a mike; a director repeatedly snaps his fingers; and a technical director madly slaps at buttons. Behind them all, in the tallest chair, the supervising producer sits like the captain of the Starship *Enterprise*.

A Day on the Set

A typical twenty-four-hour day in the life of *Days of Our Lives*:

6:30 A.M. The first actors arrive, along with makeup artists and wardrobe personnel. Actors continue to arrive throughout the morning and early afternoon. Some will finish their scenes as early as ten in the morning. Others will stay until this day's taping ends, or "wraps," sometimes as late as midnight or later, if a special night shoot is planned.

7:00 A.M. Today's director (one of three staff and two backups) arrives. Accompanied by members of the props and art departments, he "walks the sets," pointing out any changes that must be made to fit his plan for the day's taping.

8:00 A.M. Hands-on creative and technical personnel arrive. The TD (technical director), audio and video technicians, music director, and a PA (production associate) head for the control booth to complete their prep. Meanwhile actors, a director, and associate director are in the studio to begin "dry block"—mapping physical movement—of the morning's scenes.

8:30 A.M. Production, casting, editing, and writing personnel arrive and begin work on upcoming shows, including all the intricacies of scheduling, story development, personnel requirements, script breakdowns, etc. Planning and coordinating a daily one-hour drama is a bit like governing a small nation.

9:00 A.M. The supervising producer takes his place in the control booth. On the intercom, the TD gives the call: "May we have pictures and booms, please!" and a stage manager summons the cast of the first scene. Actors, crew, creative technicians, and others converge on the first set. "Block-and-tape," a system of rehearsing and taping one scene at a time rather than rehearsing the whole show before taping it from start to finish, has begun.

10:00 A.M. By now, the executive producer has read the lastest flimsy—a preliminary script, with dialogue—and sends it on to the writers with his final editorial comments.

10:30 A.M. A writers' assistant faxes the changes on the flimsy to the appropriate dialogue writer, who may live next door or across the continent.

11:00 A.M. Upstairs, in the second-floor production area, another set of artists and technicians (director, TD, lighting designer, etc.) meet to discuss and plan tomorrow's show. A PA has typed and made 200 copies of tomorrow's taping schedule and starts to call or fax tomorrow's actors with their call (arrival) times.

11:30 A.M.   A typing service delivers the final version of the script that was edited and faxed to them yesterday, and which will be taped in about a week. A PA distributes copies to the director, cast, and crew.

1:00 P.M.   Lunch. Everyone troops off to various watering holes, especially the famous NBC Commissary. Most will return at 2:10, but the actors, director, and AD return earlier to dry-block the afternoon session.

1:30 P.M.   Afternoon dry block begins while tomorrow's taping schedules, call sheets, etc., are distributed to appropriate persons.

2:00 P.M.   By now the dialogue writer has usually faxed in changes and the writers' assistant types and copies a final flimsy.

2:10 P.M.   Block-and-tape continues until the show wraps. By now, taping in one of the two studios likely has been completed and the scenic crew starts to break down the morning's sets. After that, they start to construct the sets for tomorrow. Rome wasn't built in a day, but Salem is rebuilt *every* day.

2:30 P.M.   The coordinating producer reviews the final flimsy and an assistant breaks it down for certain detailed information and produces a six-page report that becomes the blue pages of the finished script, which lists sets, cast, and personnel involved in that day's shoot.

4:00 P.M.   The assistant faxes the cover pages and flimsy to the script service, which types them in final script format.

6:00 P.M.   Most of the production staff, cast, tape-editing and writing personnel have gone home.

8:00 P.M.   Eventually the TD announces over the speakers, "That's a wrap!" Everyone, except the night crew and cleaning staff, heads home. Each episode has its own unique problems. If a show has been straightforward, it might wrap at 5:00 P.M. Some demanding shows can wrap at 1:00 A.M., or even later.

MIDNIGHT The lighting designer and his crew arrive to begin the process of lighting tomorrow's (now today's) sets. Because they must be on hand to make subtle adjustments throughout taping, they won't go home until today's new show wraps.

6:30 A.M.   Another set of sleepy cast and crew arrives.

Who's Who and What's What Around the Set

With Ken Corday at the helm as President, CORDAY PRODUCTIONS oversees the entire show from a business and financial perspective. Gary Fogel, Executive Vice President, oversees and coordinates the negotiations with the network, with *Days of Our Lives'* distributor Columbia Pictures Television, Inc., and with all agents and lawyers for writers, producers, directors, and actors. Greg Meng, Vice President, supervises the overall budget of every aspect of the show's production.

EXECUTIVE PRODUCER has the final say in every area of production including, but not limited to story development, casting, budget, and studio relations. They determine what appears on screen and shape life in the city of Salem.

SUPERVISING PRODUCER is the final arbiter of creative and technical decisions during taping. He/she is present in the control booth throughout the day. The prime responsiblility is to maintain the standards, style, and tone demanded by the executive producers. During breaks, the supervising producer is often found reading outlines, viewing rough cuts, and conferring with other producers.

SENIOR COORDINATING PRODUCER is responsible for hiring most technical and staff personnel; preparing and analyzing budgets; planning and scheduling of sets; supervising location shoots; and functioning as liaison with the network.

COORDINATING PRODUCER is responsible for final review of scripts before they are sent out for printing. This producer researches archived scripts and tapes for flashback scenes, clips, etc., and has much interaction with the writers for the selection of cuts and taking care of changes that often occur during taping and on short notice.

ASSOCIATE PRODUCER is responsible for creation and processing of the daily taping schedule, including coordinating the demands and needs of personnel in all areas of production.

HEAD WRITER creates the primary elements of the long-term storyline, refines it with the executive producers, and supervises the team of associate head writers and dialogue writers who produce outlines and finished scripts.

ASSOCIATE HEAD WRITER translates the head writer's ideas into detailed outlines, on which final taping scripts are based. The associate head writer sometimes participates in story development meetings with the head writer and executive producers.

DIALOGUE WRITER takes the script outline and gives the drama words, presenting a final taping script.

DIRECTORS work for several days before taping, analyzing and breaking down the script into scenes and cuts. They apply visual imagination to the script's demands and meet with various technical and creative personnel to solve any potential problems. Throughout the taping process, the director must communicate his/her vision to the actors and crew. The director sits in the control booth, calling the shots by snapping fingers as different camera compositions come onscreen.

ASSOCIATE DIRECTOR (AD) is responsible for coordinating music, audio, the studio floor, and the control booth throughout the taping process. This person

Supervising Producer
Steven Wyman

has creative input as well, pointing out problems and possibilities to the director and supervising producer. At *Days*, the ADs alternate as editing supervisors, overseeing the process of transforming raw tape into a polished transition of scenes for the air show.

TECHNICAL DIRECTOR (TD) is responsible for most communication and coordination between various technical personnel; preparing shot cards, based on the director's shooting script, for the camera operators; and switching between cameras during taping in response to the director's finger-snaps.

PRODUCTION ASSOCIATES (PAs) are responsible for typing and distribution of daily schedules, call sheets, and breakdowns; pretiming of scripts; distribution of script cuts and changes; and timing and script supervision in the control booth during taping.

PRODUCTION DESIGNER creates sets, helps to coordinate their planning and placement, and makes adjustments after the morning walk-through. The designer produces daily blueprints showing studio layouts in detail; assists in design and set dressing; and produces sketches and elevations.

STAGE MANAGER is responsible for calling actors to the set and keeping track of their comings and goings. Stage managers are the communicators between actors and the control booth. They cue actors, block and supervise atmosphere players, and generally manage all activities involving actors while in the studio. There are always three stage managers working during a taping day at *Days*.

MUSIC DIRECTOR researches new music, works with composers, and acquires rights to use already recorded music. He must also be on hand during taping to see that the proper cues are provided. When changes are needed, he must produce them on the spot from the music library. He reviews edited show tapes and makes final adjustments.

LIGHTING DIRECTOR designs lights for each set and scene, bearing in mind considerations of the season and time of day in Salem, the emotional climate, etc. This director and staff arrive at midnight to hang and focus the lights, and they remain until the show wraps in order to make the many adjustments necessary during taping.

MAKEUP SUPERVISOR attends various production meetings, studies outlines and scripts to determine future makeup and hair styling needs, and orders needed materials. The makeup supervisor's staff applies makeup and styles hair for all the players. Some staff members serve specific actors. At least one staff member remains in the studio during taping to touch up makeup and solve any problems that may arise.

WARDROBE SUPERVISOR coordinates and supervises the wardrobe department. He/she attends production meetings and studies outlines and scripts to determine future costuming needs and shops for clothes, fabrics, and accessories. The wardrobe supervisor's staff creates, repairs, maintains, and distributes all costumes.

Coordinating Producer
Janet Spellman Rider and
Senior Coordinating
Producer Jeanne Haney

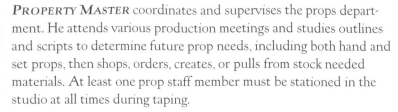

ABOVE: Casting Director Fran F. Bascom and Casting Assistant Ronald Sperber

BELOW: Associate Casting Director Linda Poindexter and Casting Assistant Rick Lorentz

PROPERTY MASTER coordinates and supervises the props department. He attends various production meetings and studies outlines and scripts to determine future prop needs, including both hand and set props, then shops, orders, creates, or pulls from stock needed materials. At least one prop staff member must be stationed in the studio at all times during taping.

SOUND EFFECTS TECHNICIAN manipulates keyboard, synthesizer, and an extensive audio library to create everything from door slams (hard, soft, wooden, metallic), to the natural sounds of Salem (crickets, wind, rustling leaves), to the occasional gunshot (any caliber), and whatever else the script demands.

EDITORS are responsible for cutting tape and transforming a multitude of "takes" into a sequential, rhythmic presentation that fits neatly into the time limits of a one-hour format.

HEAD CARPENTER supervises the night crew that dismantles and erects the sets.

HEAD ELECTRICIAN and his crew are responsible for cabling, power, and all the juice that keeps the studio humming.

AUDIO MIXER is responsible for balancing and combining everything heard on Days with the visual taping.

CAMERA OPERATORS are the three, and sometimes four, technical experts who run the cameras that capture the action, following the shot cards prepared by the TD. The director relies heavily on their experience and instinct for composition.

CASTING DIRECTORS supervise the selection of contract or lead actors, day players, and most "under-fives." Another casting director handles the remaining under-fives and all extras.

DAY PLAYERS are actors who have speaking roles of more than five lines hired for a single show or limited series of shows.

UNDER-FIVES are actors hired to speak five or fewer lines in a single show.

The following information is called the "crawl" because of the way it appears to crawl up the television screen at the end of the show. This is the 1995 crawl:

Executive Producer
KEN CORDAY

Co-Executive Producer
TOM LANGAN

Supervising Producer
STEPHEN WYMAN

Head Writer
JAMES E. REILLY

Associate Head Writers
MAURA PENDERS
DENA HIGLEY
MARLENE CLARK
POULTER
KATHERINE PENDERS
SHAWN MORRISON
DOROTHY ANN PURSER

Dialogue Writers
FRAN MYERS
PEGGY SCHIBI
VICTOR GIALANELLA
MARALYN THOMA

Directors
PHIL SOGARD
HERB STEIN
RANDY ROBBINS

Senior Coordinating Producer
JEANNE HANEY

Coordinating Producer
JANET RIDER

Associate Producer
TOM WALKER

CAST

starring
FRANCES REID
as *Alice Horton*

Mickey Horton
JOHN CLARKE

Victor Kiriakis
JOHN ANISTON

Jennifer Rose Devereaux
MELISSA REEVES

John Black
DRAKE HOGESTYN

Maggie Horton
SUZANNE ROGERS

Caroline Brady
PEGGY MCCAY

Shawn Brady
FRANK PARKER

Abe Carver
JAMES REYNOLDS

Vivian Alamain
LOUISE SOREL

Bo Brady
PETER RECKELL

Carrie Brady
CHRISTIE CLARKE

Samantha Brady
ALISON SWEENEY

Jonah Carver
THYME LEWIS

Lexie Carver
RENEE JONES

Lucas Roberts
BRYAN DATTILO

Kristen DiMera
EILEEN DAVIDSON

Ivan Marais
IVAN G'VERA

Tony DiMera
THAAO PENGHLIS

Laura Horton
JAIME LYN BAUER

Jamie Caldwell
MIRIAM PARRISH

Peter Blake
JASON BROOKS

Mike Horton
ROARK CRITCHLOW

Hope Williams Brady
KRISTIAN ALFONSO

Celeste
TANYA BOYD

Jack Devereaux
MARK VALLEY

Stefano DiMera
JOSEPH MASCOLO

Austin Reed
AUSTIN PECK

and DIEDRE HALL *as*
Marlena Evans-Brady

Theme by
CHARLES ALBERTINE
TOMMY BOYCE
BOBBY HART

Music Composed by
KEN CORDAY
CORY LERIOS
JOHN D'ANDREA
DOMINIC MESSINGER
D. BRENT NELSON

Music Directors
AMY BURKHARD
STEVE REINHARDT

Production Designer
CHIP DOX

Associate Directors
ROGER INMAN
SHERYL HARMON

Production Associates
DAVID N. KOHN
DEBBIE WARE BAR-
ROWS
ROY FRIEDLAND

Production Manager
TIM STEVENS

Property Master
TOM TROUT

Special Effects
PETE TRZEPACZ

Art Director
WADE BATTLEY

Assistant Art Director
TOM EARLY

Assistants to the Producers
NANCY LEWIS
TERRY ANN HOLST
STUART W. HOWARD

Continuity Coordinator
JOYCE ROSENBLAD

Writers' Assistant
JEANNE M. GRUNWELL

Stage Managers
FRAN BELLINI
JERRY MASTERSON
JOSEPH LUMER
GARY WENTE

Casting by
FRAN F. BASCOM, C.S.A.

Associate Casting Director
LINDA POINDEXTER

Casting Assistants
RONALD SPERBER
RICK LORENTZ

Publicist
PAULETTE COHN

Costume Design
RICHARD BLOORE

Wardrobe
SHERRELL BIGGERSTAFF
FLORENCE CALCE
SAL LICON
SHARON NICHOLS
JIM PFANNER
CONNIE SECH

Makeup Artists
GAIL HOPKINS
NINA WELLS
JOHN DAMIANI
CORINA DURAN

Hairstylists
ZORA SLOAN
TERRIE VELAZQUEZ

Technical Directors
WAYNE MCDONALD
JOHN C. O'NEILL

Lighting Directors
DON DESIMONE
TED POLMANSKI

Audio
BRUCE BOTTONE

Boom Operators
RALPH CRUSE
PAT STITES

Senior Video
ARNOLD SHAPIRO

Video Tape Editors
MASON DICKSON
BRUCE BRINKERHOFF

Camera
MICHAEL CARUSO
MIKE MECARTEA
JOHN D. SIZEMORE

Sound Effects
TOM KAFKA

Production Executive
GREG MENG

*Executive in Charge of
Production*
GARY FOGEL

**A CORDAY
PRODUCTIONS, INC.
PRESENTATION**

Interviews:
Co-executive
Producer
Tom Langan
and Head
Writer
James E. Reilly

Ask Tom Langan, Co-executive Producer, what makes *Days of Our Lives* so special and he immediately points to its quick pacing and its mix of adventure and romance.

"The pace of this show is faster than any other daytime drama. We may have as many as thirty-two to thirty-five items, or scenes, in each show while others have about twenty-five. The maximum time for most scenes on this show is two and a half to three minutes, unlike the five or six minutes per scene on other shows. This certainly appeals to the MTV appetite. Young people today are very acclimated to hearing a story told in a two-and-a-half-minute song and they get it. They don't need things explained, overexplained, and explained over again. They want to move on and see the next step. We're in a generation of sound bites.

"At *Days* we go for the young audience's emotional jugular vein," Langan explains. "In our own lives, we have relationships and each one will have a certain number of road blocks. If we don't get beyond those road blocks, we are going to have a very lonely life. Often scenes with lovers pulled apart have more emotional impact than when the lovers were together. Jim will put such a major issue in a relationship that it seems it can never be mended, but, of course, that makes us root all the more for them to get back together. The lesson that comes through our show is that we need to learn love and forgiveness. Love is the one most powerful thing we've got.

"I loved my experience on *Y&R*. Bill Bell is a genius in daytime. He has such a talent for delineating character. You can watch the show and your best friend will always be there. He keeps characters so distinct, intact, and each is unique. That was the show that made me fall in love with what I do."

Much of the personal joy Langan finds in his work on *Days* comes from the camaraderie of working with long-time friend, head writer James E. Reilly.

"First, working with Jim in terms of storytelling is a delight. In my eyes, he's the new genius in daytime. I enjoy the rapport that we have, which is so important in discussing characters, how we mold them and shape them. He writes the character and I must direct the actors on stage. The conversations with Jim are just very rewarding because we really understand each other. We speak the same language and have known each other most of our lives, since we were both in our early twenties. We were really tight friends before we worked together. I encouraged Jim to get involved in daytime writing because I felt he would be perfect for it. He loves it."

It's certainly a big plus that the two are friends, since, according to Langan, "We are on the phone seven days a week, five and six times a day. We joke about it a lot. We just can't imagine people who can write and/or produce a soap and who have any other life. Although we talk all the time, we don't even have time for dinner together."

Langan carries the job with him virtually from the moment he rises to the time he goes to bed. Recently, his sister was visiting. "She was trying to talk to me while I was having breakfast at 6:30. She noticed I wasn't really listening or responding. She was right. My mind was already on the job. It was Monday, and I had our outline meeting to look forward to that morning. I just wasn't with it in conversation with her. Most evenings, I come home and watch *Jeopardy!* for a half-hour of R&R while I'm having dinner and then I'm on the phone with Jim."

Tough job but someone's gotta do it and love it too.

TOM LANGAN

Head writer James E. Reilly has been writing soap opera for almost fifteen years. He's been a consultant or writer on the majority of shows currently on the air.

The Fordham University graduate (1974) decided to take a ten-year "retirement" before settling into a career. He was on his seventh year of world travel when he came to Los Angeles en route to China. He met Ed Scott and John Conboy, who were producing *The Young and the Restless* at the time. He impressed everyone with his delightful storytelling ability and finally gave in to suggestions that he should write. Reilly bought a house in Palm Springs and in 1980 found himself happily writing soap opera. His career is a joy for him.

Since Jim started writing, the medium has changed, perhaps most notably in pace. "It's much faster now," says Reilly. "Every scene accounts for something. We keep the continuity and pace without losing the threads of what's happening, and viewers have to watch several days a week in order to keep up. In general, viewers are exposed to faster pace in movie, television, and music. It doesn't matter whether it's an action or psychological thriller or a romantic comedy.

"At the same time," Reilly reminds, "the audience likes the stretch of a story that has an energy to it. It cannot go so fast that they can't savor the flavor of how delicious it is to see so-and-so walk into the room. Moments are built up to. Our audience must be psychologically prepared for what's about to happen. For example, Maison Blanche paved the foundation for the Stefano-Marlena infatuation and the middle of the night visits through her armoire in Salem. DiMera's passions, his interest was aroused as never before. It didn't pay off for about six or seven months, but it made sense when it did. Likewise, Gina was introduced over a year before she was revealed as Hope. We had to have the audience fall in love with her while the Bo and Billie wedding excitement had to hold. The energy must be up, but every beat of story must be played. Anticipation must be played where it counts, not over everything. And there's always focus on the emotions."

Asked to pick some of his favorite characters, stories, and times, Reilly gasps, "That's like picking one child over another!" But concedes, "I've had fun with all of them. Some are so great and out there, like the buried-alive story and the Satanic possession. I like the things that make people talk. And the one I like because of the nice slow development and there were lots of twists: Bo-Billie-Hope. That had all the elements of romance, sex, passion, surprises, friendship, and a triangle without a bad person. People didn't do evil things to each other."

Even lesser characters with short-term runs can be pivotal. Curtis Reed, for example, was important so that the audience understood that "because of her background, Billie does things that a totally honest, noble person would not. Then she goes back and tries to undo the bad she may have done, even at great personal risk to her own emotional life. Billie is different in that regard because at the end of everything, she will be true to herself. She emerges without defining herself in terms of the man in her life. Her attitude is 'I had this great love . . . I am a better person for having loved and lost.' There's more equality for women in this kind of a story."

The uniting element of love is the undercurrent in all relationships in Salem. "Family love and unity is so important too. I enjoy seeing family, from grandparents to newborns, brought together in story and scenes. It starts with love between individuals.

"Love is the answer, always," Reilly notes. "The women on *Days of Our Lives* are loved by men who will do anything for them. When a woman is loved, she is his queen. He will walk through fire for her. Love is that important."

Location shooting was certainly a major addition to soap opera over the decades. *Days of Our Lives* has visited a number of faraway places, including Athens, London, Cancun, Puerto Rico, and New Orleans. Closer to home, the show often goes on location around Los Angeles: San Pedro Harbor, the Lake Arrowhead ski area, Beverly Hills, and even Universal City Studios in Hollywood.

Production designer Chip Dox may have to make two or more trips to a location area before the shoot begins. If that sounds like fun, he reminds, "Sometimes it means twelve or more hours on the plane to get somewhere, and then we spend our time driving around in vans scouting places we can use for filming. You don't spend much, if any, time relaxing on the beach. In Puerto Rico I literally spent two minutes in the water," he says, laughing. "I just had to do it. Get in just long enough to get wet."

The set designer's location work is not complete when the cameras come home. "I have to concurrently design the interior sets that coordinate with the outdoor scenes that were shot and have them ready to shoot when we return," says Dox.

The biggest interior design change for soaps over the years has been the scope of the scenery. Entryways and hallways have become as important as the main set. This gives the writers more areas for characters to enter and move around in more naturally.

Originally, *Days* sets didn't even have carpeting on the floor, just the studio tile, which was never shown. That's why actors could wear sneakers or slippers if they chose. That shooting style has changed.

Perhaps the largest change in the type of scene that can be shot in the studio is the "indoor exterior." The same shots that might be filmed at some location area for a nighttime show are taped right on the soundstages of NBC for daytime. Indoor exteriors include small areas like back alleys, back and front yards, Smith Island, pits, and wooded areas. Car crashes, even off a pier, can be and have been created inside the studio.

Exteriors like forests and graveyards, pits and cliffs, can be challenging. Car wrecks are hard, too. It can be difficult to match another car with the wrecked one for before-and-after shots. Sometimes the design team can make a car look wrecked if it was not, or sometimes they rent a wreck from a junkyard or theatrical car agency. It's all in the magic of storytelling!

Production designer Chip Dox has been creating *Days of Our Lives* sets for over sixteen years. He also scouts global and domestic location sites for the show.

LEFT: Puerto Rico entailed three separate preproduction planning trips and unpredictable weather, which had cast and crew dodging rain when least expected. It was a real nightmare for the lighting crew.

BELOW: Jennifer and Jack's wedding was taped a few miles away from the *Days* NBC lot at Universal Studios Hollywood. Their wedding there became a Wild West stunt show, with Jennifer swinging from a tall pole and Jack catapulting into a well.

ABOVE: Cancun, Mexico, was a joy for most everyone. There was enough time in the shooting schedule to explore the Mayan ruins in the surrounding jungles while John searched for his identity with Bo's help.

LEFT: The Kern River was Bo and Hope's greatest adventure as they battled the rapids with Shane. Hope found life with Bo to be one exciting escapade after another.

ABOVE: Chip Dox's favorite production assignment was for Patch and Kayla's Civil War–era fantasy as Emily and Gideon. Not only were the location scenes enjoyable, but redecorating their Salem house to relate to their fantasy was challenging.

RIGHT: When Renee saw an opportunity to get rid of her love rival, she planted a bomb on the boat Anna was sailing. However, she didn't know Tony would be on board, too. This location was only a few hours from home in Southern California.

Dressing up or dressing down, costume changes are an integral part of daytime's overall look. The right apparel can enhance a trip to a different time period, transform a leading man into a leading lady, embellish a lovely actress's figure, or—with a little padding and thrift shop attire—make a performer look his absolute worst!

Makeup artistry and a hairdresser's teasing comb can top the creation to complete the look. Salem residents, *Days* actors, and viewers all have a great time when wardrobe wizards and makeup magicians unleash their talents.

ABOVE: **C**ostume designer Richard Bloore heads a department of wardrobe wizards who outfit actors in everything from elegant evening wear to barely-there lingerie. Bloore has created wedding gowns from a sketch, added baubles and beads to off-the-rack frocks, and matched just the right designer label to an actor's character and personal style.

LEFT: **D**aytime Emmy Award–winning hair and makeup department staff: clockwise, makeup artists Gail Hopkins, Nina Wells, John Damiani, Corina Duran, and Lucia Bianca; seated, hairstylists Zora Sloan and Terrie Velazquez.

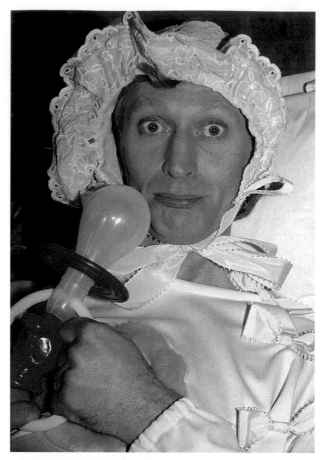

ABOVE: Vivian escaped Pine Haven Sanitarium and followed Laura and Jennifer right into a party filled with friends and foes. Taking no chances of being recognized while on the loose, Vivian left her sophisticated lady look at the asylum and donned a dashing gentleman's facade.

ABOVE RIGHT: Oh baby! After Vivian's sidekick and confidant Ivan helped her give birth to a healthy baby boy with the help of a magnum of champagne, she had quite a cute hallucination.

RIGHT: After the asylum burned down, Vivian was thought dead. She took advantage of the situation and came up with a multitude of disguises to keep her identity under wraps. Her bag lady attire was a perfect ploy.

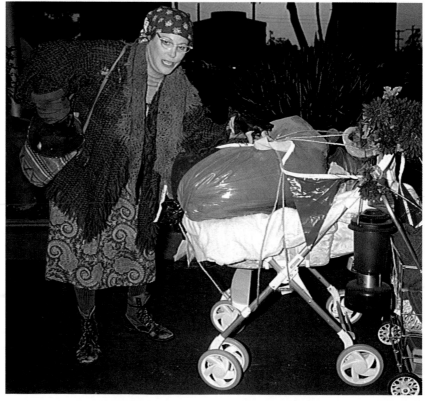

She's just the devil in disguise. . . . When Isabella
returned from the dead to tempt Fr. John Black
from his exorcism duties, she first appeared lovely
and angelic. Then, rebuffed, she let her true character materialize.

LEFT: Hats off to Calliope, who donned more chapeaux than gossip queen Hedda Hopper. Her wacky persona brought lots of color to Salem.

BELOW LEFT: Fantasy sequences provided Scott and Eve dream-come-true romance and celebrity. Viewers loved the musical strolls down memory lane.

BELOW CENTER: Roman Brady was transformed with makeup magic—and lots of putty and padding—to become Mr. Snow when he worked as an undercover agent cracking a local cocaine ring.

BELOW RIGHT: In 1987, Dr. Neil Curtis and Grace Forrester personified European elegance when they dressed as Marie Antoinette and a Russian czar.

ABOVE LEFT & RIGHT: In 1992, Alice, Tom, and Marlena enjoyed Vivian's masquerade ball, but for John Black and Isabella Toscano it would evoke new mystery regarding John's past as the jewel thief Romulus.

FAR LEFT: Steve and Kayla brought a western flair to the 1988 Halloween party. He personalized his outfit with his pumpkin "patch."

LEFT: Jack Devereaux always had an antic or ploy to get himself out of a scrape. This one was a real drag.

OPPOSITE & ABOVE: Fairy tales came true against a rich make-believe backdrop that shed a medieval spell on Salem residents: Shane, Kimberly, and their son Andrew; and Victor, Jack, and Kayla.

ABOVE RIGHT: Marlena was bedazzling as Cleopatra; however, Mark Antony was nowhere in sight. So she settled for John's Count Dracula.

RIGHT: For Halloween 1994, Caroline and Shawn Brady had fun playing a gunslinger and saloon floozy.

ABOVE: In 1994, a charity ball at Maison Blanche was the splendid setting for mystery and intrigue that would change the lives of best buddies Billie, Kristen, and Jennifer. It also earned the show a Daytime Emmy Award for hairstyling.

RIGHT: Halloween 1993 provided another colorful soiree. Mickey and Maggie were dashing as Rhett Butler and Scarlett O'Hara.

ABOVE: Jennifer and Peter made love for the first time at this romantic inn on the bayou. It was a night they would never forget.

RIGHT: After a long and chivalrous courtship, Bo proposed to Billie with all the heightened emotion of lovers united at last.

Our Days in Salem

Interviews:
Frances Reid, Deidre Hall, Drake Hogestyn, and Kristian Alfonso and Peter Reckell
Special Tribute: Macdonald Carey

FRANCES REID
(Alice Horton)

Frances Reid is eighty, but don't bother telling her she doesn't look her age because her likely retort will be, "I don't know what it means to look or feel eighty." A few years ago she traveled to China. This year she plans to trek through South Africa. No wonder Alice Horton has such spunk. She's inherited it from Frances.

ABOUT FRANCES'S CHILDHOOD

"I was born and raised in Wichita, Texas, at a time when there were three school districts, separate ones for white, black, and Hispanic. There was no room for me at the local public school so I didn't start until the second grade, and then I went to Miss Barrow's one-room schoolhouse. During the first year of my education away from the classroom, my parents read to each other every night. So I always heard poetry, H. G. Wells, everything. I'm certain my education was really quite advanced at that point."

HIGHER EDUCATION

"Shakespeare and Dickens were my favorite authors in high school. In my senior year, I dated college men. One took me to the Stanford prom. I quit college, where I was not considered academically serious, to go to the Pasadena Playhouse School of the Theater."

FRANCES'S EARLY CAREER

"In grammar school, I played a man in a thirty-minute play. In the late 1930s I played an ingenue in the West Coast company of *Tovarish* with Osgood

Perkins, a wonderful actor who was Tony Perkins's dad. My first movie role was in *Stage Door* with Katharine Hepburn and Lucille Ball. I was the new girl they took up the stairs at the very end of the movie. My first radio job was at NBC before WWII. No one timed the radio scripts. We were the only thing on. I played Ann Rutledge in *Prologue to Glory*, and starred as Mrs. Moonlight in 'Mrs. Moonlight,' and did Charlotte Corday in 'Charlotte Corday.' I did those things, probably because no one else would do them for that pay. All the lead players on those shows received fifty dollars for ten days' work. I do remember so many years later when someone got one thousand dollars per show here and we were all aghast. 'I don't believe that!' we all murmured. We thought it incredible. My very first soap opera role was in 1954 in the fifteen-minute soap, *Portia Faces Life*. I quit after six months because I was exhausted. Now I've been doing this show for thirty years and I'm still going strong."

ABOUT FRANCES'S START ON *DAYS*

"I took the role thinking it would be all right for a year. Suddenly when I reached twenty years here I realized I had spent two decades in the theater and half my professional life doing this. Now I'm way beyond that. Most of my professional life has been as Alice Horton, and I have no regrets. I knew Ted Corday when he was stage manager in New York and Betty was casting radio at NBC. We all knew the theater community in New York. It was a wonderfully small little world where everyone knew everyone."

ABOUT ALICE'S EARLY DAYS

"I've always been among the 'old folk' on the show. I was already a grandmother when we started. In three decades, I think Tom and Alice had one story line. Julie got sick. She was an evil child! But she almost died and then seemed to become a dear child. Anyway, there was some ecology problem or someone was poisoning the water system of Salem. Some people threw rocks through the Hortons' kitchen windows. The story didn't work. It was dropped quickly and without explanation, but I used to enjoy playing coy in the supermarket when people asked about it. They'd ask, What happened to the story? And I'd question back, 'You missed it? It was wonderful, a wonderful resolution!' as I managed to move on."

MORE ABOUT ALICE

"Alice has evolved wonderfully over the decades. She's certainly outside of the house, asserting herself as head of the volunteers at the hospital. It's wonderful to see a person mature socially. Even before Tom's death, after the children and grandchildren who came to live in the Horton home were on their own, Alice asserted herself more and became involved with the volunteer program at the hospital, with the youth center, and with the community in general. She matured socially a bit later in life. Alice was a mom for the better part of her life."

ABOUT ALICE'S LOVE

"Taking in granddaughters Julie, Sandy, Hope, Jennifer, and Jessica for a short time gave Alice the greatest pleasure. She loved a houseful of kids. She would have loved to have all her grandchildren live with her if they could. Alice has an expanding unconditional love. Alice kept her door open. She was genuine in her welcome. She was not taking them in out of a sense of responsibility alone; she really felt it was so nice to have them around. And she let them be their own people. She took care of them but did not try to dominate them or tell them what to do."

ABOUT HER FEISTY SPIRIT

"Alice always loved her children, whether she had to go to a prison or a sanitarium to visit them. She also helped Roman Brady escape from prison with doughnuts laced with some drug that made it look as if he'd had a heart attack. That was heaven. I played detective with Bo and we had this insane scene, but we got Roman out of jail and I got to ride Bo's motorcycle, too."

WHAT FRANCES LIKES MOST/LEAST ABOUT ALICE

"She doesn't see evil in anyone. This is an extraordinary quality that my mother had as well. It really just exuded from her. I so miss my mom. Everyone was always just fine. My friend K. T. Stevens was like that too. I think she's a little free with her advice. That's something one just doesn't do. I learned that from my mom, too."

ABOUT ALICE'S KEEPING IN STEP WITH THE TIMES

"She's been amazing in the way she's kept up with the times. Imagine, she goes along with people living together out of wedlock. Certainly, at the beginning, that would have been unthinkable to her. Now she understands that it's a rule of society. She moves with the times and yet keeps her own values.

"Her advice to Jennifer was always precious. When Jennifer asked about making love, Alice responded with, 'I can only tell you from my experience. I loved Tom, and that was it. We were married and it was good.' Alice responded in terms of her own history, not dogmatically. The show even got awards for the way we handled teaching responsibility to the young and dealing with issues for youth. It was during a period when abstinence was not considered the popular thing to do. It's come back in style now."

ABOUT ALICE'S FUNNY HABITS

"Alice could never remember the names of her children. Well, I really thought that should be written into the scripts as a personality trait. I remember my mother looking me straight in the eye and saying, 'Now look, Mildred . . .' and I'd remind her I'm not Mildred. 'All right, Dorothy . . .' No, Mother. 'Well, you know who I mean . . .' I think all parents do that. And I think most children get incensed at that. I remember looking straight at Mickey and saying, 'Now look, Tommy . . .' They would stop tape. Mac would reprimand me, 'You're looking at your own child, don't you know who it is?' Well, of course, I do, I just don't remember his name."

ABOUT ALICE'S SEXY SCENES

"She never had a sexy scene, but Tom thought she did. An old boyfriend appeared and Tom was absolutely incensed about it all. Tom would go crazy if I even danced with him. The only other bed scene I remember was with Patch. I think I was in the hospital or someplace. There was the sound of gunshots and Patch was nearby and came over to the bed and threw himself over me with so much force he knocked the breath out of me. And at one point, Alice thought Tom was much too interested in Calliope. He kept going to her place to do poetry readings and Alice thought he was just interested in her."

"Drake brought it to my attention that I have a habit of looking straight at people when I talk. Well, Alice would never conceive of *not* looking at the person she's talking to with absolute attention.

"Neither would Frances."

On *Days of Our Lives* since 1976 (with some time out for other projects and trying to become pregnant), Deidre Hall has played Marlena Evans Brady longer than she's done anything else in her life, including being married, having her children, going through school, and living at home with her parents. "It's my longest-lived relationship and certainly a home," Deidre points out.

In many ways, for the viewers and actors alike, it's a home environment of times gone by. "Salem offered me a multigenerational environment that most people never have because we're now a community of single parents and latch-key kids," says Deidre. "We're lucky if we ever spend time with one or two of our grandparents. I think that's one of the things that's so comforting about the show."

Deidre shared other insights too.

ON TURNING DOWN THE ROLE OF DR. MARLENA EVANS

"I thought there had been a mistake, or everyone else turned it down because there was something about this part, the show, or something that everybody knew that I didn't know. So I turned it down. A few months later it was offered to me again. Now I was certain something really must be wrong if they couldn't find anyone to accept the role. Then they made it clear that there was no one else who they wanted and were very surprised by what I had thought. So I came on board."

ON WORKING WITH MACDONALD CAREY AND FRANCES REID

"Their sense of propriety, dignity, and regard for their profession was so present. I learned stage manners from them. How important it is to come on stage respectful of each other, learning the names of the crew, being courteous, cordial, and cheerful regardless of your mood. That's a great lesson to be learned. I cared about earning their respect, becoming a peer. People say don't take yourself too seriously. I do take myself seriously on stage. I learned that too from Mac and Frances."

ON JOHN CLARKE AND SUZANNE ROGERS

"John Clarke was one of my first co-stars, and he's magnificent to this day with even the smallest of scenes. He brings so much value to every moment. He's engaging, entertaining, and captivating as the character. I love him with all my heart. There are reasons he's lived so long on the show. Suzanne is the same way. These four are my heroes."

WHAT WORKING WITH HER SISTER TAUGHT DEIDRE

"I worked with my twin sister, Andrea. It was a magnificent time and fun watching her do something she didn't know was hard to do. She had a very difficult scene: a short phone call and burst into tears. You can cry anywhere but on

DEIDRE HALL
(Dr. Marlena Evans Brady)

stage . . . well, she simply said, 'I can cry.' At that point, three years on the show, I could not cry on stage. She hung up that phone, and I'll be darned if she didn't burst into tears. I looked at her and figured, if she can do it, it can't be that hard. After that, I never had a problem crying. I had been making it harder than it really is. It was like when she first came on and I was telling her about all the marks, overlaps, sound, and so many things. Her reaction was, 'I can do it. I've seen you do it. How hard can it be?' We taught each other a lot in those moments."

WHAT DEIDRE TAUGHT HER SISTER

"Her character Samantha had to testify at her sanity hearing. She had her script, I reminded her to study it. She shrugged it off because it was just one page. Later, she realized the lines 'made no sense.' Of course not. Samantha was emotionally disturbed, ranting, dissociating. I helped her work on that scene. She couldn't memorize it, so we created a dialogue in her head that the audience wouldn't hear. It gave her a subtext to relate to. The next day on the set she was breathtaking. The crew burst into applause, and that only happens about once a year on a set."

WHY DEIDRE LOVES ACTING AND HOW SHE DOES IT

"I enjoy the exploration of a character, yet I don't give any character a pre-life. I find a universal reality. I don't personalize it myself. I know other actors do. If I'm a woman whose husband has left, what are the levels and beats of the emotions I would go through. I sit down and sort that through. For example, on the news, a woman's son has just been killed by a drive-by shooter. She's not crying, not raising her voice, not looking at the interviewer. She looks at her hands a lot, keeps her eyes away from human contact. I study that emotion completely and go on stage and repeat it in detail without feeling it. I show up in the moment and relate to the person I'm with. The situation will provide the emotion. I want to know how that emotion will manifest. I don't have to imagine that my baby died in order to show you how somebody felt when that happened to them. I don't go there; I think that's too dangerous."

ABOUT WAYNE NORTHROP

"Wayne was even tempered, infectiously gentle, with never a malicious moment. He could tease anyone on any topic because everybody knew that he was completely benign. It never came out of anger, prejudice, rage, or resentment. It came from a place of absolute humor. For example, when we used to share dressing rooms, Jed Allan and Robert Clary shared. One day Wayne went to the prop department and got a doorknob and attached it to their door, two feet off the ground. I laughed so hard I thought I would need oxygen. Robert, who is about 4'7", laughed too because it had been Wayne who did it. And there was the time I had an emotional scene with John around the holidays. Wayne came out in a raincoat and flashed me with Christmas ornaments hanging from every part of his body . . . he did have shorts on. It was funny, totally goodhearted. We all miss him enormously."

AND ABOUT DRAKE HOGESTYN

"I'm crazy about him! He's very bright, with a background in dentistry studies before baseball and acting. We asked him about a concussion once and he had chapter and verse. He just knows about many, many things. And he's funny. I

love what a great father he is. Of course, he's been taught by a great mother, his wife, Victoria, who is extraordinary."

ABOUT HER FAVORITE STORY LINES

"I was particularly interested in Sami's bulimia story. I've been around it a bit and realize it's tough to spot. I've had few stories I haven't loved. I didn't love the Kellam Chandler story. But I did love the Johnny story. And I loved the Mickey-in-the-sanitarium story. It was my first introduction to 'sweet acting,' sitting with a co-star who shows you by example how to communicate real tenderness. John is a very deep-feeling, tender man. It comes through in his work. John, as Mickey, sat across from me discussing his son and Laura with such incredible sweetness. I remember thinking, 'I want to be here for you.' He evoked something deep from me. And I loved working with Elaine Bromka. I really love her. The first day we worked together I knew I wanted to work more with her, so I went to Tom and asked for a story on grief therapy. After all, Stella's son had died and Marlena's infant son, Don Jr., died of sudden infant death syndrome. Well, we got a story together. Stella threw me in a pit!"

ON THE DAY MACDONALD CAREY DIED

"When Mac died, I was washing my hair at the studio and felt John walk in. I remember raising out of the shampoo bowl and going into his arms without much being said. We held each other with water running down my face, down my back, across his shoulders, the two of us just crying. So often after that we spent so much time saying, 'Do you know how much I love *you*? Do you know how much you do for me? Do you know how much I get from you when I walk in and get to see your face here, what a comfort and source of strength you are for me, what goodness you bring to my life?' Those are the important conversations with people. I just love him with all my heart."

WHAT DEIDRE LOVES MOST ABOUT MARLENA

"I love that she has deep relationships, a fierce sense of loyalty. I love that Marlena is blind to her daughter Sami's deceptions. She loves her so thoroughly. In a scene recently I was emotionally torn between reaching for Sami and reaching for Carrie. The director said reach for Sami and Ali said, of course, I'm her natural daughter, you know. I had to laugh because that is always my natural instinct, to reach for her. I'm mad for her. I think she's an extraordinary actress."

WHAT IRKS DEIDRE ABOUT MARLENA

"She has no sarcasm, no guile. I think she needs that. In my own life I have plenty of sarcasm, guile, mystery, and raucous, raging humor. I *loved* playing a devil because I got to play that side with Tony, John, my girls, and Celeste. Tom Langan, co-executive producer, had to keep pulling me back. When I first laughed as the devil and I slapped a Bible out of a priest's hand, it shocked everyone. It was a little bit frustrating to hold myself in. I only wish the voice hadn't been computerized."

WHAT'S SEXY . . . WHAT'S NOT

"We did a scene with John in my office talking out all his feelings about Isabella. He took off the collar and left. I said a prayer for his comfort and guidance. Then I took the collar and caressed my face with it and smelled it. I love him so much. That was sexy. Taking clothes off is not sexy. No one really likes it. No one is comfortable doing that. Empathic scenes are sexy because they're so deeply felt. We're grown up. I don't want to see tongues on camera, thighs and breasts and lower backs."

ABOUT JOHN AND MARLENA ON THE PLANE

"It was incredibly hard. It was necessary for us to both break down to a point where we were both emotionally out of control. We tried it again and again and again. Drake and I don't hold back much. We work with dials on 10 whether fighting, screaming, kissing, etc. Finally, after about eight takes, Tom came out of the booth and said to me, 'I'm sick and tired of you playing safe. I'm sick of it!' He verbally beat me up a bit. 'I know you love Drake. I know you love Wayne. If anything happened to either one you would die a million times. This is goodbye, babe. I want to see some guts! Don't give me this safe stuff. I'm sick of it!' I was so angry and so confused. I always give everything. Well, I trust him so much I played out of me. Afterward, I cried so hard I just couldn't stop that convulsive, choking kind of cry after Drake had just grabbed me, threw me on bed, pulled off my coat . . . really pushing an actress beyond what anyone would dare do to me. I thought the audience would die seeing her do this. But it worked."

ABOUT CHANGES IN HER CHARACTER

"Until head writer Jim Reilly and Tom Langan got together, Marlena was never tarnished. They knew they could bring me back from the conference table, from the airplane and the devil. Jim wrote cleverly. There's great storytelling. I love putting my character in their hands."

A man for the 1990s, Drake Hogestyn offers a perfect balance of strength and sensitivity, rugged good looks, and easy charm. He's garnered a long list of awards as a much swooned-after soap opera hero—quintessential lover, husband, father, demon conqueror.

Over the last decade, Drake has been or was suspected of being: The Pawn, John Black, Roman Brady, Romulus, John Stevens, Forrest Alamain, and Fr. John Black, a Roman Catholic priest. No other character in all of soap history has gone though the incredible transitions that Drake has.

After he exorcised the devil from Marlena, Drake's character reached another important transition point: an encounter with the spirit of his dead wife. "Isabella was saddened that John was not emotionally able to move on," Drake points out. "That's why she came back. He had felt so helpless when she was dying. He wasn't able to save her and had always wanted to know if she was at peace, in heaven."

Keeping the John-Isabella love story memory alive for three years was quite unusual. Isabella's angelic return was great closure for this couple, a writing choice that the actor applauds, noting, "It would have been terribly unfair if Isabella had come back only as a devil and not something so much closer to the wonderful person she was. She was really quite an angel, always."

Isabella's message was quite touching, too. "She promises that we will be together for eternity, but for now John has a life to live and needs to share his life with someone here on earth."

John has now left his priestly career and persona behind, and as a secular John Black will be off on new adventures.

That's what this medium is all about. "The show is like a book you pick up and read a chapter a day," says the actor. "You lose yourself in it and get away from whatever madness is in your life. I am an entertainer. I provide entertainment."

Drake started what he thought would be a three-month role and gives credit to its longevity simply to "the luck of the draw."

"The audience really wanted to see Roman Brady resurrected. I happened to be around at the right time and was reading a Robert Ludlum novel, *The Bourne Identity*. It intrigued me that John Black was somewhat patterned after Jason Bourne. That sounded good to me."

For all the changes the character has gone through, however, the one thing that has remained is the audience's loyalty. Roman has come and gone again. Hogestyn remains because the viewers want him, in spite of his protests that success is fleeting.

"I always know my name can slide easily off the dressing room door. There's no such thing as permanent," he says.

Drake's down-to-earth practicality runs as deep as his romantic streak, and without contradiction. If he has any illusions, he keeps them in the world of love, women set on pedestals, and men who must guard those positions with courage and single-focused determination.

Days of Our Lives has been Drake's only daytime show. "I realized that this is a very passionate medium," he admits. "The characters are a little bit bigger than life and quite emotional. Heroes are strong and yet vulnerable. I don't know if most men find it hard to display tenderness and sensitivity towards their wives, girlfriends, lovers. I decided to follow my instincts and play the emotions. That was not difficult

for me to do that. It's who I am. And this show is about love.

"I've always been a romantic," says Drake. "I really believe in the flowers, surprise gifts, lots of hugs, and saying 'I love you' thirty times a day. It's clichéd, but it's truly important to stop and smell the roses. I do that even more often than I'm aware. With children especially. It's easy to dismiss children if you're involved in another activity. But you must look into their faces. It is really important to stop what you're doing and look at them, hear them, be with them in that moment of communication."

Emotional generosity and essential honesty are unmistakable. As NBC tour groups are led through the exterior halls of the *Days* studios, Drake gives a wave. If he's not immersed in his script and on the tether of a tight shooting schedule, he's likely to join the fans for ten, fifteen, or more minutes. If there are fans waiting at the studio gate, it's not unlikely to see Drake pull over and sign autographs from his rolled-down car window while other castmates wave and smile as they head toward the freeways and home after a full day of work. At personal appearances, Drake signs autographs until the fans are gone, not until the time is up. Even impromptu hospital visits or house calls are not out of the question.

Why does he go out of his way?

"It just seems right" is his answer.

This year Drake was chosen to receive the Red Jacket Award at the Mad Anthony Celebrity Pro-Am Golf Tournament in Fort Wayne, Indiana, his hometown. It's a lifetime achievement award presented to the Hoosier who has brought national recognition to that state and city. Other honorees have included: former Vice President Dan Quayle, astronaut Neil Armstrong, pro golfer Fuzzy Zoeler, and Wendy's founder Dave Thomas.

"I used to cut the grass and sit on the tractor watching people like that go into the golf tournament. Now I was standing beside them," says Drake. "I'm not sure I'm altogether worthy of being onstage with these people, who have made tremendous contributions in other fields. It's the same with my former career in baseball. I'm grateful."

The show, and soap opera stardom, "changes your life financially for the good and bad. There are times I long for the days when I lived in an apartment on the beach with my dog and had five bills to pay each month. That was it. I remember when the restaurant where I worked got washed away. I helped them rebuild, not getting paid, so I would have a job to go back to.

"Now, financially, things are quite different," he concedes. "I can provide for my children. Present them with opportunities. That's all a parent can hope to do. I can't shield them from life's horrors. I can do my best. If I can provide a cornucopia of things that may stimulate them, maybe they'll find something really important to them."

The show shoots an hour episode each day. The rigors of the medium are well known. But Drake points out that the difficult part has to do with "the emotional levels you have to reach and maintain. For example, the exorcism and

Marlena's death. Although it was one night on the air from the time Marlena died to the next night when I carry her into the church, it was actually ten days from the time she died to the church. To stay on that emotional edge is very difficult. We're telling a story, but the body doesn't know the difference. Your mind sends the signals and body reacts. I'm sure this work just peels the years off."

Raw emotions have to have a place to spill. "I go through huge boxes of tissues at the movies," Drake admits. "I buy popcorn and take wads of napkins. All that buildup releases.

"That's what actors do," he points out from an audience member's perspective. "We give hope. We express emotions, love. Everyone has walls protecting ourselves for one reason or another. Actors, the emotions we evoke, help us break through."

Clearly, Drake is satisfied with his life's choices.

"Things happen to lead me in a direction," he underscores. "I've been taken care of. As I worry about what to do, it's decided for me. It's happened often like that for me, so I've learned not to fight it."

And like his loyal viewers, he's "looking forward to seeing where my character leads me next."

O ver the decades, *Days of Our Lives* has focused on the love between people and how it grows, comes apart, meets with stress, and either survives or dies.

Hope Williams Brady, the great-granddaughter of Horton family matriarch Alice Horton, and Bo Brady bring the core Salem families together. The DiMera family, specifically Stefano, has tried time and time again to manipulate and destroy these two. They keep coming back, conquering all obstacles with an enduring love that brings a sense of promise to all lovers.

Recently, Bo and Hope were reunited again. Their chemistry on and off the scene is clear. Their respect for each other is strong and the delight they share in working together gives the audience pleasure.

KRISTIAN ALFONSO: What makes them so magical is that they don't seem to take anything too seriously. It's that bantering back and forth, that one-upmanship that makes them fun and unpredictable. They have a lot of tender moments, but they have genuine fun and can laugh. A fan recently sent me a tape of Bo and Hope's greatest comic moments. I loved it. It's really not until you look back that you see such variety of humorous moments. There was a scene right after Hope had gotten shot and she was in a coma. He gave her an engagement ring and, of course, it brought her back to consciousness. A few days later we were sitting on the Horton sofa and were listening to everyone getting into making our wedding plans for us. We just got so hysterical at the silliness of it somehow that we started laughing. They kept the cameras rolling because it was such a real moment between Bo and Hope. It was truly real. I think that's what keeps the magic going. They can have a good time. They spar, but they are peers.

PETER RECKELL: I think that's the core of any amazing relationship. Two strong people who are certain about themselves. And when they come together there will be a lot of sparks. They may be intertwined in their romance, but

KRISTIAN ALFONSO
AND PETER RECKELL
(*Hope Brady and Bo Brady*)

they never lose their individuality. We could butt heads and come together again. I think people enjoy seeing that and I know we enjoy doing that.

The last time we came back together, Kristian was pregnant, but it was not in the story so we couldn't see that on camera. We were doing this scene in a hot tub. Kristian was so disappointed that she couldn't enjoy it. She kept popping up.

KA: This poor man could hardly fit in there with me. He was like up against the wall, and I was fighting so hard to stay down.

PR: We laughed so much. It was so hard to do it.

KA: I was about eight months pregnant at the time.

PR: Another time that was great fun was the hot air balloon. I jumped in and tried to comfort her. My stunt double grabbed hold of the ropes and went up into the sky with us. It's up. He's hanging on and we cut. The stuntman had a hook that protruded from his long sleeve. It connected to a harness. But he was holding on just by his own hand to a part of the rope about two feet below where the hook would have connected. We were about three hundred feet in the air and this guy is just hanging on to the rope. I was shocked. We had to get that balloon down in a hurry before we both died. Me from shock and . . .

We were doing the Kern River.

KA: I ended up going down the river without a boat by accident.

PR: The guide, or the technical advisor, told us that if we were in the water for more than forty-five seconds without a wet suit, we would likely go into hypothermia. It was that cold.

KA: Luckily, I did have on a wet suit, but there I was going down backward, screaming. They were all saying I was doing such a great job, but I really was out of control. I needed help. The water would pull me back down every time I'd get back up.

PR: I had gone right off the back of the boat, and every time I tried to come up, the boat itself was over me. It took some doing to come through that.

In London we had to be in a muddy moat.

KA: Eeuugh.

PR: And in Florida we had to do some scuba diving.

KA: You couldn't see your hand. You couldn't see anything.

PR: And we were under that shooting.

KA: I was really scared. I couldn't see anything. My eyes were getting bigger and my heart was pounding.

PR: We were trying to make the shots work in this really murky water. Somehow we always manage to pull each other through those moments.

KA: There's an incredible trust there. We listen to each other and have a great deal of respect for each other.

PR: We know how to take care of each other. And in general, ideas just pop back and forth between us for scenes and takes. It's great.

KA: There was a bed scene and we were supposedly in New Orleans. Well, we were in bed. Bo reaches over Hope to turn the light on, but I wouldn't let go of my covers and he went THUD! fell out of bed, I fell on top of him, and the light fell on top of both of us.

KA: Another fun time was in New York and they wouldn't close down any streets for us, but we were doing the shoot anyway. I think we were on Fifth or Sixth

Avenue, and there was enough traffic we had to dodge. It was pretty busy and we had to try to wait for the just the right moment and run down the avenue in spite of the traffic. We'd just wait for the stage manager's signal and run like crazy.

I was in high heels and dress, running blindly on someone else's cue. It was frightening. Whether in location scenes, intimate ones, or just working together every day, the relationship we share is like fitting pieces of a tough puzzle together. With patience, it all fits, but it takes some doing.

PR: In flashbacks, I take her away from the Larry Welch wedding and there's a scene where we're away from the church at the park, but she's still resisting me. We're both stubborn and strong, coming at each other. But we come from a place of love.

KA: There's always a little anger, a little fire underneath everything they do together. Playful competition.

PR: She does things her way. He does things his way. Somehow, in spite of that, it works out.

KA: We're both very opinionated and argumentative characters. And it's great.

PR: The absolute very first scene we ever had started that way. Argumentative and right at each other.

KA: Everything's a challenge between them.

PR: In that scenes she's trying to act older than her years, be someone special. She's just come back from boarding school.

KA: And he's calling my number, asking: How old are you? You don't need to know. What's your name? I didn't say.

PR: We don't come at each other and repel. We immediately lock into each other's core. We just have that incredible rapport between us, between Bo and Hope.

So Bo and Hope Are Fated to Be Together?

KA: We don't completely know yet.

PR: Certainly the timing of me coming back to the show right now seems quite fateful. So many things just came together to make it all quite perfect. We're ecstatic about doing this story line together again after eight years.

KA: I find it remarkable how as characters and actors we've come and gone together and individually in those years. The chances of this all happening like this seem, to me, absolutely remarkable. It's fate.

PR: For Bo, Hope is definitely the love of his life. Bo's relationship with Dr. Carly Manning was quite different. It was based on need. I had a son and a need for love and a family. I'm still getting clear on the Billie thing. There's a bit of similarity between Billie and Hope. I think perhaps Bo has been trying to redo, rediscover Hope through

Billie, who has a similar look and energy. Part of the difficulty that Bo is experiencing right now in accepting that Gina is truly Hope is that once he does, he also has to acknowledge that he left her.

KA: That's a problem for Hope, too. She basically feels that you gave up trying to find her, help her.

PR: That would mean that I was weak. Not a man. At first I believed that Hope was not dead at . . .

KA: When we came back last time and we were on the cruise of deception, I kept having those nightmares of something happening. I kept telling Bo that I was certain something was going to happen. She seemed to know that something bad was going to happen and that they were going to be separated.

PR: After all that happened, I believed she was dead, but looked for her and in my heart thought she was still alive. Still, at some point, I gave up and went on with my life without her. There's got to be a lot of guilt and pain over that. There's been genuine feeling for Billie, but I think the saving-someone aspect really came into that relationship.

KA: Billie was someone who could be rescued from the circumstances around her. You couldn't rescue Hope, but you could rescue Billie. The character stood by Billie through the murder trial and when all the truth about her father and their incestuous relationship came out.

PR: When Bo and Hope come together they become something greater than either one alone. I think that's what we all long to have in our lives, and why it works so well with us. Because people would love to have that. I would love to have that in my life. It's really an attractive goal.

MACDONALD CAREY

Although the late actor Macdonald Carey is best known to most television viewers as Dr. Tom Horton, a role he originated in 1965, he had an outstanding career prior to devoting himself to Salem and the small screen of television. Landing the celebrity to take the starring role on *Days of Our Lives* was quite a victory for Ted Corday. Until that time, no other major motion picture star had ever made such a move.

At the time, Mac agreed to stay with the show for only a few years. No one knew how long the show would last, and Mac never imagined it would become the longest running role of his career. In a funny twist, Mac agreed to do the opening voice-over for an additional fee. Today, several years after his passing, Mac's wonderful voice still introduces the show each day. He is still a very real, very warm part of Salem as viewers tune in and hear Mac announcing, "Like sands through an hourglass, so are the days of our lives . . ."

The man most *Days* fans knew was Mac was born Edward Macdonald Carey on March 15, 1913, in Sioux City, Iowa. He launched his acting career at the age of six, playing Simple Simon in a Mother Goose play.

After graduating from the University of Iowa, he became affiliated with the famed Globe Theater in London, England, returning to the States in 1937 to begin his long relationship with NBC, as a radio performer.

Mac's first radio soap opera performance was in 1937 in "Women in White." He played a young doctor in a script written by Irna Phillips. That was followed by "Young Hickory," in which he starred as a country doctor. Other radio soaps included the legendary "Stella Dallas," "John's Other Wife," "Just Plain Bill," and "Ellen Randolph."

A popular stage actor, Mac was seen on Broadway with performances in the hit shows *Anniversary Waltz* with Kitty Carlisle and *Lady in the Dark* opposite Gertrude Lawrence.

World War II intervened and Mac signed on for duty in the United States Marine Corps. After returning stateside, Mac appeared in more than 60 films such as the Alfred Hitchcock classic *Shadow of a Doubt*, followed by *The Great Gatsby; Streets of Laredo; Let's Make It Legal; Blue Denim; The Lawless; Copper Canyon; Comanche Territory; Song of Surrender; Excuse My Dust; John Paul Jones; Wake Island; Suddenly, It's Spring; Dream Girl;* and *Stranger at My Door.*

Mac's long relationship with television began in the 1950s during its Golden Age with performances in the classics, *Climax, Playhouse 90, U.S. Steel, Your Show of Shows,* and *Alcoa Playhouse,* as well as *Police Story, Mr. Novak, Burke's Law, Outer Limits,* and *Ben Casey, M.D.* He also appeared in the memorable miniseries *Roots,* and starred in the series *Dr. Christian* and *Lock Up.*

Family and career were the two most important things in Mac's life. Mac was married for 26 years to Betty Hecksher, with whom he had six children: Lynn, Lisa, Mac Jr., Steve, Theresa, and Paul. The marriage ended in 1969 because of Mac's self-admitted dependence on alcohol, which he detailed with disarming candor in his autobiography *The Days of My Life.* "Drinking stalled my advancement," he said in 1993. "At 69 I stopped drinking, well past the age of 'retirement,' but that's when my life really started." Before Mac's death in 1993, he celebrated 12 years of sobriety and prided himself on a prolific output of creative literature that included three volumes of poetry: *A Day in the Life, That Further Hill,* and *Beyond That Further Hill.*

A devout Catholic, Mac was among the ranks of Knights of the Holy Sepulchre and Knights of Malta. Mac expanded his family to include community, especially in his later years. He was very involved in the fight against mental illness on both the state and national levels. A recipient of an honorary Ph.D. from the University of South Carolina, Mac was honored by the San Fernando Valley Mental Health Center in 1993 when it named its North Hollywood facility the Macdonald Carey East Valley Mental Health Center. He also worked with the University of California in Los Angeles' Center for Aging. It's no wonder that he was delighted that, in storyline, the Horton house was turned into a community center.

Less than three months before his death, Mac admitted, with clear enthusiasm: "I personally feel more motivated and productive every minute of my days right now than I ever did in my entire life. I'm happier now every second of my life than I ever was. My life is so rich."

Macdonald Carey's long career made him a role model for actors, but more than that, his life and courage remains an inspiration to us all. Hearing his voice each day at the start of the show is a loving reminder that his spirit still touches many hearts in Salem and viewers everywhere.

Vignettes

JOHN CLARKE

(Mickey Horton)

JOHN ANISTON

(Victor Kiriakis)

Many current cast members share their favorite scenes and more.

At the start I was told, "Mickey is the only character in this play who is pretty well adjusted." By the early seventies it was fun to play insanity, but I have always liked that Mickey seemed most often to be the calm in the middle of the storm. He would try to help people around him decipher their emotions. He was always the logical attorney.

After Bill came back from prison, Mickey seemed to get straighter, taller, and perhaps less approachable. Laura kicked him out of the house because he was being so uptight and suspicious over what he thought was going on between her and Bill. As far as I knew, Mickey had no plans to sleep with Linda Patterson. As a matter of fact, it wasn't until the next day I found out I had. I remember telling the producers, "You can't do that to me! I didn't get a chance to enjoy last night!" It was an off-camera affair. It was funny, but I was a bit upset about not being able to enjoy it.

My favorite scenes were on the farm. Playing guitar, painting the mailbox, baling hay, shearing the sheep, going to square dances . . . There was no soap about rural life. It was different and I loved those scenes. In those days I had two daughters who were riding horses and we had a little ranch in San Juan Capistrano, California. It was a lovely pastoral time on and off the screen.

I auditioned for the part of Doug Williams and it was the last time I shaved my mustache. They wanted me to test without it. So I shaved, tested, and they must have hated it. I didn't get the role. A few weeks later, however, they called and asked that I grow back my mustache and I played Dr. Eric Richards for about a year. He was a prison doctor in scenes with Bill Horton and Doug Williams.

Luckily, I was a dancer. When I started, they wanted me to run a household on crutches, which I did. Then there was one day when there was something wet on the floor. I didn't see it. I wasn't looking down, but I didn't slip. Quite the contrary. The crutches acted like suction cups and stuck to the floor and as I fell I left them behind. They just stayed as my momentum kept me going forward. I about died when I turned around and saw those crutches standing there on their own.

Of course, as far as the story setting, it was very Waltons and I liked that because it was so different for daytime, and because it's close to my own Virginia background. It was also rather sweetly coincidental that the red shoes became

significant. I had seen the movie *The Red Shoes* as a young person and became a dancer. My character, who was still unable to walk, also had an attachment to that production and the character of Mickey used the red shoes as a way of encouraging Maggie to walk. It was quite a coincidence.

The sexiest scene Maggie ever had was dancing an adagio with an athlete, Kyle McCullough, whom she helped at the hospital. It was a fantasy sequence, because he had developed a crush on me during therapy sessions. It was a delightful scene, and sexy too. I must say I was a bit surprised that the actor, Rick Hill, who was quiet athletic and buff in build was so wonderfully graceful.

I like that Caroline is not submissive. She's strong and outspoken. When Shawn played favoritism between her two sons, Roman and Bo, she wouldn't stand for it. She walked out and left him. It wasn't fair to Bo; it hadn't been his fault that Victor was his father.

I think the exorcism storyline was powerful, imaginative, interesting, and well done. My favorite scene during it was sitting in the chair that shook every which way. That was rather frightening. It felt out of control. Once we shot it, I had to laugh and told the crew, "You better send this lounger back. There's something wrong with the massage unit."

At the beginning they wanted me to wear dresses that were like Ma Perkins's. I refused to wear little lace collars and wrap-around shirt-maker dresses—the kind they dig up for commercials. What would Victor Kiriakis see in this? I brought my own simple tailored clothes that were more sophisticated. Caroline was always fearless with this man. She slapped him and told him he shouldn't be living life as a crime boss. Caroline really was the one love of his life.

Victor and Caroline really loved each other. It tore her up because, really and truly, she wanted to go with Victor but she made a sacrifice for her children. Caroline went to the hotel to run away to San Francisco with

Victor. Yet she carried a gun. She had very mixed emotions and thought of killing him rather than have the truth come out. Then, after the truth was known, there was no point in killing him.

Sammy Davis, Jr., was a fan. We met when we guest-starred on "Give Me a Break." He even remembered me from *General Hospital.* I was pleased he thought I was a great actress. Tammy Wynette and Loretta Lynn are fans. And I'm fans of theirs.

BRYAN DATTILO
(Lucas Roberts)

I thought I had blown my audition. I totally reversed my last line. It was something like, "You get ready, and in five minutes, I'll be downstairs." Instead I said, "I'll be getting ready and you be downstairs in five minutes." I just kept going and tried to be cool. I finished and walked out of the room thinking I was ruined and I felt just awful. But they liked that I didn't stop, I just kept going.

I love the fact that if Lucas likes you he'll do anything for you. If you go away on vacation with him, you know everything will be first class, VIP treatment all the way. He knows how to live right. On the downside, unfortunately, he's a little wrapped up in his own world. He's self-centered.

Whenever Lucas gets in a bind or a tough situation, getting cornered, he puts his hands in his back pocket or hooks his fingers through a back belt loop. It's rather a submissive position. A kind of "aw shucks" position. It's not something I would do. It's part of Lucas, though.

During the Curtis Reed murder trial, the court scenes were tough when I had to get really emotional and really hysterical, actually lose it. That was the first time I did that.

IVAN G'VERA
(Ivan Marais)

When I first came to the show, the character had a different name. I don't remember what it was. They kept calling for the character over the loudspeaker, but I couldn't get used to it. The name never connected with me and I would miss my cue. People would come looking for me. Finally, they decided that since I couldn't seem to get it right, they made it simple for this foreigner. They called the character by my name to make it easier. I also had trouble moving around. I'm from the theater, where an actor uses space quite differently. On set here in the first few days I kept missing my mark. The cameramen complained because they kept losing me because I moved too much. They finally put down, as a joke, a couple of large sandbags to indicate my marks so I could not possibly miss them.

This was not my first character on the show. About a year earlier, I played Carly Manning's father, Anthony Von Leuschner, in a flashback.

I enjoy playing sidekick to a wealthy and mischievous woman. I've had the most fun when dressed as a baby, or woman. But I've discovered I'm very uncomfortable in panty-hose that keeps crawling down to my knees.

I'm not sure what I like most about Ivan. He's kind of neurotic. He has such a love for Vivian and status, and needs to be a member of that blueblood society in any way he can. I love the way he always tries to stay in total control, but when he loses it, he loses it so completely and falls apart in a funny way.

The day of Carly's wedding I got into some trouble. Just about everyone in Salem was in that scene and I had one line. It was the first scene after lunch break. On my way back I got lost somehow in the bowels of NBC. I opened the wrong door and found myself in some boiler room and couldn't get out. I traveled the tunnels down there getting sweaty and more anxious every moment. Sweaty and wearing shorts, tee shirt, and sneakers, I finally got out and back to the set with barely enough time to grab a tuxedo shirt, jacket, and clip-on bow tie. I did the scene without more than a dab of makeup, wearing those shorts and the tee-shirt underneath, and tennis shoes on my feet. I caught a little trouble for that.

Pranks? Well, at the country fair scene, Vivian got duped into having pies thrown at her face. I told Louise that the pie was really delicious. The cream was wonderful. I held it out toward her and she took a healthy fingerful and put it in her mouth only to discover it was shaving cream. Everyone present *loved* her expression.

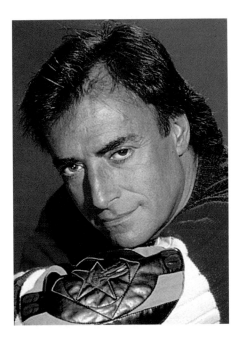

Scenes with Leann Hunley (Anna) were so light-hearted and bad, in a good way. I could be a bit of a rogue and I remember a woman in the supermarket who said, "I love hating you." I remember some of the sexiest scenes I did were with Leann. Anna had gotten into the shower and tub with her clothes on. It was very sensual. There we were in the tub with the rubber ducky and the water was coming out all over. Leann had on a body stocking kind of thing, but as we were doing the scene, her left breast started to come out. I tried to create more bubbles so we wouldn't have to do the scenes over again. We were already sitting in that thing for a

THAAO PENGHLIS
(Tony DiMera)

long time. The water was cold, you don't look great with bubbles all over your face, your skin is getting pruny . . . doing naughty tickling with my feet underneath and all.

Joe, like some already very tall men around here, likes to wear boots with heels. Well, we were doing some photos for something and I figured it would be a torso shot and so I stood on my toes to be the same height as Joe in his high heels. Well, when the photo was published, there I was looking a bit funny as I stood on my toes. It was a full-length shot. Joe had such a scream at my expense.

A reporter had mentioned he had just interviewed Jean Simmons and I said I really enjoyed her work. He told me she enjoyed mine, too. She always watched the show. And there was Jean Peters. I once was sitting next to her. I told her that my family, especially my sister, would be so thrilled when I told them I was sitting next to Jean Peters. She replied I love you on *General Hospital*, which is what I was doing at the time.

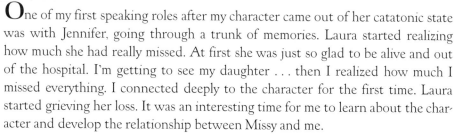

JAMIE LYN BAUER
(*Laura Horton*)

One of my first speaking roles after my character came out of her catatonic state was with Jennifer, going through a trunk of memories. Laura started realizing how much she had really missed. At first she was just so glad to be alive and out of the hospital. I'm getting to see my daughter . . . then I realized how much I missed everything. I connected deeply to the character for the first time. Laura started grieving her loss. It was an interesting time for me to learn about the character and develop the relationship between Missy and me.

My sexiest scene had to be when Clark (Jack) sweeps me off the floor into his arms and places me gracefully on the bed and makes mad, passionate love to me, not once but four times in the same evening. Laura would never want anyone her own age again; not after being catatonic for eighteen years.

My funniest scene was with Vivian when I got approval for several line changes to have a few "one-ups" on her. She was quite taken aback and surprised. It was the day of the ambulance escape. Vivian rescued me from being taken back to the asylum. They wheeled me into the foyer of her house. She says, "Why don't you just rest now," and I came back with "Strapped on a gurney in your foyer?!" She wasn't expecting that line, and I finally got her. I could see the reaction in her eyes. "Unstrap me right now!" I followed up. Of course, she passed it off to Ivan, who was afraid to unstrap this crazy person.

That scene was the same day I did the ride in that ambulance. I had the flu. During taping, I was under blankets in the back of the ambulance with the key light and camera operators in this tiny little space. Then guys on the outside were shaking the ambulance to make it look like it was dodging and speeding. It was bouncing all over. My head was bouncing and bopping. My temperature soared. We were finished with the scene and I was the last one out and barely able to move. I remember asking, "Can someone get me out of this?" One of the guys unstrapped me. I got out and started to pass out and went to the ground. They touched me and realized I was burning up. They brought icepacks and eventually I was all right, enough to get home.

Jimmy Stewart and his wife are fans. My husband, a makeup artist, came home from work and said, "So you had these passionate scenes on the show today." All the girls at *Price Is Right* watch the show. And all the people on

Models, Inc., Full House, etcetera. I remember the day Jeremy told me that one of my biggest fans is Audrey Meadows. From the *The Honeymooners!* Later one time she called to hire him for something and she and I talked. It was great.

JAMES REYNOLDS
(Abe Carver)

In the last few years, Abe has become more involved with the community. Certainly as chief of police he's more visible. He's completely his own man now. Before he was reactive to other people's pain and joy. Now Abe's a catalyst.

Once, on a cocaine bust, Roman and Abe were hiding down in the backseat of the bad guy's car. It was tense. In dress rehearsal Wayne and I were to poke our heads up. Well, when we did, we had dusted ourselves with flour. It definitely got a good laugh out of the rest of the cast and crew.

There's a gold Hamilton watch Abe wears that's significant to him because it had been an anniversary gift from Lexie. It originally came from the wardrobe department, of course, but I've taken charge of it now and I make sure I wear it whenever I become Abe.

MIRIAM PARRISH
(Jaime Caldwell)

Certainly, the most satisfying storyline has been dealing with the issue of sexual abuse of my character by her father. The incest issue is not a class-defined problem. Billie's background was quite different. She had been abused by a father who was a con man, a liar, a thief. Jaime's background is upper middle-class. Her dad is a successful and respected lawyer. At the beginning, Billie is the only one who would even suspect that something was going on. It was a shock to everyone else in Salem. I think it got the point across that it's something that can happen to anyone, anywhere. My most challenging scenes were through that storyline, too. Several took place in his office. Jaime had to hide when Billie came in. In acting out those scenes, I had to convey extreme fear, shame, and guilt. Powerful emotions. Powerful moments. I still get mail from young girls in similar situations. They're grateful for the way the show handled the issue. It makes it easier for them to deal with the problem.

Perhaps the funniest scenes were when I finally tell Sami that she's losing it. It's so obvious that Sami is very troubled, but as a best friend I rarely tell her to straighten up. Jaime got wise for a scene or two.

Funny in a different way was a scene in which Brandy, a bulimic model, was in the restroom throwing up and Sami and I overhear. While we listen through the door, we naturally pretend to hear the sounds of someone vomiting. So we're listening quietly, and at that moment, over the loudspeaker, are the sounds of someone being ill and the flush of a toilet. It was an overpowering gross noise. Everyone cracked up.

JASON BROOKS
(Peter Blake)

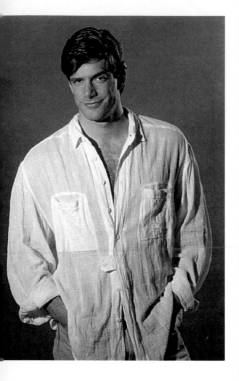

I really loved the Maison Blanche storyline because it appealed to the romantic in me. We dressed up for the ball. It was also the first time Jennifer and I consummated our relationship. I professed my love to her. And I loved skiing in the nighttime episode. I held Missy in my arms as we went down the slope. I loved it. I'm not sure Missy did. And I also liked the roof rescue. I like romance, togetherness. I don't go anywhere without my wife, Corinne. I guess I'd really like being a complete romantic hero if I could be. I always loved John Wayne and Errol Flynn movies.

I have some odd habits, like wearing *really* old and messy clothes when I'm not on the set. Onscreen I'm almost always wearing suits and good clothes, so that now, off set, I'm more apt to wear even messier old clothes than I would normally.

And I break down my scripts in a very meticulous way. Most actors have one corner fastener on the script, roll it up, and stick it dog-eared in their back pocket. I like to double-fasten my script, keeping it flat. I break down each of my scenes by page number, in the order of the shooting schedule, and give it a stick-on tab. I use symbols to denote what I need to do: triangle—one line or one sentence; black star—no lines, I just focus on motivation and subtext; red star—I have to learn the scene right before I go on, or the morning of the shoot; if it has no symbol I have to learn it the night before. Probably the most annoying thing I do is remove the tab after each scene. I stick them on cameramen, the boom, etcetera. At some point they'll tell me to quit it. If I lay down my script I can bet someone will try to steal and hide it just to get a rise outta me.

ROARK CRITCHLOW
(Mike Horton)

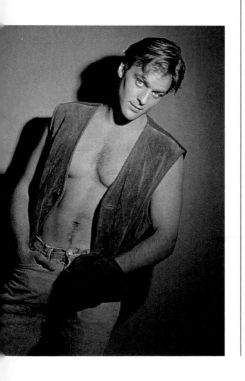

I think my character Mike is a workaholic because I think he's afraid to deal with his life. Smuggling bombs, having his heart busted, being an accessory to murder, as far as he's concerned. Then he was blackmailed by Stefano. He's very competent, very concerned, and cares about people. I like that about him, but he doesn't allow himself to be vulnerable. He seems to have a bit of a shell around himself; allows his caring and concern to go out from him, but he doesn't allow it to come in, he doesn't accept that for himself. I'd like to see him taking care of his own needs. It's all about love. I think if he were to try to love again it would scare the hell out of him.

There have been funny moments. Peter came rushing into the hospital with Jennifer all wrapped up in a blanket and I'm supposed to take her pulse. She's like in a cocoon. I couldn't even find her body. Second take, we agreed he'd not have her quite so wrapped up. But the next take came and she's still wrapped up. So I grabbed her ankle and Missy started to chuckle. Then I grabbed his wrist for a pulse, and we all cracked up.

I remember a favorite line. I'm a doctor; I deal with technical medical jargon all the time. In one scene, I come in and my assessment of the situation is that my mother is having a "paranoid freakout." We all cracked up.

Tough scenes? When I have to look up and see Marlena floating in the air and I have to believe that she's possessed. I'm a bit of a cynic. I'm a doubter of the paranormal.

Lisa Rinna did the screen test for this role with me. At the end of the scene I was supposed to kiss her. I did, but it was really awkward and fumbly. I apologized to her afterward. Why? Out of practice, in a way, because in the six years prior I had not kissed any other woman but my wife. Geez. I felt I had to learn to do this again.

I like showing a softer side of Celeste with Alexandria. Celeste would not call her Lexie any more than she would call her husband Abe. His name is Abraham. I refused to use those nicknames, and now they write it that way for me. It also gives Celeste and Alexandria a bond and keeps Celeste different from the others.

I still haven't seen all of Celeste. She still throws me different things. I like her sense of power, control. She even has that with Stefano although she lets him think he has it. That form of manipulation is a woman thing. She uses womanly wiles on Stefano to get what she wants. With anyone else, well, they're not important. I haven't gotten bored with her. Every day I go out onstage and don't know how she is going to react. I learn my lines and make my choices and let her take over.

I'm still learning the technical aspects of TV work. In theater you have the whole stage, so you don't think in technical terms, like my frame or camera angle. When I first came to the show I was pretty meek around Stefano. But not long ago we were doing a scene and we're facing each other and then he turns his back to me a bit. I'm over his left shoulder. In the middle of my talk to him he starts scratching his head. His arm is completely blocking my face. I blew his mind when I just said, "Will you get your arm outta my camera!" Right in the middle of the scene. I had never done that before. I think that was a part of Celeste that just popped out. He cracked up and commented, "See what happens. They come on the show nice and sweet and now listen to her!" We all had a good laugh. His reaction, his facial expression was priceless. Then he goaded me a bit with, "But I'm acting . . ." I told him, "Yeah, right. Act with your other arm."

TANYA BOYD
(Celeste)

I was with Burt Reynolds and Charles Nelson Reilly doing a Neil Simon play in Houston, Texas. My agent called to ask if I would test for this role on daytime TV. I refused. They asked that I read. I refused. Would you come to talk? When I came back to Los Angeles, I agreed to talk. Afterward, I told my agent to find out who the highest paid person on the show was and tell them I want a dollar more. I thought for sure they'd tell me to go away. I realized I was being a little difficult. I was having fun with it. The headwriter at the time, Pat Falken Smith, had seen me in a miniseries called "Gangster Chronicles" and wanted me for

JOE MASCOLO
(Stefano DiMera)

Stefano. It was her call. She stuck to her guns. She wanted me for the role in spite of what others said and in spite of my protests. I gave her a few books on power and discussed what I would like to see in this role. The music, the chess, opera, art, culture, sense of power, family loyalty, and love. The bad guy cannot be totally dark. I particularly like the fact that if he gives his word to do something, he will not stop at anything. For the people he loves he will go to the end of the world.

MARK VALLEY
(Jack Devereaux)

There have been so many scenes in which I'm begging Jennifer to forgive me and Jennifer saying no, she can't. One day Jennifer had to get worked up to a pretty high level of that and was going at it, saying what an awful guy I'd been. She was totally committed to it, but then I had to say "Forgive me" just one too many times. I couldn't help myself, I started laughing. I lost it for a little bit. I wish they had Stuart Smalley at the Meadows. I would love to bring a little more humor into Jack's personality. I've added some, I'd like to add more.

MELISSA REEVES
(Jennifer Horton Devereaux)

I miss working with Macdonald Carey. I love working with Frances to this day. From the first days, she treated me like a friend. I would sit in her dressing room every day when I started and she'd tell me everything about the business, soap operas, and so on.

I like the scenes and story lines that bring everyone together like the "Cruise of Deception" and Maison Blanche. And now Aremid. I love those times when we're together as a group because we always seem to have the most fun.

I sort of invented this person Vivian. What I like most about her is her absolute lack of rules. She's so full of life, joy, ferocity. No matter what happens to her, she survives: she buried Carly, but they dug her up; she killed people and ended up in a mental hospital with a shaved head, but she escaped. You really cannot judge her by anyone else's rules. She has nothing of her own—no man, no money, no home. But she sure has spirit and a great sense of humor!

LOUISE SOREL
(*Vivian Alamain*)

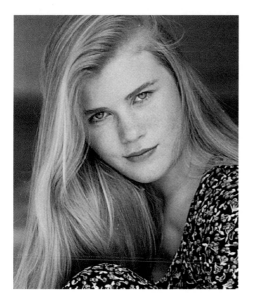

I'm really grateful that I've been able to be involved in some very important storylines and issues. I got a lot of mail from girls who have suffered with bulimia and anorexia. The date rape was another important story. That really put Sami over the edge. She had her troubles before, but this emotional trauma was so intense. It's really contributed to her need for control and power. The pregnancy at a young age is an important storyline too. I've been lucky to have such meaningful issues.

ALISON SWEENY
(*Sami Brady*)

It was interesting to play being a devil when Marlena, who was possessed, changed shape to try to seduce John. I wore a very scanty outfit and I had to feel comfortable, ready. The devil would not feel the least bit inhibited. So I couldn't afford that luxury either, even as a character. It was appropriate to be very sexual. It was fun to play Satan, to play with people's heads, to be a tease, a bitch, a vixen, all those things I haven't done so much on the show. I had a good time!

EILEEN DAVIDSON
(*Kristen Blake DiMera*)

CHRISTIE CLARK
(Carrie Brady)

One of my favorite times was playing a street hooker when Austin and Carrie went to look for Sami. It was great for Carrie, this very, very good girl to dress up in sexy, trampy clothes. I loved playing the sexuality in such an overt way. It was fun, and I'd love to do it more often.

FRANK PARKER
(Shawn Brady)

Every scene with my daughters Kimberly and Kayla was always special to me. Even when it's your make-believe kid, you can't help but feel the fear, love, and it's as real in your scene as it would be in your real life. It broke my heart and often brought me to tears to watch Kimberly going through blindness and split personalities.

TOM TROUT
(Property Master)

Burying Carly alive was fun. We bought a coffin but it wasn't until a few weeks later that we realized it needed to have oxygen, and lights. We installed a little portable bar and had a string of disco lights that just didn't work when she turned on the switch. It just looked too silly. The gaffaws were so loud!

Another time, I was on my knees at 5 A.M. on Hollywood Boulevard coloring in the names of the Graumann's cement autographs so they would show up on camera at that hour when it wasn't sunny enough otherwise. I used water-soluble eyebrow pencil.

Another time, during the runaway train and Tanner-Molly's trek-through-the-woods episodes, what was supposed to be a wild dog became a wolf and then finally, they wanted a grizzly bear. Those changes came on pretty short notice. The actors had a torch that they were using to drive the bear back and it set the trees afire on the set. We didn't want to panic the bear either, so we stationed several people within the trees with fire extinguishers to put out the flames while we continued to tape.

After a scene with fire we usually take a five {-minute break} to let the smoke clear out. After one particular fire scene, the smoke still had not cleared, but the director wanted to keep going, so he insisted we get everyone in the next scene cigars. It was in 1983 with Don Craig, Neil Curtis and Chris Kositchek sitting around a table discussing some business.

The hardest one was the recent bee attack. Anytime you turn 250,000 live bees loose indoors, you're asking for trouble. There's potential for lots of pain. But only one person got stung, and that was the very next day, when a crew member was adjusting a lamp and a bee flew out and stung him on the hand. To do the scene, the swarming was accomplished rather naturally. Bees instinctually swarm around the queen. So the beekeepers took the queen and put it around the neck of the stunt man. When it came time to get them in their hive again, they put the queen inside.

Memory Lane

Interview:
Bill and Susan Seaforth Hayes

Sweethearts of the seventies Bill and Susan Seaforth Hayes graced the January 12, 1976, cover of *Time* magazine with a headline that read: SEX AND SUFFERING IN THE AFTERNOON. It was a new era of soap opera popularity and acceptance. *Days of Our Lives*, specifically, had reached a new pinnacle.

"It was a scary and joyful experience," Susan recalls. "I remember once having said that I would consider myself successful if I ever got on the cover of *Time*. I believed the people on the cover of that magazine were movers and shakers."

Bill remembers, "I was amazed by the cover and a beautifully done article."

Ironically, with all the attention soaps were receiving, the demographics of the audience were shifting. The viewers were younger, wanted more action and adventure in their hour, and changes in virtually all soap operas of the time were made.

"Salem was beautiful," Bill points out. "It was a real gem, and a part of the mystique of the seventies and early eighties. It was America's hometown, a part of everyone's family throughout America."

Some of the changes brought new people to Salem, and long-time residents jetted and cruised to farflung places. For the most part, it was exciting for everyone involved. Doug and Julie traveled more, too. And helped solve murders and intrigues involving secret rooms and underground tunnels.

"We were lucky to have had so many kinds of stories together," says Susan.

"We became something like the Thin Man and his wife," Bill points out. "We had funny things to sleuth, and it was often fun, but it just wasn't who we were."

The Julie and Doug of the 1970s were the soap opera epitome of lovers who loved and lost, then loved and conquered—several times over.

As actors, they started on the show separately, Susan in 1967 and Bill two years later for what was to have been a seven-month run as Brett Douglas.

What was attractive to Julie about Doug?

"Doug was not a doctor, lawyer, or a plastic man. He was a lively rogue," Susan says with enthusiasm. "When Bill was cast in the role, everyone was delighted he had so many facets. Julie took risks. She needed a man with more dimensions, and one more sexy than any other man on the show, up to that point."

Of course, what made Doug attractive to Julie made him very appealing to other women in Salem as well. Bill remembers, "I think, if Joan Van Ark had stayed as Janene Whitney [Bill Horton's girlfriend] there may have been some hanky-panky there. After all, Susan Martin [played by Denise Alexander] and Bill could've been a possibility.

"But when Susan and I began to work together, headwriter Bill Bell saw something going on between the two of us and wanted to explore it," Hayes recalls. "Bell built on the chemistry he saw between us."

The first screen kiss between Bill and Susan was memorable for many reasons. "We were to kiss and start to dance as the music came on an old-fashioned record player," Bill says. "The machine would not turn on. It was a half-hour show and there was no editing. We had to go back to the beginning of the scene and start over. We had to kiss, and kiss, and kiss, and kiss. We must have done the scene about six times and got to know each other quite well!

"Meanwhile," Bill continues, "Addie, Julie's mother, returned from Europe after being widowed, came into the picture to keep people who love each other apart. Julie had dates with Bert, Bob, Don. And Doug became very fond of Addie. I think Addie changed him in a positive way."

Susan is certain of it, both on and off the screen. She remembers that "the week Doug married Addie a woman in a local grocery store came up to Bill, shook his hand profoundly and said, 'You'll never regret it dear.' She was a bit of an older, character-type woman, much like Addie. I think Bill made a lot of fans with that marriage."

Did Bill think Doug changed that much?

"At first," the actor muses, "Doug was still an opportunist. He and Julie were planning their escape to Portofino and suddenly Julie insisted we had to take her young son along. Doug said no. Then, when Addie came in and offered marriage, he simply went. She influenced him over the course of several months. He did care for Addie. Always respected her."

The story always pulled Doug and Julie one way or another, but rarely together for long. Doug's first wife Kim came back and came between them after Addie died. Then a manipulative gold-digger, Lee Dumonde, arrived.

Those on-camera splits were agonizing for the couple.

"It was all very meaningful to us because we were still not married," Susan says. "Working together and spending time together had become very important to us. To be put together and pulled apart hurt us as well as it pained Julie and Doug."

Married twice on the show, Susan favors the second ceremony because "Bill sang to me and we contributed a great deal, like the quartet from our church leading the choir. And Patty Weaver sang 'The Rose,' which was the theme of the wedding. Bill recited poetry to me."

Bill mentions that the first was more traditional but also romantic for him because they used the same vows they had exchanged in their real-life wedding.

The overlapping of real and screen life was "both a blessing and a curse," says Susan. "It was sometimes very strange not to be able to get away from the show either professionally or personally. I never expected life to be like that. It was a situation that Bill and I had never experienced in our professional lives before. It was a lot of fun and rather a grave responsibility. I'm sure we never had children together because we had the show. It took over so much. I really knew there was not enough of me to be a good wife, a good mother, and Julie, too. Other people have done it, but they're not married to their co-star."

In more recent years, Susan has worked on the show without Bill and noted that she had always felt a sense of incompleteness. "I appreciate that the two characters were never recast," the actress says. "I never quite understood why Julie came back without Doug, and Julie attempted to find other partners, but my character had neither the impact nor the importance that we as a couple had."

During one of those periods, Susan particularly liked working with Matthew Ashford (Jack) and Missy Reeves (Jennifer). "And I loved the 'cruise of deception' with the whole adventure on the island. I loved my breakaway red evening gown that I selected myself. I loved the fact that crew members took pieces of my dress and had it hanging on their cameras. It was like being in a war movie!"

Doug and Julie were of another generation. The foundation of the show had always been family, its growth and its enduring love. How fitting that their daughter Hope would keep the Horton family moving forward, in step with the times.

For Susan, the reality was bittersweet. "I think the casting of Kristian Alfonso as Hope was the beginning of the end for Doug and Julie as attractive people. The new Hope ushered in another time. There was a climate of change. Kristian as Hope has been very important to the show."

Bill concurred, saying, "That happened about '82," and notes his sorrow for the changes in Doug. "Our last few years there, our characters changed drastically. Doug became a negative, overbearing, reactive father. Totally unlike the Doug who had been in Salem all the years before."

He also observes that, unlike the kind of love Doug and Julie shared, there may now be too many "one-and-only fantastic loves" for everyone, all the time, and they never stay the same.

However, Hope is back in Salem and reunited with Bo. Through the next decade viewers will see if the Horton loyalty and passion for one-and-only true love will conquer all again.

F

ormer cast members fondly recall *Days* past.

It was a wonderful ten years of my career. One of the funniest scenes I can still remember was when Don and Marlena were wallpapering the apartment, I guess 1976. We were using real paste and it was hysterical trying to handle it. We had glue in our hair, on our faces, in our mouths. It was funny and messy and wonderful. And we did a telethon to raise money for the Salem hospital CAT-scan unit. I played Margaret Dumont and Frances Reid played Groucho. I wore a big bosom and a dress. It was so campy—it was real fun and a great show.

I liked the fact that Don had a great sense of humor and was a good man. He was always there for you and would never turn his back on you. That's a quality that few men have and I've tried to emulate.

JED ALLAN
(Don Craig)

I was on the show for a six-year period when we went through five headwriters and six supervising producers. It was a time of great flux and change. My first days were in the middle of a writers' and crew strike. There were production assistants and management running the cameras and booms—and where the scripts were coming from, I never did find out. It was chaos, but in the midst of that chaos was the potential for great things.

Marybeth Evans (Kayla) and Stephen Nichols (Patch) were the first people I worked with. We shot eleven shows that day, with Marybeth nine months pregnant. There was a tremendous connection between those two actors. Jack could accept that in his heart, but not his head. That was his character flaw, which I used in my work many times. It still intrigues me that so many people have such different ideas of who my Jack was—villain, clown, lover, guy. He was all these things at different times to different people, and I'm glad he didn't fit into any one mold. Most human beings don't. After playing one-sided characters in the past, I was grateful to get a chance to play with a larger palette.

Melissa Reeves was such a tremendous support and has the ability to go with the moment to make whatever outrageous thing I was doing look normal to Wayne Heffley's irascible Vern, Jack's newspaper editor and fallible sidekick. I

MATTHEW ASHFORD
(Jack Devereaux)

always felt I was better when I worked with these two. Wayne's enthusiasm for working on scenes that seemingly had nothing to go on always encouraged me to do my best. It was the best of times . . . it was the worst of times, and I wouldn't change a minute of it.

EILEEN BARNETT
(Stephanie Woodruff)

There are a few scenes I remember with amusement. I was killed in an auto accident and brought DOA to the hospital. I had a sheet over my head. One of the doctors took the sheet from my head and started shaking my body and doing all sorts of things that just didn't seem the way to tell if a person was dead. Maybe they were sorry to see me go. Maybe he thought he could shake me back. Maybe he was an actor who wanted more to do in the scene.

I had a scene with Quinn Redecker playing Alex. I was on booze and drugs and I had to throw a glass of water in his face during a screaming fight we had with each other. Every time I threw the drink, I missed. Sometimes I missed completely, other times, it hit his chest or neck. After about four or five takes, I finally got him just right.

As for actors I loved recognizing me, I was at a formal charity and Caesar Romero came up to me and enthused, "Stephanie! I love you!" That was a sweet moment.

PETER BROWN
(Dr. Greg Peters)

Getting married to Amanda on the show was very stressful. In rehearsal I almost passed out. You see, I had just finalized a divorce after a bad marriage and the very *thought* of getting married again so soon—even if only on the show—was just too scary for me to handle.

CRYSTAL CHAPPELL
(Dr. Carly Manning)

For me, Salem was always full of mystery and intrigue. Nothing was ever simple, but that was part of the fun of being there. My storyline was always about some loss and dwelling upon loss. Afterward, it was like a hangover. I had to rest and recover, get my bearings. So I played a lot, found my youth again and lightened up. It took about three months before I felt I had recuperated.

Overall, for me, aside from being part of a couple who were very popular, I got to play a woman who was incredibly independent and bright and passionate. I loved her will to continue, carry on. She never gave up. She was always fighting for something. I loved her drive, her passion.

There were amusing and funny moments always. There's always that wonderful look that comes across an actor's face when they've forgotten their lines and start to make things up. Some of those witty remarks come out of moments of desperation. Of course, when I went up on a line, I'd do something very intelligent like my Porky Pig imitation! And lying in the coffin, buried alive, was gruesome. But I'd lie there and sing "Sweet Mystery of Life I Have Found You," or some other weird stuff like that. Music and a sense of humor got me through.

When I was in the coffin, Lawrence was desperately hurrying to dig me out. When he did finally open up the coffin I was wearing a baseball cap and mustache and holding a baseball bat. That was because, at the time, someone had the scene from "Magnum, P.I." in which Tom Selleck was in a coffin in a cap, too. That was from a fantasy episode of his show. Anyway, everyone was so freaked out about me in a coffin because they actually had to close it and put dirt on top of it for a few minutes. It was tense, so to break the mood, I got silly.

And there was a silly moment when Robert (Bo) and I were in bed together. My leg was to slip from under the sheet as I put my foot on the floor in a rather sultry, easy move. They wanted to see my leg. I taped a lot of long hair to it so it looked more like a gorilla leg. Everyone, as expected, had a good laugh.

MARIE CHEATHAM
(*Marie Horton*)

My personal favorite story was falling in love with my brother who had amnesia and extensive plastic surgery. That storyline upset my mother. "You and your brother! Oh, but it was all right, sugar, you never touched." She was right, in a way. We never saw any onscreen touching, although it was implied. Whenever there was a kiss, they'd pan the camera to something else as you heard some heavy breathing. Often, it would be a standing kiss. We'd move to the kiss, but the camera would pan to our feet. That always cracked me up, because we were the same height. I supposedly stood on tiptoes to reach him for a kiss. Maybe I was kissing the top of his head! We really laughed a lot over that.

In those early days, I was talking about being a medical research technician. I was supposed to say "I'm going to do such good work. I'm going to be just like Madame Marie Curie." Instead I said, "I'm going to be just like Madame Bovary." Quite another type of character.

My toughest scenes were always those that had to show pain. I had been brought up with the stiff-upper-lip attitude. On the show, I had a nervous breakdown and went into a decline. I had to wear far too much forest green and other dark earth-tone colors. I wasn't a redhead at the time, so I really looked quite drab. I was depressed, all right. Then I (Marie) read about a medical missionary group and I decided to join them in Africa. While there, I decided to become a nun. At least I got to choose the habit to wear, so I chose the habit of the order of the Sisters of the Immaculate Heart. They were the nuns I grew up with at St. Mary's when I was in a Catholic orphanage in Galveston, Texas. I wore my boots and jeans underneath the long skirt. It was strange that when dressed that way, that's when many crew members were compelled to tell me blue jokes and tease me suggestively. There was just something about it. They didn't do it when I wasn't in the habit.

Cannonball Adderly, the jazz musician, told me he used me as his alarm clock while he was on the road. He'd have the TV on and when he'd hear my voice, he'd open his eyes long enough to come awake. I was his favorite character on the show. And Beverly Sills, the opera singer, was standing next to me at some charity function and we all sang "The Star Spangled Banner." I remember turning to her and saying, "I can't believe I sang with Beverly Sills!" and she graciously responded, "I can't believe I sang with Marie Horton!"

WAYNE HEFFLEY
(Vern Scofield)

It was an easy job because the character was so close to who I am. It was likely the best job I had in forty-five years and more enjoyable than the over six hundred films I've done. I really liked the quick pace and fairly regular job, which ran almost six years on and off, although I never was contract.

There were many memorable scenes. One, in a bar with my son Tanner, who was trying to track his mother's history. Vern is trying to dissuade him. They sat and talked. Vern recalled a Christmas when the boy was very young. He described him with his little hatchet and going out to get a Christmas tree, stepping in his dad's footprints. It showed a very moving father-son relationship. They had become very uncommunicative until now. Vern told Tanner he always loved him, loved him now and hopes that whatever he needs to do will turn out fine. Vern gives him sanction to do what he must do.

The funniest scenes included one in which we were at an embassy and we dressed as a couple of Tyrolean crackpots. We were in strange outfits and had handlebar mustaches. We made up some insane accent. I laughed my head off when I saw myself in that outfit. Matt looked even worse. I laughed harder realizing that millions of people were watching this.

ED MALLORY
(Bill Horton)

When my wife Laura was having a mental collapse, my sister Marie and several doctors finally realized that Laura was doing too many peculiar things. Bill had been in a state of denial about it all. He started to realize what was going on, I guess. Although the language didn't necessarily call for it, I found I burst into tears. The moment took over, very charged and real. He was still in denial. His words were saying one thing and his emotions were expressing the truth.

On a lighter note, there was a scene in the hospital, and I was taking heart rate and vital signs. The director's voice came over the loudspeaker to remind me to put the stethoscope I had around my neck into my ears. I also once took a temperature, removed the thermometer from someone's mouth, shook it down, and then read it as 104 degrees. And, in another scene, when Dr. Greg Peters called, he audibly said, "Dr. Spencer, this is Peter Brown . . ." Susan Flannery never missed a beat and replied, "It's Peter Brown, the actor from Hollywood, calling Bill." She did this whole improvisation and Peter kept getting redder and redder.

ANDREW MASSETT
(Larry Welch)

I had just gotten married not much before I had a bedroom scene with Kristian Alfonso, a nice young Catholic girl who looks a lot like my wife, with dark hair, beautiful light eyes, and Italian background. So, Larry and Hope are in bed and I'm putting the moves on her. I guess I got caught up in the moment a bit too much even with everyone standing around and watching. All of a sudden, Kristian jumped up and pointed her finger at me and yelled, "I said no tongue!" Apparently, I'd gotten carried away and slipped. Everyone just went nuts in laughter. I was much better behaved in the next take. And forever after.

I was the exorcism expert when Marlena was possessed by the devil. That was quite amusing for me since I'm not particularly religious and certainly not Roman Catholic. When the script called for me to say the Lord's Prayer *in Latin*, my wife helped write it out phonetically. 'En cielo et en terra' became 'in cello et in terror.' It was a lot of mumbo jumbo. That was really tough. I had to do it in a way that suggested this character had done it for many, many years, the biggest single challenge possibly of my entire career.

ERIC CHRISTMAS
(Fr. Francis)

Chris and Savannah had a bedroom scene that was quite cozy. The director started the countdown: five, four, three, two, one, and Shannon pulled out a can of whipped cream and asked me, "Ready for the fun?" Everyone cracked up.

I still remember one of my favorite fan letters, from a woman in South Dakota. She wrote, "I want you to know that I'm seventy-eight years old. I'm sitting here with the snow up to the window and you still put heat in my feet."

JOSH TAYLOR
(Chris Kositchek)

My son had died in the hospital and I was involved in a malpractice suit against them. In a dramatic courtroom scene I had a huge outburst of anger in front of most of the residents of Salem. I was really having a big fit, threatening them and going after them. Then I stormed out. Well, for whatever reason, the floor was slippery, and on my way out I slipped and fell to the floor right at Macdonald Carey's feet. He never missed a beat. He continued with his lines like nothing had happened. After all, I had fallen out of frame.

Roger was an alcoholic and violent father and husband who did go into rehab. I was at the local mall one afternoon with my wife and girls when, from across the mall a booming voice called out, "Hey, Roger! Glad to see you sober!" It was funny, but I was really redfaced.

MARK DREXLER
(Roger Lombard)

I had gone to a brunch in Malibu and Betty Corday happened to be there. At the time, I probably went for a free meal. A few weeks later I auditioned for Eric. I'm sure I wouldn't have gotten the audition if it hadn't been for that luck of meeting Mrs. Corday that day.

As brothers, Greg and I would get so close, but never open up emotionally to each other. That was always tough. Those scenes, trying to communicate all that you want to say to an older brother but can't, was really challenging each time. There was one moment when we were sitting on the sofa together and getting a bit animated, but not real big. I got so excited, agitated, that I jumped up, totally out of frame, and then sat down again. That was in the time when tape stopped only if a wall fell down. So there were a few seconds of Eric cut off from the waist up. They never stopped taping.

As far as things that happened away from the set, I remember being in a nice upscale restaurant having dinner with friends and a woman across the room who'd had a bit too much to drink suddenly shouted, "You raped Susan!" That was my first encounter with recognition.

STANLEY KAMEL
(Eric Peters)

SCOTT REEVES
(Jake Hogansen)

I was on for about nine months and it was fun to play Jake because I was always up to no good. I was a henchman with spiky hair. Never did have a chance to justify myself. I was just bad. I ran Nick off a cliff and messed him up pretty good. It was a fun shoot because we had gone out to a studio ranch to race the cars around. It was like doing a very short action movie.

Steve Burton, who is now on *General Hospital*, was on the show then, too. We hung around together on set and worked closely together. Actually, I had gone in to audition for Steve's role of Harris on *Days*, but I got Jake. As it turned out, Jake ran lots longer so I got lucky. Now Steve's girlfriend, Tara Reid, is on *Days* as Ashley. And, of course, *Days* is where I met Missy, who became my wife in real life.

DENISE ALEXANDER
(Susan Martin)

Overall, I remember laughing a lot. It was such a happy time. Most of us enjoyed our work immensely. Lots of cast spent time together outside the work hours, which was rather unusual. I'm still most in touch with Susan Hayes. In story we were always rivals, but in real life we get along quite well. We enjoyed each other. We think we're quite similar and really quite wonderful.

Susan Martin was supposed to be a rebellious teenager but soon evolved into a character who was extremely sympathetic. One of the times I liked best, however, was the period of time when she tried to hire Doug Williams to ruin Julie's romance with Scott Banning. I was able to be caustic and sarcastic and, I thought, quite terrific. I had great fun. I remember scathing put-downs to David Martin, too. I liked Susan's period of being twisted and evil. I got to do that so seldom. She baked far too many cookies. I wanted so desperately for her to break out and be wild, wicked, and mysterious. While I was constantly picking up baby toys, I really just wanted to have one wonderful romance after another. I wanted to be the evil, irresistible slayer of men. I yearned for a life of magic, mystery, and sophistication. I even circulated a petition around the set saying the character would be much more beneficial to the show if she got kissed every once in a while. I got everyone, cast and crew, to sign it. It helped me to do that, but it didn't get my character anywhere.

The funniest moments were with Susan Hayes off the set. We got each other's sense of humor better than anyone else did. We'd play weird word games in hair and makeup. We were telepathically in tune with each other. Then there was the time we went to a coffee shop in Beverly Hills for dinner and there were about a dozen people grouped near the entrance waiting to be seated. A woman at the far end of the group looked at Susan and screamed, "I can't stand it! I have to know! Are you going to have the abortion?" Things like that would happen to us all from time to time.

Personally, one of the most fun times was when we got heavily into water pistols. We would go up and down those studio hallways shooting at each other. It would go on for weeks at a time and we usually ended up ganging up on one of the directors. Who was the best shot? I was!

It's funny, the memories that come back. I remember the houndstooth sofa and how I loved one really stupid caftan. I wasn't even pregnant in story at the time. I kept the caftan for years, then gave it to Mother [Elizabeth Harrower], a head-writer on *Days* for a short time and later took it back again. I remember Laura's wedding shower scene. The women came through the door, and one, not known for being particularly graceful, slipped and fell down on her entrance. Everyone began to laugh, a lot. I mean, with great gusto. We all laughed so heartily that one of the other women peed. Then word got around and everyone laughed some more and it was impossible to shoot. We had to absolutely stop completely. Al Rabin, supervising producer at the time, came down from the booth and tried to be calming. He said NBC had seen the work and was now considering a spinoff. We laughed some more!

SUSAN SEAFORTH HAYES
(*Julie Olson Banning Williams*)

Playing Isabella helped me grow up. I was young, naive, shy, and anxious to please. I got to grow up in a pretty nurturing environment, and for the first time financially support myself, which was very nice. I remember how different it had been. The first day on the job I had to roll dimes to have enough money to buy gas to get to the studio.

I loved coming back from the dead to give such sweet closure to the John-Isabella story. They had been such a wonderful couple. I loved playing the character who was so very special that people who never related to me before the story, did, during and after. Isabella transcended personalities. At the original time of Isabella, when she died, Ken [Corday] gave me an original instrumental piece, "Isabella," which he wrote for me. It was such a lovely gift.

STACI GREASON
(*Isabella Toscano Black*)

My audition for *Days* in 1983 was the very first one I had in Hollywood. After the screen test with John Delancie, John came running after me to the parking lot. He was telling me I had gotten the job. I was *so* excited. I went home and called my agent and told him that the actor I tested with told me I had landed the role. When my agent called the producers, however, they said they hadn't yet made a decision. I had been so naïve. It was over two weeks later, long after I thought I had lost the role, that they called my agent, and I had, indeed, gotten the role. It was a tender and touching time between us. John played the zany guy and I was the rather demure flower just waiting to blossom and he was nurturing and tending me. It was lovely, but short. I was on for ten months and then killed off during the Salem Slasher period. My friend Philece Sampler was the first to go. I think I was number four. It was very sad.

BARBARA CRAMPTON
(*Trista Evans Bradford*)

Telling my brother Austin that I had been raped by our father was probably the best, most challenging, and satisfying scene. I loved the intimate, emotional scenes with Patrick as my brother, especially since I don't have a brother. Patrick will always be like my brother. And I loved the fight scenes with Deborah Adair.

LISA RINNA
(*Billie Holliday Reed*)

Funniest scenes . . . any scene where I get pies and other food thrown at me like I had at the country fair scenes not long ago. I was in a raincoat in heat over one hundred degrees. On the other hand, just the other day there was a scene in which Peter sprayed champagne all over us and that was really quite sexy, as well as funny. I liked that scene. We were soaked.

WALLY KURTH
(Justin Kiriakis)

Days was my first professional television gig. The first year was magical. I loved the part of the story when rich Justin was pretending to be a construction worker while courting Adrienne. The scenes just sitting on park benches and talking were very sweet. I really liked the scene where I put the engagement ring in a little paper boat and pushed it across a pond for her to find the ring inside. I also sang her a love song I wrote, "In Paradise."

I had set fire to the emergency center so I could buy up the property. Adrienne was still inside, so I had to rush in to rescue her. The funny part was that I couldn't lift her. She was lying on the floor and the angle plus the dead weight—and she was *not* heavy—worked against me. I was too weak. It was funny for us both when she had to help me get her up. Later, I had been paralyzed, and I guess one day the writers simply decided enough was enough and in an inspired moment, I miraculously got up and walked. Within twenty-four hours Adrienne and I were running around in the snow, falling down and making snow angels.

ARLENE SORKIN
(Calliope Jones)

When Shelly Curtis, one of the producers, saw a Cyndi Lauper concert, she came to the writers and designed a Calliope character. I loved playing Calliope. I especially loved the wedding gown with lights I wore on Calliope's New Year's Eve wedding to Eugene. Many months later, in a magazine, Cyndi Lauper commented that she was watching "some soap opera," she didn't remember which one, and fell in love with a wedding gown with lights all over it. That's exactly the gown I want for my wedding. Of course that was my gown! I thought it was really funny how the Cyndi Lauper thread came full circle.

Leann Hunley (who played Anna) came over to me during my first day on the set. I thought she was going to give me some piece of acting advice. Instead, she just wanted to remind me, "Always bring a sweater. It gets really cold out here on the set sometimes." Leann always took care of all of us, right to the point of knowing our lines and camera blocking for us when we forgot them.

I went to the wedding of Rosemary Clooney's son. I was surrounded by a lot of important show business people and entertainers I adored. When I got off the elevator, the whole room cried, "Calliope! I'm so glad you're here!" Rosemary was a fan. She made me feel like a star. We've been good friends ever since then.

One of my favorite lines was one word, "Huge!," when, in our first love scene, a naked Eugene let the pillow hiding his privates fall.

Awards

In 1995, Executive Producer Ken Corday proudly accepted the Lifetime Achievement Award for his parents, the late Ted and Betty Corday.

1994/1995

Lifetime Achievement Award for Extraordinary Contributions to Daytime: the late Ted and Betty Corday.

Outstanding Daytime Drama series (nomination): *Days of Our Lives.* Ken Corday, Executive Producer; Tom Langan, Co-executive Producer; Stephen Wyman, Supervising Producer; Jeanne Haney and Janet Spellman-Rider, Senior Coordinating Producers.

Outstanding Achievement in Music Direction & Composition (nomination): Amy Burkhard, Music Director; Stephen Reinhardt, Music Director; Ken Heller, Ken Corday, Cory Lerios, John D'Andrea, Dominic Messenger, D. Brent Nelson, Composers.

Outstanding Achievement in Hairstyling (WIN): Zora Sloan and Terrie Velazquez, Hairstylists.

Outstanding Achievement in Makeup for a Drama Series (nomination): Gail J. Hopkins, Nina Wells, John Damiani, Lucia Bianca, Makeup Artists.

1993/1994

Outstanding Drama Series Writing Team (nomination): James E. Reilly, Headwriter; Maura Penders, Dena Higley, Ethel M. Brez, Mel Brez, Marlena Clark Poulter, Dorothy Ann Purser, Associate Headwriters; Fran Myers, Maralyn Thoma, Peggy Schibi, Michelle Poteet Lisanti, Dialogue Writers.

Outstanding Original Song (nomination): Ken Corday, Composer; Tom Langan, Lyricist, Composer.

Outstanding Achievement in Music Direction & Composition (nomina-

tion): Stephen Reinhardt, Music Director; Amy Burkhard, Music Director, Composer, David Leon, Music Supervision; Ken Corday, D. Brent Nelson, Marty Davich, Cory Lerios, John D'Andrea, Ken Heller, Dominic Messenger, Composers.

1992/1993

Outstanding Drama Series Directing Team (nomination): Susan Orlikoff Simon, Herb Stein, Stephen Wyman, Directors; Sheryl Harmon, Roger W. Inman, Associate Directors.

Outstanding Achievement in Makeup for Drama Series (nomination): Carol Brown, Keith Crary, Lucia Bianca, Gail Hopkins, Nina Wells, Robert Sloan, Makeup Artists.

Outstanding Achievement in Hairstyling (nomination): Zora Sloan, Janet Medford, Michelle Jennings, Hairstylists.

1991/1992

Outstanding Younger Actress in a Drama Series (nomination): Melissa Reeves as Jennifer Horton Devereaux.

Outstanding Achievement in Makeup for a Drama Series (WIN): Carol Brown, Head Makeup Artist; Keith Crary, Gail Hopkins, Lucia Bianca, Robert Sloan, Makeup Artists.

Outstanding Achievement in Hairstyling for a Drama Series (nomination): Zora Sloan, Head Hairstylist; Sandra Rubin, Michele Jennings, Hairstylists.

1990/1991

Outstanding Younger Actress in a Drama Series (nomination): Charlotte Ross as Eve Donovan.

Outstanding Achievement in Makeup for a Drama Series (WIN):

Carol Brown, Head Makeup Artist; Keith Crary, Robert Sloan, Gail Hopkins, Lucia Bianca, Makeup Artists.

Outstanding Achievement in Hairstyling for a Drama Series (nomination): Zora Sloan, Head Hairstylist; Diane Shinneman, Voni Hinkle, Hairstylists.

1989/1990

Outstanding Juvenile Female in a Drama Series (nomination): Charlotte Ross as Eve Donovan.

Outstanding Achievement in Music Direction and Composition for a Drama Series (WIN): Marty Davich, Music Director/Composer; Amy Burkhard, Music Supervisor; Ken Corday, Composer.

Outstanding Achievement in Costume Design for a Drama Series (nomination): Lee H. Smith, Costume Designer.

Outstanding Achievement in Makeup for a Drama Series (nomination): Carol Brown, Head Makeup Artist; Keith Crary, Robert Sloan, Gail Hopkins, Lucia Bianca, Makeup Artists.

1988/1989

Outstanding Supporting Actor in a Drama Series (nomination): Joseph Campanella as Harper Devereaux.

Outstanding Supporting Actress in a Drama Series (nominations): Arleen Sorkin as Calliope Bradford; Jane Elliot as Anjelica Curtis.

Outstanding Juvenile Male in a Drama Series (nomination): Darrell Utley as Benjy.

Outstanding Achievement in Music Direction and Composition for a Drama Series (nomination): Marty Davich, Music Director/Composer;

Ken Corday, Composer; Amy Burkhard, Music Supervisor.

Outstanding Achievement in Makeup for a Drama Series (nomination): Carol Brown, Head Makeup Artist; Keith Crary, Robert Sloan, Gail Hopkins, Lucia Bianca, Makeup Artists.

Outstanding Achievement in Lighting Direction for a Drama Series (nomination): Jeff Barr, John Nance, Lighting Directors.

1987/1988

Outstanding Lead Actor in a Drama Series (nomination): Stephen Nichols as Steve "Patch" Johnson.

Outstanding Supporting Actress in a Drama Series (nomination): Arleen Sorkin as Calliope Bradford.

Outstanding Younger Leading Man in a Drama Series (WIN): Billy Warlock as Frankie Brady.

Outstanding Drama Series Directing Team (nomination): Joseph Behar, Susan Orlikoff Simon, Herb Stein, Stephen Wyman, Directors; Becky Greenlaw, Gay Linvill, Sheryl Harmon, Associate Directors.

Outstanding Achievement in Costume Design for a Drama Series (WIN): Lee H. Smith, Costume Designer.

Outstanding Achievements in Makeup for a Drama Series (WIN): Carol Brown, Head Makeup Artist; Keith Crary, Robert Sloan, Gail Hopkins, Lucia Bianca, Makeup Artists.

Outstanding Achievements in Hairstyling for a Drama Series (WIN): Zora Sloan, Pauletta Lewis.

Outstanding Achievement in Lighting Direction for a Drama Series (nomination): John Nance, Art Busch, Carl Pitsch, Lighting Directors.

1986/1987

Outstanding Lead Actress in a Drama Series (nomination): Frances Reid as Alice Horton.

Outstanding Supporting Actress in a Drama Series (nomination): Peggy McCay as Caroline Brady.

Outstanding Younger Leading Man in a Drama Series (nomination): Billy Warlock as Frankie Brady.

Outstanding Drama Series Directing Team (nomination): Joseph Behar, Susan Orlikoff Simon, Herb Stein, Stephen Wyman, Directors; Becky Greenlaw, Gay Linvill, Sheryl Harmon, Associate Directors.

Outstanding Drama Series Writing Team (nomination): Leah Laiman, Sheri Anderson, Thom Racina, Headwriters; Anne M. Schoettle, Dena Breshears, Richard J. Allen, Associate Headwriters; M. M. Shelley Moore, Penina Spiegel, Associate Writers.

Outstanding Achievement in Costume Design for a Drama Series (nomination): Lee H. Smith, Costume Designer.

Outstanding Achievement in Live and Tape Sound Mixing and Sound Effects for a Drama Series (nomination): Frank Jackson, Davey Cone, John Machea, Production Mixers; Bob Mott, Sound Effects Mixer.

1985/1986

Outstanding Lead Actress in a Drama Series (nomination): Peggy McCay as Caroline Brady.

Outstanding Supporting Actress in a Drama Series (WIN): Leann Hunley as Anna DiMera.

Outstanding Drama Series Directing Team (nomination): Susan Orlikoff Simon, Joseph Behar, Herb Stein, Stephen Wyman, Directors; Gay Linvill, Sheryl Harmon, Becky Greenlaw, Associate Directors.

Outstanding Achievement in Costume Design for a Drama Series (nomination): Lee H. Smith, Costume Designer.

Outstanding Achievement in Makeup for a Drama Series (nomination): Carol Brown, Makeup Supervisor; Keith Crary, Robert Sloan, Gail Hopkins, Makeup Artists.

Outstanding Achievement in Hairstyling for a Drama Series (nomination): Zora Sloan, Hairstylist.

Outstanding Achievement in Live and Tape Sound Mixing and Sound Effects for a Drama Series (nomination): Tom Ruston, Frank Jackson, Dave A. Cone, Production Mixers; Bob Mott, Sound Effects Technician.

1984/1985

Outstanding Daytime Drama Series (nomination): Al Rabin, Betty Corday, Executive Producers; Ken Corday, Shelley Curtis, Producers.

Outstanding Actress in a Drama Series (nomination): Deidre Hall as Dr. Marlena Evans Brady.

Outstanding Ingenue/Woman in a Drama Series (nominations): Kristian Alfonso as Hope Williams; Lisa Trusel as Melissa Anderson.

Outstanding Directing in a Drama Series (nomination): Al Rabin, Joseph Behar, Susan Orlikoff Simon, Stephen Wyman, Herb Stein, Directors; Gay Linvill, Sheryl Harmon, Becky Greenlaw, Associate Directors.

Outstanding Writing in a Drama Series (nomination): Sheri Anderson, Head writer; Leah Laiman, Margaret De Priest, Maralyn Thoma, Dana Soloff, Anne Schoettle, Michael Robert David, Leah Markus, Thom Racina.

1983/1984

Outstanding Daytime Drama Series (nomination): *Days of Our Lives:* Betty Corday, Executive Producer; Al Rabin, Supervising Executive Producer; Ken Corday, Shelley Curtis, Producers.

Outstanding Actress in a Drama Series (nomination): Deidre Hall as Dr. Marlena Evans.

Outstanding Writing in a Drama Series (nomination): Margaret De Priest, Sheri Anderson, Maralyn Thoma, Michael Robert David, Susan Goldberg, Bob Hansen, Leah Markus, Dana Soloff.

1982/1983

Outstanding Daytime Drama Series (nomination): Betty Corday, Executive Producer; Al Rabin, Supervising Executive Producer; Patricia Wenig, Supervising Producer; Ken Corday, Producer.

1979/1980

Outstanding Supporting Actress in a Drama Series (nomination): Deidre Hall as Dr. Marlena Evans.

Outstanding Guest/Cameo Appearance in a Drama Series (WIN): Hugh McPhillips as Hugh Pearson.

1978/1979

Outstanding Daytime Drama Series (nomination): Betty Corday, H. Wesley Kenney, Executive Producers; Jack Herzberg, Producer.

Outstanding Actor in a Drama Series (nominations): Jed Allan as Don Craig; John Clarke as Mickey Horton.

Outstanding Actress in a Drama Series (nomination): Susan Seaforth Hayes as Julie Williams.

Outstanding Supporting Actor in a Drama Series (nomination): Joe Gallison as Dr. Neil Curtis.

Outstanding Supporting Actress in a Drama Series (WIN): Suzanne Rogers as Maggie Horton.

Outstanding Supporting Actress in a Drama Series (nomination): Frances Reid as Alice Horton.

Outstanding Directing in a Drama Series (nomination): Al Rabin, Joe Behar, Frank Pacelli, Directors.

Outstanding Writing in a Drama Series (nomination): Ann Marcus, Michael Robert David, Raymond E. Goldstone, Joyce Perry, Elizabeth Harrower, Rocci Chatfield, Laura Olsher.

Achievement in Design Excellence for a Drama Series (nomination): *Days of Our Lives* Design Team.

1977/1978

Outstanding Daytime Drama Series (WIN): Betty Corday and H. Wesley Kenney, Executive Producers; Jack Herzberg, Producer.

Outstanding Actress in a Drama Series (nomination): Susan Seaforth Hayes as Julie Williams.

Outstanding Individual Director for a Drama Series or Single Episode (nomination): Al Rabin, February 21, 1978.

Outstanding Writing in a Drama Series (nominations): William J. Bell, Kay Lenard, Bill Rega, Pat Falken Smith, Margaret Stewart; Ann Marcus, Ray Goldstone, Joyce Perry, Michael Robert David, Laura Olsher, Rocci Chatfield, Elizabeth Harrower.

1976/1977

Outstanding Daytime Drama Series (nomination): Betty Corday, Executive Producer; H. Wesley Kenney and Jack Herzberg, Producers.

Outstanding Individual Director for a Drama Series or Single Episode (nomination): Al Rabin, Julie and Doug's Wedding; Joseph Behar.

Outstanding Writing in a Drama Series (nomination): William J. Bell, Pat Falken Smith, William Rega, Kay Lenard, Margaret Stewart.

1975/1976

Outstanding Daytime Drama Series (nomination): Betty Corday, Executive Producer; Jack Herzberg and Al Rabin, Producers.

Outstanding Actor in a Drama Series (nomination): Macdonald Carey as Dr. Tom Horton; Bill Hayes as Doug Williams.

Outstanding Actress in a Drama Series (nomination): Susan Seaforth Hayes as Julie Olson.

Outstanding Writing in a Drama Series (WIN): William J. Bell, Kay Lenard, Pat Falken Smith, Bill Rega, Margaret Stewart, Sheri Anderson, Wanda Coleman.

1974/1975

Outstanding Daytime Drama Series (nomination): Betty Corday, Executive Producer; Ted Corday, Irna Phillips, Allan Chase, Creators; Jack Herzberg, Producer.

Outstanding Actor in a Drama Series (WIN): Macdonald Carey as Dr. Tom Horton.

Outstanding Actor in a Drama Series (nomination): Bill Hayes as Doug Williams.

Outstanding Actress in a Drama Series (WIN): Susan Flannery as Dr. Laura Horton.

Outstanding Actress in a Drama Series (nomination): Susan Seaforth as Julie Olson.

Outstanding Individual Director for a Drama Series or Single Episode (nomination): Joseph Behar, November 20, 1974.

Outstanding Writing in a Drama Series (nomination): William J. Bell, Pat Falken Smith, Bill Rega.

1973/1974

Outstanding Daytime Drama Series (nomination): Betty Corday, Executive Producer; Ted Corday, Irna Phillips, Allan Chase, Creators; H. Wesley Kenney, Producer.

Best Actor in Daytime Drama (WIN): Macdonald Carey as Dr. Tom Horton.

Best Individual Director for a Drama Series (WIN): H. Wesley Kenney.

Outstanding Technical Direction and Electronic Camerawork (nomination): Gordon C. James, Technical Director; George Simpson, George Meyer, John Kullman, Cameramen.

Outstanding Sound Mixing, Daytime (WIN): Ernest Dellutri.

Outstanding Lighting Direction (nomination): Alan E. Scarlett.

1972/1973

Outstanding Achievement by Individuals in Daytime Drama (nomination): Macdonald Carey, Performer, Series; H. Wesley Kenney, Director.

Program Achievement in Daytime Drama (nomination): Betty Corday, Executive Producer; H. Wesley Kenney, Producer.

1967/1968

Outstanding Achievement in Daytime Programming, Individual (nomination): Macdonald Carey as Dr. Tom Horton.

Soap Opera Digest *magazine initiated the Soapy Awards in 1977. After seven years, the kudo was renamed in 1984 and the award was redesigned from its former spire to a heart shape. They are now known as the Soap Opera Awards.*

1995

Outstanding Show: *Days of Our Lives*

Hottest Male Star: Drake Hogestyn as John Black

Outstanding Lead Actress: Deidre Hall as Marlena Evans

Outstanding Villain: Jason Brooks as Peter Blake

Outstanding Female Scene Stealer: Louise Sorel as Vivian Alamain

Hottest Soap Couple: Robert Kelker-Kelly and Lisa Rinna as Bo Brady and Billie Reed

1994

Outstanding Show: *Days of Our Lives*

Outstanding Lead Actor: Robert Kelker-Kelly as Bo Brady

Hottest Male Star: Drake Hogestyn as John Black

Hottest Female Star: Melissa Reeves as Jennifer Devereaux

Outstanding Supporting Actress: Deborah Adair as Kate Roberts

Outstanding Female Newcomer: Lisa Rinna as Billie Reed

Outstanding Child Actor: Scott Groff as Shawn-Douglas Brady

Outstanding Villain/Villainess: Louise Sorel as Vivian Alamain

Outstanding Male Newcomer: Patrick Muldoon as Austin Reed

Outstanding Musical Achievement: *Days of Our Lives*

Outstanding Storyline: "Who Fathered Marlena's Baby?"

1993

Outstanding Show: *Days of Our Lives*

Outstanding Supporting Actor: Richard Biggs as Marcus Hunter

Outstanding Comic Performer: Matthew Ashford as Jack Devereaux

Hottest Female Star: Crystal Chappell as Carly Manning

Favorite Song: "One Dream" from *Days of Our Lives*

1992

Outstanding Show: *Days of Our Lives*

Outstanding Comic Performer: Robert Mailhouse as Brian Scofield

Best Wedding: Matthew Ashford and Melissa Reeves as Jack and Jennifer

Best Love Story (Daytime or Prime Time): Matthew Ashford and Melissa Reeves as Jack and Jennifer

1991

Outstanding Show: *Days of Our Lives*

Outstanding Super Couple: Matthew Ashford and Melissa Reeves as Jack and Jennifer

1990

Outstanding Villainess: Jane Elliot as Anjelica Curtis

1989

Outstanding Show: *Days of Our Lives*

Outstanding Supporting Actress: Joy Garrett as Jo Johnson

Outstanding Hero: Stephen Nichols as Steve "Patch" Johnson

Outstanding Villain: Matthew Ashford as Jack Devereaux

Favorite Super Couple: Stephen Nichols and Mary Beth Evans as Steve and Kayla

1988

Outstanding Show: *Days of Our Lives*

Outstanding Actor: Stephen Nichols as Steve "Patch" Johnson

Outstanding Comic Actress: Arleen Sorkin as Calliope Bradford

Outstanding Comic Actor: Michael Weiss as Mike Horton

Favorite Super Couple: Charles Shaughnessy and Patsy Pease as Shane and Kim

No awards were presented in 1987 by Soap Opera Digest.

1986

Outstanding Show: *Days of Our Lives*

Outstanding Actress: Patsy Pease as Kimberly Brady

Outstanding Actor: John Aniston as Victor Kiriakis

Outstanding Supporting Actor: Stephen Nichols as Steve "Patch" Johnson

Outstanding Younger Leading Actor: Peter Reckell as Bo Brady

Outstanding Villain: John Aniston as Victor Kiriakis

Outstanding Comic Performer:
Arleen Sorkin as Calliope Jones

Favorite Super Couple: Charles
Shaughnessy and Patsy Pease as Shane
and Kim

1985
———

Outstanding Show: *Days of Our
Lives*

Outstanding Actress: Deidre Hall as
Marlena Evans

Outstanding Actor: Peter Reckell as
Bo Brady

Outstanding Supporting Actress:
Arleen Sorkin as Calliope Jones

Outstanding Supporting Actor: John
de Lancie as Eugene Bradford

Outstanding Male Newcomer:
Charles Shaughnessy as Shane
Donovan

Outstanding Actress/Mature Role:
Frances Reid as Alice Horton

Outstanding Actor/Mature Role:
Macdonald Carey as Tom Horton

Outstanding Villainess: Cheryl-Ann
Wilson as Megan Hathaway

Outstanding Villain: Joseph Mascolo
as Stefano DiMera

Outstanding Youth Actress: Andrea
Barber as Carrie Brady

Outstanding Youth Actor: Brian
Autenrieth as Zach Parker

1984
———

Outstanding Show: *Days of Our
Lives*

Outstanding Actress: Deidre Hall as
Marlena Evans

Outstanding Actor: Peter Reckell as
Bo Brady

Outstanding Supporting Actress: Lisa
Trusel as Melissa Anderson

Outstanding Supporting Actor: John
de Lancie as Eugene Bradford

Outstanding Female Newcomer:
Kristian Alfonso as Hope Williams

Outstanding Male Newcomer:
Michael Leon as Pete Jannings

Outstanding Actress/Mature Role:
Frances Reid as Alice Horton

Outstanding Actor/Mature Role:
Macdonald Carey as Tom Horton

Outstanding Villain: Joseph Mascolo
as Stefano DiMera

Outstanding Youth Actress: Andrea
Barber as Carrie Brady

F*ollowing are the Soapy Award
winners:*

1983
———

Outstanding Actress: Deidre Hall as
Marlena Evans

Favorite Villain: Quinn Redeker as
Alex Marshall

1982
———

Outstanding Actress: Deidre Hall as
Marlena Evans

*In 1980 and 1981 there
were no* Days *nominations.*

1979
———

Favorite Soap Opera: *Days of Our
Lives*

Outstanding Actor: Jed Allan as Don
Craig

Most Exciting New Actress: Tracey
Bregman as Donna Temple

Favorite Actress/Mature Role:
Frances Reid as Alice Horton

Favorite Actor/Mature Role:
Macdonald Carey as Tom Horton

1978
———

Favorite Soap Opera: *Days of Our
Lives*

Outstanding Actor: Jed Allan as Don
Craig

Most Exciting New Actress: Andrea
Hall-Lovell as Samantha Evans

Most Exciting New Actor: Josh
Taylor as Chris Kositchek

Favorite Actress/Mature Role:
Frances Reid as Alice Horton

Favorite Actor/Mature Role:
Macdonald Carey as Tom Horton

1977
———

Favorite Soap Opera: *Days of Our
Lives*

Outstanding Actress: Susan Seaforth
Hayes as Julie Williams

Outstanding Actor: Bill Hayes as
Doug Williams

Favorite Heroine: Susan Seaforth
Hayes as Julie Williams

Trivia

Did you know that. . .

■ Drake Hogestyn's (John) dressing room once belonged to Jack Klugman during the filming of Jack's *Quincy* series.

■ Renee Jones has held down two roles on the show: first, spoiled rich girl Nikki Wade; second, cop-turned-doc Lexie Carver.

■ Gloria Loring (Liz) and Al Jarreau struck gold with their duet single, "Friends and Lovers." The song served as Kimberly and Shane's love theme. It rose to Number 2 on the record charts in 1986.

■ Mike Farrell of *M*A*S*H* fame played Scott Banning from 1968 to 1970. Joan Van Ark of *Knots Landing* played Janene Whitney from 1969–1980.

■ Speaking of *M*A*S*H*, two of Alan Alda's relatives appeared on *Days*. His dad, Robert Alda, played Stuart Whyland; his half-brother, Antony Alda, played Johnny Corelli.

■ The special contacts that turned Deidre Hall's eyes yellow for her devil possession story were custom-designed by Andrea LeVine of Body Tech, who created similar lenses for Brad Pitt in *Interview with the Vampire*.

■ Shannon Sturges, who played Molly Brinker, is the real-life grand-daughter of renowned filmmaker Preston Sturges.

■ Michael Easton (Tanner) was named one of *People* magazine's Most Beautiful People in 1992.

■ One of Robert Mailhouse's (Brian) best pals is film star Keanu Reeves. The guys even perform in a band together.

■ Two *Days* alumni now play dads on *Beverly Hills 90210*. Jed Allan portrays Ian Ziering's pop, while Josh Taylor plays Luke Perry's father.

■ Christie Clark (Carrie) was the homecoming princess of El Dorado High School in Placentia, California, in 1989.

■ Edward Mallory, who played Bill Horton, ended up marrying his *Days* daughter-in-law, Suzanne Zenor (Margot) in real life.

■ Liz Chandler's older woman–younger man affair with Carlo Forenza led to the real thing off-camera for Gloria Loring and Don Diamont.

■ Back in 1985, future *Days* star Karen Moncrieff (Gabrielle) represented the state of Illinois in the Miss America Pagaent.

■ Before turning to acting, Suzanne Rogers (Maggie) was an accomplished dancer who once kicked up her heels with the Radio City Music Hall Rockettes.

■ The Fifth Dimension's Marilyn McCoo joined *Days* in 1986 as Tamara Price, a friend of Marlena's who came to sing at her wedding to Roman.

■ Since exiting daytime, Arleen Sorkin (Calliope) has turned to scriptwriting. She's currently a writer on the NBC comedy *Pride and Joy*.

⚁ The accent Joseph Mascolo uses for Stefano DiMera is a takeoff of Rossano Brazzi's in the film *South Pacific*.

⚁ West Point graduate Mark Valley (Jack) served in Operation Desert Storm.

⚁ George Jenesky's (Nick) given name is Conrad Dunn.

⚁ Drake Hogestyn once played third base for a New York Yankees farm team.

⚁ Although James Reynolds has played Abe for over a decade, it was his short role as business tycoon Henry Marshall on *Generations* in 1991 that earned him his only Daytime Emmy nomination for Best Actor.

⚁ Roark Critchlow's (Mike) first TV role was as a male prostitute who beat up Richard Grieco on *21 Jump Street*.

⚁ When he's not on-camera, Peter Reckell (Bo) *always* sports a pinkie ring, a birthday gift from his mother.

⚁ James Reynolds (Abe) was a journalist in the Marines during his tour of duty in Vietnam and, in his civilian career, interviewed celebrities like Jack Nicholson, Peter Fonda, and Mike Douglas.

⚁ Before joining *Days*, Alison Sweeney (Sami) was a major fan of the show. Her favorite couple was Bo and Hope.

⚁ Joe Gallison (Neil) invested some of his acting residuals in a Studio City, California, bar called Residuals. The pub is frequented by actors, directors, and other showbiz folk.

⚁ Joseph Mascolo (Stefano) is good buddies with Burt Reynolds. Not only has he starred in productions at Burt's dinner theater in Jupiter, Florida, but also in Reynolds' films, *Sharkey's Machine* and *Heat*.

⚁ Kristian Alfonso (Hope) was a successful model with the Wilhelmina Agency and graced the cover of some thirty international magazines, including *Vogue* and *Bazaar*, by the age of fifteen.

⚁ Before striking it big as Shane Donovan, Charles Shaughnessy made his daytime debut playing Emma Samms's cousin, Alistair Crawford, on *General Hospital*.

OPPOSITE: **D**uring *Days* location shoot in Chichén Itzá, Mexico, Crystal Chappell suffered a gash to her head, when she collided with a paddle boat. Once doctors stitched her up, she bravely continued taping.

RIGHT: **I**n 1987, when Calliope discovered her pet pooch was going to have puppies by playboy poodle Reggie, she orchestrated a shotgun wedding true to her zany style. Dr. Neil Curtis led Martha down the aisle to the tune "How Much Is That Doggie in the Window."

⌛ *Days* employed its very first father-daughter acting team in 1989, when Mindy Clarke (Faith), John Clarke's daughter, joined the cast.

⌛ Andrea Barber, who originated the role of Carrie Brady in 1982, went on to nighttime fame as Kimmy in *Full House*.

⌛ Peter Reckell's (Bo) favorite junk food is Häagen-Dazs Rum Raisin ice cream.

⌛ In 1987 Deidre Hall had her own nighttime show. She co-starred in *Our House* with Wilford Brimley, and Shannen Doherty played her daughter.

⌛ Writer Quinn Redeker (Alex) was nominated for an Academy Award for his work on the screenplay for the film *The Deer Hunter*.

⌛ Shannon Tweed (Savannah) was *Playboy*'s Miss November in 1981 and Playmate of the Year in 1982.

A wall in Louise Sorel's dressing room displays a ten-by-five foot trompe l'oeil painting of the Tuileries in Paris by renowned muralist Lou Marek.

⌛ Before landing the role of sassy Eve Donovan, Charlotte Ross tested for Kelly Bundy in *Married with Children*. Ross placed first runner-up to Christina Applegate.

⌛ Peggy McCay (Caroline) was cast as a regular on the *Lou Grant* television series for six years as Marion Hume.

⌛ Two *Days* stars have penned autobiographies: Macdonald Carey, *The Days of My Life*, and Jay Robinson, *The Comeback*.

⌛ *Days* took its first location shoot out of California in 1994, when Peter Reckell, Kristian Alfonso, Frances Reid, and Stanley Brock headed for New Orleans.

⌛ One of macho Josh Taylor's (Chris) hobbies is collecting music boxes.

⌛ Tonya Boyd (Celeste) has worked as a backup vocalist for Lou Rawls, Anita Baker, and Natalie Cole.

⌛ Bryan Dattilo (Lucas) grew up "in the know," when it came to gossip. His mom, Peggy, was a reporter for *The Enquirer*.

⌛ Susan Flannery (Laura) appeared in the film *The Towering Inferno* with Faye Dunaway.

⌛ Two weeks after leaving *Days*, Patrick Muldoon (Austin) was scooped up by Aaron Spelling and signed to *Melrose Place*.

⌛ During Thaao Penghlis's (Tony) days as an apprentice art dealer in New York, his celebrity clientele included Jacqueline Kennedy and the Rockefellers.

⌛ Lisa Rinna (Billie) shared her first ever onscreen kiss with Jason Bateman, when she was cast as his girlfriend on *The Hogan Family*.

⌛ Mary Beth Evans's (Kayla) all-time favorite TV series is *I Love Lucy*.

⌛ Stephen Nichols (Patch) learned how to play the harmonica when he was 15; his grandfather, Earl, taught him.

⌛ In 1986 Peggy McCay (Caroline) was honored with two Emmy nominations: a daytime nod for Best Actress and a nighttime one for her guest-starring role on *Cagney and Lacey*.

⌛ For years Wayne Northrop (Roman) held the title as the *Days* resident backstage prankster, constantly pulling gags on his co-stars.

⌛ Leann Hunley (Anna) was named after actress and former Miss America, Lee Anne Meriwether.

⌛ Eileen Davidson (Kristen) insists her "first love" has always been writing; she's kept a journal since she was fourteen.

⌛ Patsy Pease (Kimberly) once shared the big screen with two-time Academy Award–winner Tom Hanks. They both appeared in *He Knows You're Alone*.

⌛ Real-life twins have been cast as twins on *Days* twice. Deidre Hall and Andrea Lovell Hall played Marlena and Samantha, while Camilla and Carey More portrayed Gillian and Grace Forrester.

Do You Remember. . .

⌛ Tom and Alice Horton had five children (Tommy, Addie, Mickey, Bill, and Marie), nine grandchildren (Julie, Mike, Sandy, Jennifer, Hope, Steve, Jessica, Melissa, and Sarah), three great-grandchildren (David, Shawn Douglas, and Abigail), and one great-great-grandchild (Scotty).

Samantha Evans brought her dog, Phaedra, with her on one of her several visits to her sister Marlena in Salem. The sisters' hometown was Boulder, Colorado.

☒ After a bout with amnesia Mickey Horton began calling himself Marty Hansen, a name he concocted from the initials on his belt buckle.

☒ Before Celeste, Stefano had a right-hand man named Petrov.

☒ The DiMeras' devoted maid was Delia Abernathy.

☒ Hope's first pet was a kitten given to her on Christmas, 1976.

☒ The Salem Slasher left a raven's feather next to each of his victims.

☒ The song "Up Where We Belong" was played at Marlena and Roman's wedding.

☒ When George Jenesky first appeared as pimp Nick Corelli, he was dubbed Nick Bartelli.

☒ Madam Foxy Humdinger once set her sights on Doug Williams, much to his wife Julie's chagrin.

☒ Calliope Jones once bought a baseball team named the Salem Sky Hawks.

☒ Roman Brady's middle name is Augustus.

☒ Bo and Hope wed on May 23, 1985, in London, England.

☒ Eugene Bradford met his second wife, Trista, when she answered his note, found in a bottle thrown in the river.

☒ Calliope Jones's favorite soft drink was strawberry soda.

☒ Eugene Bradford ran a singles' support group in Salem: The Lonely Hearts Club.

☒ On Hope's eighteenth birthday Bo gave her an old book of poetry that his father, Shawn, had once bestowed upon him.

☒ Pete Curtis originally ran with a gang called The Vipers; later he operated a club called JUMP!

☒ When Liz Chandler was convicted of shooting Marie, she was sent to Reinhart Prison.

☒ Jack Devereaux debuted on the show suffering from Hodgkin's disease. He's been in remission ever since.

☒ Steve and Kayla's first encounter wasn't exactly heaven-sent—he was hired by Victor Kiriakis to terrorize her.

☒ Frankie Brady turned out to be Francois Von Leuschner, the long-lost brother of Katerina, a.k.a. Dr. Carly Manning.

☒ When filthy-rich Justin Kiriakis met poor girl Adrienne Johnson, he pretended he was a construction worker.

☒ Although Steve was the love of her life, Kayla lost her virginity to Chris Kositchek.

☒ The Brady sisters, Kimberly and Kayla, both lost senses due to story twists: Kimberly went blind following a trip to England, and Kayla was left deaf and mute after an explosion.

☒ Alex Marshall nicknamed Anna DiMera "Saddle Shoes."

☒ The specialty at Brady's Fish Market was homemade clam chowder.

☒ Originally called Sergio's, Salem's finest dining establishment changed names over the years to Doug's Place, Blondie's, and Wings.

☒ The full names of Marlena and Roman's twins are Eric Roman Brady and Samantha Jean Brady.

☒ Steve Johnson was shown *sans* his famous eye patch on June 21, 1989, when he went undercover as Daniel Lucas.

☒ All the Brady siblings—Roman, Bo, Kim, and Kayla—have resided in the loft apartment where honorary Brady, John Black, currently resides.

☒ Art imitated life when real-life poet Macdonald Carey recited poems at The Beat Bar on *Days*. Tom's alias: Norm de Plumme.

☒ Alice Horton's culinary specialty is her homemade donuts.

☒ During Bo and Patch's Merchant Marine days, they both fell for a gal named Britta. The inseparable trio even had their own slogan: "Three together, together forever."

☒ Both Lucas Roberts and Justin Kiriakis debuted in similar fashion. In bed, making love to a woman.

☒ When Kimberly suffered a split personality her aliases were Claire and Lacy.

☒ Bo and Hope first kissed at a Fourth of July fair's kissing booth.

⊠ Although Austin Reed was introduced as a talented pianist, he hasn't tickled the ivories in years.

⊠ Jack and Jennifer's wacky wedding turned out to be part of the Wild West stunt show at Universal Studios.

⊠ The Civil War diary Kayla found in her house told the love story of Emily and Gideon.

⊠ When amnesiac Tommy Horton returned to Salem, no one recognized him because of his plastic surgery. But in the hospital laboratory, his former pet monkey instinctively responded to him the first time he came back in the lab.

⊠ Marlena and John's daughter, Belle, is named after John's late wife, Isabella.

⊠ Shane's ISA boss was Nickerson.

⊠ The cat Tony DiMera gave Renee was named Moonshine.

⊠ Vivian was shaved bald and prepped for a lobotomy at Pine Haven Sanitarium after discovering the nurse and administrator were bilking patients' families out of thousands by keeping them overmedicated.

⊠ Mike Horton nicknamed April Ramirez "Boom Boom."

⊠ Jack and Jennifer's daughter, Abigail, suffered from aplastic anemia.

⊠ Steve Johnson and Marcus Hunter met as children in an orphanage.

⊠ Jack Devereaux bought *The Spectator* from Diana Colville.

⊠ Roman met his first wife, Anna, in a library; three months after their wedding she disappeared.

⊠ Anna DiMera once dated a prince named Nicholas, who presented her with a Rolls-Royce.

⊠ When Eve Donovan arrived in Salem, she went by the name Eve Baron.

⊠ Mama Jo Johnson has a favorite dish she prepares for her kids: tuna noodle casserole.

⊠ Kayla's favorite flower was always the yellow rose.

⊠ Private eye Howie Hoffstedder donned Hope's wedding dress and walked down the aisle to her awaiting groom, Larry Welch.

⊠ Tom and Alice Horton were wed twice. They exchanged "I do's" a second time upon learning their first marriage wasn't legal.

⊠ When Frankie and Eve left town, they headed to Africa.

⊠ Billie treasured her first gift from Bo: a brass ring he snared from a merry-go-round ride they took together in Hollywood.

⊠ Marlena stripped for Stefano at Maison Blanche to get the keys to the dungeon where he was holding John captive.

⊠ The three powerful prisms were eventually tracked down by Stefano DiMera. One was around the neck of a native girl named Jasmine by Tony, on an island in the Bermuda Triangle; another in a Louisiana bayou where Kate Honeycutt got it back from alligator poachers who found it in the belly of one of their kills; and the third from the USSR when it was smuggled to Salem by an ice-skating troupe. The prisms were invented by Victor Chorvat, Larry Welch's father.

⊠ In spite of renovations to the Horton home over the last three decades, the original front door to the house remains.

⊠ In 1985 two very dissimilar men wore women's clothing in Salem: Stefano DiMera as Mrs. Lafferty and Eugene Bradford as Bettina Lovecraft.

⊠ Bill Hayes's character began as Brent Douglas, who then changed his name to Doug Williams. Bill also played a dual role when he portrayed his older half-brother, Byron Carmichael, in 1979.

⊠ Tommy Horton Jr. was originally named Danny in the *Days* story bible, and the character who had been called Mark Miller in the bible, came to Salem as Dr. Mark Brooks.

⊠ Julie Olson's son by David Martin was called Brad Banning when adopted by Scott and Janet Banning.

⊠ Game show host Pat Sajak appeared on *Days* as Kevin Hathaway, and Ruth Buzzi played Letitia Bradford the same year, 1983.

Cast List

TOM HORTON	Macdonald Carey	1965–1994
ALICE HORTON	Frances Reid	1965–
MICKEY HORTON	John Clarke	1965–
MARIE HORTON CURTIS	Marie Cheatham	1965–1968; 1970–1973; 1994
	Kate Woodville	1977
	Lanna Saunders	1979–1985
JULIE OLSON BANNING ANDERSON WILLIAMS	Carla Doherty	1965–1966
	Catherine Dunn	1967
	Catherine Ferrar	1967–1968
	Susan Seaforth Hayes	1968–1984; 1990–1993; 1994
ADDIE HORTON OLSON WILLIAMS	Patricia Huston	1965–1966
	Patricia Barry	1971–1974
BEN OLSON	Robert Knapp	1965
STEVE OLSON	Flip Mark	1965
	James Carroll Jordan	1972
	Stephen Schnetzer	1978–1980
CRAIG MERRITT	David McLean	1965–1967
	Harry Lauter	1966
TONY MERRITT	Richard Colla	1965–1966
	Don Briscoe	1966
	Ron Husmann	1966–1967
DETECTIVE JIM FISK	Robert Stevenson	1965
	Burt Douglas	1965
DIANNE HUNTER	Jane Kean	1965–1966
	Coleen Gray	1967–1968
BILL HORTON	Paul Carr	1965–1966
	Edward Mallory	1965–1980; 1991; 1992
	Christopher Stone	1987–1988; 1994
LAURA SPENCER HORTON	Floy Dean	1966
	Susan Flannery	1966–1975
	Susan Oliver	1975–1976
	Rosemary Forsyth	1976–1980
	Jaime Lyn Bauer	1993–
SUSAN HUNTER MARTIN	Denise Alexander	1966–1973
	Bennye Gatteys	1973–1976
RICHARD HUNTER	Terry O'Sullivan	1966–1968
DAVID MARTIN	Steven Mines	1966
	Clive Clerk	1966–1967
HELEN MARTIN	K. T. Stevens	1966–1967; 1969
JOHN MARTIN	Ed Prentiss	1966
	Robert Brubaker	1966–1971
TOMMY HORTON	John Lupton	1967–1972; 1975–1979
KITTY HORTON	Regina Gleason	1967–1969

SANDY HORTON	Astrid Warner	1967
	Heather North	1967–1971
	Martha Smith	1982
	Pamela Roylance	1983–1984
DAVID BANNING	Chad Barstad	1967–1970
	Jeffrey Williams	1970–1973
	Steve Doubet	1975
	Richard Guthrie	1975–1981
	Gregg Marx	1981–1983
SCOTT BANNING	Robert Carraway	1968
	Mike Farrell	1968–1970
	Robert Hogan	1970–1971
	Ryan MacDonald	1971–1973
MICHAEL HORTON	Kyle Puerner	1968–1969
	Wade Holdsworth	1969
	Craig Bond	1969
	Brian Andrews	1970
	Bobby Eilbacher	1970
	Eddie Rayden	1970
	Alan Decker	1970–1971
	John Amour	1971–1973
	Dick DeCoit	1973
	Stuart Lee	1973
	Wesley Eure	1974–1981
	Paul Coufos	1981–1982
	Michael Weiss	1985–1990
	Roark Critchlow	1994–
JANET BANNING	Joyce Easton	1967–1968
MEL BAILEY	Richard McMurray	1968–1969
PETER LARKIN	Gene Peterson	1968–1969
CLAIRE LARKIN	Catherine McLeod	1968–1969
SARAH FREDERICKS	Kay Peters	1969
JANENE WHITNEY	Mary Wilcox	1969
	Pat Hornung	1969
	Joan Van Ark	1969–1970
DOUG WILLIAMS	Bill Hayes	1970–1984; 1985–1987; 1994
LINDA PHILLIPS PATTERSON ANDERSON	Margaret Mason	1970–1971; 1975–1980; 1982
	Elaine Princi	1984–1985
MELISSA PHILLIPS ANDERSON JANNINGS	Joseph Trent Everett	1971
	Kim Durso	1976
	Debbie Lytton	1978–1980; 1982
	Lisa Trusel	1982–1988
	Camilla Scott	1990–1991
CLIFF PATTERSON	John Howard	1971

JIM PHILLIPS	Victor Holchak	*1971; 1974–1975*
DON CRAIG	Jed Allan	*1971–1985*
GREG PETERS	Peter Brown	*1972–1979*
ERIC PETERS	John Lombardo	*1971*
	Stanley Kamel	*1972–1976*
KIM WILLIAMS	Helen Funai	*1971–1972; 1976–1977*
ANNE PETERS	Jeanne Bates	*1972–1975*
ANNIE PETERS	Andreana Marie Chutuk	*1972–1973*
	Lisa Lynch	*1974*
	Elizabeth Hoy	*1975–1976*
PHIL PETERS	Herb Nelson	*1972–1975*
ROBERT LECLAIR	Robert Clary	*1972–1973; 1975–1980; 1981–1983; 1986*
MARY ANDERSON	Brigid Bazlen	*1972*
	Karin Wolfe	*1972–1975*
	Nancy Stephens	*1975*
	Carla Borelli	*1975*
	Susan Keller	*1980*
	Kim Durso	*1975–1976*
	Barbara Stanger	*1975–1981*
	Melinda Fee	*1981–1982*
BOB ANDERSON	Mark Tapscott	*1972–1980*
	Dick Gittings	*1978*
PHYLLIS ANDERSON CURTIS	Nancy Wickwire	*1972–1973*
	Elizabeth MacRae	*1977*
	Corinne Conley	*1973–1982*
DAVE, THE WAITER	Don Frabotta	*1973–1993*
NEIL CURTIS	Joseph Gallison	*1974–1991*
	Ben Archibek	*1973*
AMANDA HOWARD PETERS	Mary Frann	*1974–1979*
MAGGIE SIMMONS HORTON	Suzanne Rogers	*1974–*
TRISH CLAYTON BANNING	Patty Weaver	*1974–1982*
JERI CLAYTON	Kaye Stevens	*1974–1979*
JACK CLAYTON	Jack Denbo	*1974–1977*
DON CRAIG	Jed Allan	*1975–1985*
HOPE WILLIAMS BRADY	Kristina Osterhaut	*1974*
	Kimberly Joy Weber	*1974–1975*
	Natasha Ryan	*1975–1980*
	Tammy Taylor	*1981*
	Kristian Alfonso	*1983–1987; 1990–1991; 1994–*
REBECCA NORTH LECLAIR	Brooke Bundy	*1975–1977*
JOHNNY COLLINS	Paul Henry Itkin	*1975–1977*

BROOKE HAMILTON	Adrienne LaRussa	*1975–1977*
	Eileen Barnett	*1978–1980*
NATHAN CURTIS	Tom Brown	*1975–1976*
VALERIE GRANT	Tina Andrews	*1975–1977*
	Rose Fonseca	*1977–1978*
	Diane Sommerfield	*1981–1982*
DANNY GRANT	Michael Dwight-Smith	*1975–1978*
	Hazzan Shaheed	*1976*
	Roger Aaron Brown	*1981–1985*
HELEN GRANT	Ketty Lester	*1975–1977*
PAUL GRANT	Lawrence Cook	*1975–1976*
ADELE WINSTON HAMILTON	Dee Carroll	*1975–1976*
ROSIE CARLSON	Fran Ryan	*1976–1979*
JANICE BARNES	Martha Nix	*1976–1977*
	Elizabeth Storm	*1987*
JIM STANHOPE	William Traylor	*1976–1977*
KAY STANHOPE	Doris Singleton	*1976*
	Sandy Balson	*1976–1977*
GINNY STANHOPE	Janet Wood	*1976–1977*
JENNIFER ROSE HORTON DEVEREAUX	Maren Stephenson	*1976–1977*
	Jennifer Petersen	*1977–1978*
	Melissa Brennan Reeves	*1985–*
JACK CLAYTON	Jack Denbo	*1976–1977*
SHARON DUVAL	Sally Stark	*1976*
KARL DUVAL	Alejandro Rey	*1976*
MARLENA EVANS CRAIG BRADY	Deidre Hall	*1976–1987; 1991–*
BARBARA RANDOLPH	Elizabeth McRae	*1977*
JEAN BARTON	Jocelyn Somers	*1977*
FRED BARTON	John Lombardo	*1977*
LARRY ATWOOD	Fred Beir	*1977–1978*
DR. KATE WINOGRAD	Elaine Princi	*1984–1985*
SAMANTHA EVANS	Andrea Hall-Lovell	*1977–1980; 1982*
CHRIS KOSITCHEK	Josh Taylor	*1977–1986; 1987*
AMY KOSITCHEK	Robin Pohle	*1978–1979*
TONY JOHNSON	Chip Fields	*1978–1979*
SCOTTY BANNING	Erick Petersen	*1978–1980*
	Dick Billingsley	*1981–1983*
	David Hearst	*1989–1990*
LORRAINE TEMPLE	Francine York	*1978*
DONNA TEMPLE CRAIG	Tracy Bregman	*1978–1980*
AMELIA CRAIG	Loretta Fury	*1978–1979*
MARGO ANDERMAN HORTON	Suzanne Zenor	*1977–1980*
PETE CURTIS	Meegan King	*1978–1979*
STEPHANIE WOODRUFF	Eileen Barnett	*1978–1980*

ARLO ROBERTS	Nathaniel Christian	1978
JOANNE BARNES	Corinne Michaels	1979–1980
THERESA HARPER	Elizabeth Brooks	1979
JORDAN BARR	George McDaniel	1979–1980
BYRON CARMICHAEL	Bill Hayes	1979
MIMI GROSSET	Gail Johnson	1979
LEE DUMONDE	Brenda Benet	1979–1982
ALEX MARSHALL	Quinn Redecker	1979–1987
STAN KOSITCHEK	Thomas Havens	1979
MARTY, PIANO PLAYER	Marty Davich	1979–1993
DOUGIE LeCLAIR	Mikey Martin	1979–1980
LESLIE JAMES	Dianne Harper	1980
	Pamela Bowen	1980–1981
FLORA CHISHOLM	Meg Wyllie	1980
JOSHUA FALLON	Stephen Brooks	1980–1981
	Scott Palmer	1981–1982
JESSICA BLAKE FALLON	Jean Bruce Scott	1980–1982
KELLAM CHANDLER	Bill Joyce	1980–1981
LIZ CHANDLER CURTIS	Gloria Loring	1980–1986
TOD CHANDLER	Brett Williams	1980
	Paul Keenan	1980–1981
	David Wallace	1985–1986
SUNNY CHANDLER	Sandy Elliott	1980
	Jody Gibson	1984
MAXWELL JARVIS	Charles Bateman	1980–1981
RENEE DUMONDE BANNING	Philece Sampler	1980–1984
CASSIE BURNS	Deborah Dalton	1980–1981
BRENT CAVANAUGH	Perry Bullington	1980–1981
	Frank Ashmore	1981
DON CRAIG, JR.	Matthew Paul Bischof	1980
CAROL WELLES	Tyler Murray	1980
KYLE McCULLOUGH	Richard Hill	1980–1981
SARAH HORTON	Colin Lewis	1981
	Anthony Seaward	1981–1982
	Katie Krell	1982
	Lisa Brinegar	1985–1989
	Shauna Lane-Block	1989
	Aimee Brooks	1990
	Alli Brown	1991
ABE CARVER	James Reynolds	1981–1990; 1991–
ROMAN BRADY	Wayne Northrop	1981–1984; 1991–1994
	Drake Hogestyn	1986–1991
NICK CORELLI	George Jenesky	1981; 1984; 1986–1990
JAKE KOSITCHEK	Rene Lamart	1981
	Jack Coleman	1981–1982

STUART WHYLAND	Robert Alda	1981
EVAN WHYLAND	Lane Davies	1981–1982
ANTONY DiMERA	Thaao Penghlis	1981–1986; 1993–
STEFANO DiMERA	Joseph Mascolo	1982–1985; 1988; 1993–
KAYLA BRADY	Catherine Mary Stewart	1982–1983
	Mary Beth Evans	1986–1992
	Rhonda Aldrick	1989
CARRIE BRADY	Andrea Barber	1982–1986
	Christie Clark	1986–1990; 1992–
	Tracy Middendorf	1991–1992
DAPHNE DiMERA	Madlyn Rhue	1982–1984
EUGENE BRADFORD	John de Lancie	1982–1986; 1989
LORIE MASTERS	Cynthia Leake	1982
GWEN DAVIES	Ann-Marie Martin	1982–1985
WOODY KING	Lane Caudell	1982–1983
ESTHER KENSINGTON	Dorothy Jones	1982
ANNA BRADY DiMERA	Leann Hunley	1982–1986
NIKKI WADE	Renee Jones	1982–1983
PRESTON WADE	Jason Bernard	1982
CYRIL EDWARDS	Michael Gregory	1982
ORBY JENSEN	H. M. Wynant	1982
DELIA ABERNATHY	Shirley DeBurgh	1982–1984
OLIVER MARTIN	Shawn Stevens	1982–1983
MITZI MATUSO	Livia Ginise	1982–1983
JOHNNY	Jeremy Schoenberg	1982
BO BRADY	Peter Reckell	1983–1987; 1990–1991; 1995–
	Robert Kelker-Kelly	1992–1995
SHAWN BRADY	Frank Parker	1983; 1985–1989; 1990–
	Lew Brown	1984–1985
	Frank MacLean	1989–1990
CAROLINE BRADY	Peggy McCay	1983; 1985–
	Jody Carter	1984
	Barbara Beckley	1984–1985
OLIVER MARTIN	Shawn Stevens	1983
TRISTA EVANS BRADFORD	Barbara Crampton	1983
LETITIA BRADFORD	Ruth Buzzi	1983
KEVIN HATHAWAY	Pat Sajak	1983
PETE JANNINGS	Michael Leon	1983–1986
LARRY WELCH	Andrew Massett	1983–1985
VERONICA KIMBALL	Lenore Kasdorf	1983
FOXY HUMDINGER	Diane McBain	1983
HOWIE HOFFSTEDDER	Stanley Brock	1983–1986
NOEL CURTIS	Christina Maisano	1983
	Samantha Barrows	1984–1986; 1988

SNAKE SELEJKO	Bernie White	1983
SPEED SELEJKO	Robert Romanus	1983–1985
	Tom Everett	1985
DIANE PARKER	Dana Kimmel	1983–1984
	Cindy Fisher	1984
	De Anna Robbins	1984
ZACH PARKER	Brian Autenrieth	1984–1985
MABEL	Kathryn Fuller	1984–1985
	Lieux Dressler	1988–1989
SAMANTHA BRADY	Ronit Arnoff	1984
	Lauren Ann Bundy	1985
	Jessica Davis	1985–1986
	Tiffany Nicole Palma	1986
	Christina Wagoner	1990–1992
	Alison Sweeney	1992–
ERIC BRADY	Rory Beauregard	1984
	Jesse Davis	1985–1986
	Edwood Palma	1986
	Bradley Hallock	1986–1992
OFFICER MCBRIDE	Terrance Goodman	1984–1985
JIMMY PORTERFIELD	Ron Kuhlman	1984–1985
TESS JANNINGS	Melonie Mazman	1984

BARNEY JANNINGS	Michael Dante	1984
MAXWELL HATHAWAY	Tom Hallick	1984
MEGAN HATHAWAY	Cheryl-Ann Wilson	1984–1985
CARLO FORENZA	Don Diamont	1984–1985
CALLIOPE JONES BRADFORD	Arleen Sorkin	1984–1990; 1992
JASMINE	Jolina Collins	1984–1985
KATE HONEYCUTT	Elinor Donahue	1984–1986
SHANE DONOVAN	Charles Shaughnessy	1984–1992
IVY SELEJKO JANNINGS	Holly Gagnier	1984–1986
KIMBERLY BRADY DONOVAN	Patsy Pease	1984–1990; 1991–1992; 1994
	Anne Howard	1990; 1991
	Ariana Chase	1992–1993
ROBIN JACOBS	Derya Ruggles	1985–1987; 1989
EMMA DONOVAN MARSHALL	Jane Windsor	1985–1987
PRINCE NICHOLAS ARANI II	Grey O'Neill	1985
BENNETT HART	Chip Lucia	1985
MADELINE RUTHERFORD	Sue Rihr	1985
IAN GRIFFITH	Harrison Douglas	1985
	Darby Hinton	1985–1986
JANEY RICHARDS	Candi Milo	1985
CHARLIE JANNINGS	Tommy House	1985
SAVANNAH WILDER	Shannon Tweed	1985–1986
THEO CARVER	Rusty Cundieff	1985
RICHARD CATES	Rod Arrants	1985–1986
THE DRAGON	Lawrence Trimble	1985
STEPHEN "PATCH" JOHNSON	Stephen Nichols	1985–1990
VICTOR KIRIAKIS	John Aniston	1985–
MAID JANET	Dale Kristien	1985–1986
JAKE SELLERS	Gregory Wagrowski	1985–1986
BROTHER FRANCIS	Brian Matthews	1985–1986
LIVINIA PEACH	Diane Webster	1985–1986
	Pamela Kosh	1986–1991
VERTIGO	Christopher Neame	1986
CLAUDIA HANSEN	Amber Gilbert	1986
JARED MACALLISTER	Joseph Hacker	1986
OLIVIA REED	Amy Yasbeck	1986–1987
SIMMONS	Gerry Gibson	1986–1992
GILLIAN FORRESTER	Camilla More	1986–1987
TAMARA PRICE	Marilyn McCoo	1986–1987
ANDREW DONOVAN	Robert Elliott Canko	1986–1988
	Brian Amber	1988–1989
	Skye Rumph	1989
	Justin Page	1989–1990
	Bradley Pierce	1990–1991
	Brian Davila	1991–1992

MITCH KAUFMAN	Philip Levien	1986
ELI JACOBS	S. Marc Jordon	1986–1987; 1989
FRANKIE BRADY	Billy Warlock	1986–1988; 1990–1991
BARBARA STEWART	Elizabeth Burr	1986–1987
PAUL STEWART	Gregory Mortensen	1986
	Robert S. Woods	1986–1987
BRITTA ENGLUND	Amy Stock	1986
SILVIE GALLAGHER	Belinda Montgomery	1986–1987
LARS ENGLUND	Ken Jezek	1986–1987
GLENN GALLAGHER	Rob Estes	1986–1987
ORPHEUS	George Deloy	1986–1987
DAVID HALPERN	Maurice Roeves	1986
DEREK	Brian Cole	1986–1987
SASHA ROBERTS	Julie Jeter	1986
	Danielle Brisebois	1987
	Yvette Napier	1987
JOHN BLACK	Drake Hogestyn	1986; 1991–
ADRIENNE JOHNSON KIRIAKIS	Judi Evans	1986–1991
GRACE FORRESTER	Carey More	1987
	Camilla More	1987
HANS	Henry Stolow	1987
KAI	Charles Taylor	1987
AGENT THOMAS	Tom Ohmer	1987
JUSTIN KIRIAKIS	Wally Kurth	1987–1991
HARPER DEVEREAUX	Joseph Campanella	1987–1988; 1990–1992
JACK DEVEREAUX	Joseph Adams	1987
	James Acheson	1987
	Matthew Ashford	1987–1993
	Mark Valley	1994–
EVE DONOVAN	Charlotte Ross	1987–1991
HENDERSON	Ron Leath	1987
TRENT	Charles Van Eman	1987
DIANA COLVILLE	Genie Francis	1987–1989
SERENA COLVILLE	Valerie Karasek	1987–1988
PHILLIP COLVILLE	Morgan Woodward	1987
GABRIELLE PASCAL	Karen Moncrieff	1987–1988
DUKE JOHNSON	James Luisi	1987; 1990–1992
JO JOHNSON	Joy Garrett	1987–1993
	Marilyn McIntyre	1993
ANJELICA DEVEREAUX CURTIS	Jane Elliot	1987–1989
	Shelley Taylor Morgan	1989
	Judith Chapman	1989–1990
MARCUS HUNTER	Richard Biggs	1987–1992
ETHAN REILLY	Joe Colligan	1987–1988

ALAN BRAND	Brian Green	1987
SHAWN-DOUGLAS BRADY	Noel Bennett Castle	1987
	Paul Zachary	1990
	Scott Groff	1990–1995
	Collin O'Donnell	1995–
MAX BRADY	Adrian Arnold	1987
	Ryan Brennan	1987–1988; 1990–1992
JONAH CARVER	Bumper Robinson	1987–1988; 1989
	Thyme Lewis	1993–
ORION	Sandy McPeak	1988
ELLEN	Pamela Brull	1988
JAKE	Scott Reeves	1988
APRIL RAMIREZ	Lisa Howard	1988–1991
EMILIO RAMIREZ	Billy Hufsey	1988–1990
JULIO RAMIREZ	Michael Bays	1988–1989
ROSA RAMIREZ	Silvana Gallardo	1988
HARRIS MICHAELS	Steve Burton	1988
BENJY DIMERA	Darrell Utley	1988–1989; 1990
VERN SCOFIELD	Wayne Heffley	1988–1993
NICO	Lorenzo Caccialanza	1988–1991
MONTY DOLAN	Jay Robinson	1988–1989
CHIEF TARRINGTON	Ron Barker	1988–1992
LEXIE BROOKS CARVER	Sheila Wills	1988
	Cindy James Gossett	1988–1989
	Angelique Francis	1989 1990, 1992
	Shellye Broughton	1993
	Renee Jones	1993–
JOSE TORRES	Scott Colomby	1988
MIGUEL TORRES	Al Ruscio	1988
SIMON PRESCOTT	Dominick Allen	1989–1990
YVETTE DUPRES	Lori Hallier	1989
J. J. BAGWOOD	Patti Johns	1989–1990
GAIL CARSON	Patrice Chanel	1989
COLIN LARSON	Mitchell Laurence	1989
ADAM SCOTT	Randy Reinholz	1989
ARTHUR DOWNEY	John Calvin	1989–1990
REBECCA DOWNEY	Tracy Kolis	1989–1990
COLONEL JERICHO	Steve Eastin	1989–1990
MARINA TOSCANO JOHNSON	Hunter Tylo	1989–1990
ERNESTO TOSCANO	Terrance Beasor	1989
	Charles Cioffi	1990
	Eric Mason	1990
PEGGY	Peggy Reyna	1989; 1990
JERRY PULASKI	Jason Culp	1989

HANK TOBIN	John Lavachielli	1989
	Ron Kuhlman	1989
	Rick Porter	1989–1990
FAITH TAYLOR	Mindy Clarke	1989–1990
SAUL TAYLOR	James Hampton	1989
ISABELLA TOSCANO BLACK	Staci Greason	1989–1992; 1995
CAL WINTERS	Wortham Krimmer	1989–1990
	Joseph Bottoms	1991
GRACE JEFFRIES	Sandra Canning	1989–1990
ALEXANDER KIRIAKIS	Jonathan Thornton	1989–1991
JEREMY JACOBS	Jeremy Allen	1989
MADELINE ARMSTRONG	Lynn Clark	1990–1992
LORETTA TOSCANO	Kathrine Bates	1990
STEPHANIE KAY JOHNSON	Amanda & Jessica Gunnarson	1990–1992
SHEILA SALSBURY	Kim Morgan Greene	1990
PORTER ROLLINS	Anthony Peck	1990
BARRY	Barry Watson	1990
JOHNNY CORELLI	Antony Alda	1990–1991
GAMBINA	Mark Mikita	1990
LLOYD GARRISON	Tom Ormeny	1990
HANS	Anthony DeLongis	1990
JILL BAILEY	Deborah Hobart	1990–1991
JODI	Jodi Stolove	1990
CARLY MANNING	Crystal Chappell	1990–1993
CRAIG NORRIS	Robb Curtis-Brown	1990–1991
BOB RUSH	Doug Cox	1990
DAN RYAN	David Ruprecht	1990–1992
BABY VICTOR KIRIAKIS	Jacob Iorio	1990
	Candace Mead	1990
JOEY KIRIAKIS	Benjamin Iorio	1990
	Loren Mead	1990
GLYNNIS TURNER	Felicia Bell	1990–1991
EMMY BORDEN	Susan Diol	1990–1991
TANNER SCOFIELD	Michael Easton	1990–1992
BRIAN SCOFIELD	Robert Mailhouse	1990–1992
CASSIE SCOFIELD	Melissa Baum	1990–1991
LEOPOLD ALAMAIN	Avery Schreiber	1990
LAWRENCE ALAMAIN	Michael Sabatino	1990–1993
CHAD WEBSTER	Kirk Geiger	1990
FERNANDO TORRES	Dan Zukovic	1991–1992
RAFI TORRES	David Ciminello	1991–1992
GRETCHEN LINDQUIST	Bonnie Burroughs	1991
DESIREE	Charlayne Woodard	1991–1992
DANIELLE STEVENS	Deborah Moore	1991–1992

CHIP LAKIN	Jay Pickett	1991–1992
JEANNIE DONOVAN	Hannah Taylor Simmons	1991
	Emily & Alicia Pillatzke	1991–1992
	Caitlin Wachs	1992
	Gabriella Massari	1992
MOLLY BRINKER	Shannon Sturges	1991–1992
HOWARD ALSTON HAWKINS	Ray Stricklyn	1991–1992
HOWARD HAWK HAWKINS	J. Eddie Peck	1991–1992
GABY	Karen Racicot	1991–1992
ROB STEMKOWSKI	Charley Lang	1991–1992
GINGER DAWSON	Roberta Leighton	1991–1992
IVAN MARAIS	Ivan G'Vera	1991–
FR. O'TOOLE	Dan Cashman	1992
EDNA MAY	Tricia Tomey	1992
ROGER LOMBARD	Mark Drexler	1992
STELLA LOMBARD	Elaine Bromka	1992
JESSE LOMBARD	Tony Rhodes	1992
GUS	Leonard Kelly Young	1992–1993
CASH	John Marlo	1992–1993
CHARLIE	Robert Torti	1992
BRADY BLACK	Max & Alex Lucero	1992–1994
	Eric & Brandon Billings	1994–
ABIGAIL DEVEREAUX	Meghan & Michael Nelson	1992–1994
	Paige & Ryanne Kettner	1994–
PHILIP COLLIER	Doug Larson	1992
	Richard Burgi	1992
LISANNE GARDNER	Lynn Herring	1992
TAYLOR MCCALL	J. Cynthia Brooks	1992–1993
REBECCA MORRISON	Dani Minnick	1992–1993
VIVIAN ALAMAIN	Marj Dusay	1992–1993
	Louise Sorel	1993–
NICHOLAS ALAMAIN	Erik Von Detten	1992–1993
MARIE	Harris Kendall	1993–
ANN GOLDBERG	Lee Kessler	1993–1994
FR. KYLE	Gordon Paddison	1993–1994
PAT HAMILTON	Catherine MacNeal	1993–
NURSE JACKSON	Nancy Parsons	1993–1994
AUSTIN REED	Patrick Muldoon	1992–1995
	Austin Peck	1995–
BILLIE REED BRADY	Lisa Rinna	1993–1995
BELLE BRADY	Brianna & Chalice Fishette	1993
	Brianna & Brittany McConnell	1995–
JAMIE CALDWELL	Miriam Parrish	1993–
PETER BLAKE	Jason Brooks	1993–

KRISTEN BLAKE DIMERA	Eileen Davidson	1993–
KATE ROBERTS	Deborah Adair	1993–1995
LUCAS ROBERTS	Bryan Dattilo	1993–
ALAN HARRIS	Paul Kersey	1993–1995
CURTIS REED	Nick Benedict	1993; 1995
WENDY REARDON	Lark Voorhees	1993–1994
	Tammy Townsend	1994–
BENJAMIN REARDON	Shaquille Toney	1993–1994
	Ashaneese/Nasharin Holderness	1994–
DAVID CALDWELL	Vaughn Armstrong	1994
DR. LAYTON	Milt Tarver	1994
LEO	John Pappas	1994
OLGA	Diane Delano	1994–1995
DR. HUNT	Robert Gentry	1994–1995
LYNN	Marie Alise Recasner	1994–1995
FR. TIMOTHY JANSEN	Michael O'Neill	1994–
DR. PERKINS	Janice Kent	1994–1995
PHILLIP KIRIAKIS	Thomas & Jonathan Selstat	1994–
CELESTE	Tanya Boyd	1994–
DANIEL SCOTT	Stan Ivar	1994–1995
FATHER FRANCIS	Charles Welch	1994–1995
	Eric Christmas	1995
GABE, THE ANGEL	Mark Colson	1994–1995
BOBBY LEE COOPER	Jon Huffman	1995
ASHLEY	Tara Reid	1995
SARAH	Kristi McDaniel	1995–

Biographies

KRISTIAN ALFONSO

(Hope Brady)

Birthplace: Brockton, Massachusetts

Kristian originally joined *Days* in 1983 and stayed for four years. Then, after two years as Pilar Ortega on "Falcon Crest," Kristian returned to Salem in 1994 as a woman of mystery whose true identity turned out to be the beloved Hope. Kristian has also appeared in the television movie *Starmaker* and in the recurring role of Lauren Ethridge on *Melrose Place*; the television movie *Blindfold*; and the feature film *Joshua Tree*. At age thirteen, Kristian won a gold medal at the Junior Olympics in figure skating. She lives in Los Angeles with her son, Gino.

JOHN ANISTON

(Victor Kiriakis)

Birthplace: Crete, Greece

John came to *Days* in 1985. His other daytime drama credits include *Search for Tomorrow* and *Love of Life*. He has also appeared on *Kojak*, *Toma*, and *That Girl*. His feature film credits include *Love with a Proper Stranger* and *What a Way to Go*. A graduate of Pennsylvania State University, John also holds a biology degree from California State University. He speaks fluent Greek and Spanish. He served in U.S. Navy Intelligence as a lieutenant commander. He is the father of a young son, and his adult daughter, Jennifer, co-stars on the sitcom *Friends*.

JAMIE LYN BAUER

(Laura Horton)

Birthplace: Phoenix, Arizona

Jamie made her *Days* debut on November 12, 1993. Her other television credits include the role of Lauralee Brooks on *The Young and the Restless*, and appearances on *Young Riders*, *Knots Landing*, *Fantasy Island*, and the miniseries *Secrets*. Her feature film credits include *Young Doctors in Love*, *K-God*, and *Centerfold Girls*. She has been featured in stage productions of *Plaza Suite* and *Extremities*. Jaime is married to songwriter and makeup artist Jeremy Swan. They have two sons and a daughter.

TANYA BOYD

(Celeste)

Birthplace: Detroit, Michigan

Tanya Boyd joined the cast of *Days* in 1994 as the exotic and mysterious confidante of Stefano DiMera. Tanya has appeared on numerous television series, including *A Different World* and *Parker Lewis Can't Lose*, and the television movie *Tricks of the Trade*. In addition, she is an accomplished theater actress and won a Drama-Logue Critics Award for Best Performance in the highly acclaimed *Indigo Blues*. On stage she has starred in *Cotton* and *Jelly's Last Jam* and in *No Place to Be Somebody*. Tanya's motion picture credits include *New York, New York*, *Up the Academy*, and *Jo Jo Dancer*. Currently, she is one of the staff directors/producers at the newly formed Mojo Theatre Ensemble in Los Angeles. A versatile performer, Tanya has toured as a vocalist with Anita Baker, Lou Rawls, Natalie Cole, and Bobby Lyle. She married Lyle in 1994.

JASON BROOKS

(Peter Blake)

Birthplace: Colorado Springs, Colorado

Jason joined *Days* as the dark and dangerous adopted son of Stefano in 1993. The role earned him an award as Outstanding Villain at the Soap Opera Awards in 1995. Jason has appeared in the features *Captain America* and *Bloodmatch*. His television credits include *Baywatch*, *Doogie Howser, M.D.*, *Adam-12*, *Comedy Express*, and the television movie, *I'm Dangerous Tonight*. Jason attended the University of Arizona and the University of California, majoring in business administration. He is married and lives in West Los Angeles.

CHRISTIE CLARK

(Carrie Brady)

Birthplace: Orange County, California

Christie originally played Carrie Brady from March 1986 through December 1990, then returned three years later. Her other television credits include *General Hospital*, *Life Goes On*, *Hardcastle & McCormick*, and the TV movie *Changes*. She also starred in the horror films *Children of the Corn, Part II*, and *A Nightmare on Elm Street, Part II*. In her spare time she enjoys dancing, kick-boxing, and swimming.

JOHN CLARKE

(Mickey Horton)

Birthplace: South Bend, Indiana

John has been with *Days* since it began in 1965. In addition, his credits include *Hart to Hart* and the film *It's a Mad, Mad, Mad, Mad World*. As the son of a U.S. Army career officer, he lived in twenty states, graduating from high school in Tokyo. He attended UCLA in Los Angeles and majored in television arts. Clarke is married and has a son and a daughter, Mindy, who played Faith Taylor in 1989. John loves riding his Harley-Davidson motorcycle in his spare time.

ROARK CRITCHLOW

(Mike Horton)

Birthplace: Calgary, Alberta

Canadian native Critchlow came to Salem in 1994. His other television appearances include *The Commish* and *21 Jump Street*. He also appeared in the feature film *Cadence* and in numerous stage productions including *Billy Bishop*. Critchlow studied theater at the University of Victoria and moved to the United States in 1993. He is married and has two daughters.

BRYAN DATTILO

(Lucas Roberts)

Birthplace: Kankakee, Illinois

Bryan arrived in Salem in 1993 after earning other credits, which include *Not Necessarily the News, Doogie Howser, In the Heat of the Night, Charles in Charge, Class of '96,* and *California Dreams*. He also appeared in the feature film *Arcade*. With his sister Kristin he appeared in *The Adventures of Grizzly Adams*. Bryan attended Santa Monica College, majoring in psychology. Besides acting, Bryan's other passion is baseball. Bryan is single.

EILEEN DAVIDSON

(Kristen DiMera)

Birthplace: California

Eileen was cast as Kristen in 1993. Before joining *Days*, she appeared as Ashley Abbott on *The Young and the Restless* and as Kelly Capwell on *Santa Barbara*. Her other television work was in *Broken Badges* and the television movie *Sharing Richard*. She co-starred in the feature film *Eternity*. Eileen devotes much of her spare time working with the inner-city children of Para Los Ninos.

IVAN G'VERA

(Ivan Marais)

Birthplace: Prague, Czechoslovakia

Ivan became the extremely loyal servant and confidant to Vivian Alamain in 1991, but he had already appeared on numerous television shows including *Hunter, General Hospital, Alien Nation, Murphy Brown,* and in the films *The Hunt for Red October* and *Martial Outlaw*. Ivan left Prague for the West with a degree in electrical engineering; he also holds degrees from the University of Michigan and the University of California, San Diego. He is married, writes screenplays, and plays volleyball.

DEIDRE HALL

(Marlena Evans)

Birthplace: Lake Worth, Florida

Deidre created her award-winning role in 1976, leaving the show in 1987 and returning in August 1991. Hall's awards are numerous and include the American Women in Radio and Television (AWRT) award in 1994; five Best Actress awards from *Soap Opera Digest*; nominations for two People's Choice awards and Best Actress by Viewers for Quality Television. She has appeared on numerous television movies, which include *Woman on the Ledge*, and the miniseries *Op Center* as well as *And the Sea Will Tell*. Her episodic credits include *Wiseguy, Night of a Hundred Stars,* and a Bob Hope special. Deidre appeared on the stage in A. R. Gurney's *Love Letters*. She and her husband are parents of two surrogate children.

DRAKE HOGESTYN

(John Black)

Birthplace: Fort Wayne, Indiana

Drake turned up in Salem in 1986 as the mysterious John Black who at the time was thought to be Roman Brady. Drake was chosen Hottest Male Star at the Soap Opera Awards in 1994 and 1995. A talented athlete, he was picked by the St. Louis Cardinals after high school, choosing instead to attend college on a baseball scholarship. After graduating from the University of Southern Florida, Tampa, with a degree in microbiology, he was drafted by the New York Yankees farm team in Oneonta, New York, and played there until 1978. He is married and the father of one son and three daughters.

RENEE JONES

(Lexie Carver)

Birthplace: Opalocka, Florida

Renee *(above)* first came to the show in 1982 as Nikki Wade, a secretary at the Salem Police Department. Later, she returned as Lexie Carver, the wife of her former boss, Abe Carver. Renee became the first black model to appear on the cover of *Teen* magazine. In addition to *Days*, Renee has appeared on *Star Trek, In the Heat of the Night, 21 Jump Street, Highway to Heaven, Santa Barbara, Hardcastle & McCormick, Trapper John, M.D.,* and as Diana Moses on *L.A. Law*. Other television credits include *Honeymoon Hotel, The Jeffersons, Different Strokes, WKRP in Cincinnati,* and *Night Court*. Fans also remember her from the horror movie *Friday the 13th, Part VI*. Offscreen, Renee delights in reading, dancing, and playing tennis.

THYME LEWIS

(Jonah Carver)

Birthplace: San Francisco, California

Thyme became the handsome, younger brother of chief-of-police Abe Carver in 1993. His other television credits include *M.A.D.D., Head of the Class,* and *The Disney Special*. His film credits are *Street Music*, *Robotjox*, and *Back to the Beach*. Thyme comes from a musical background and plays the drums like his dad, Art Lewis. Thyme's name is derived from rhythm and time, and pronounced with the "th."

JOSEPH MASCOLO

(Stefano DiMera)

Birthplace: West Hartford, Connecticut

Joseph has been playing this hard-to-kill villain since 1982 with only several short absences. His other television credits include *The Gangster Chronicles*, *Kojak*, *Hill Street Blues*, and *Lou Grant*. His numerous feature film credits include *Sharkey's Machine*, *Jaws II*, and *Shaft's Big Score*. He has appeared on Broadway in *Dinner at Eight* and *That Championship Season*. Joe attended the University of Miami on a musical scholarship and turned down a chance for a Fulbright scholarship to study opera in New York while playing clarinet for the Metropolitan Opera Orchestra. A street in Ocilla, Georgia, was named Mascolo Drive to honor Mascola's efforts on behalf of the state's emotionally challenged citizens. An avid tennis player and art patron, Mascolo relaxes in the rose garden and library of his hillside home.

PEGGY McCAY

(Caroline Brady)

Birthplace: New York, New York

Emmy Award–winner Peggy first joined *Days* in 1983. In addition to winning the Outstanding Guest Actress in a Drama Series for her work in *The Trials of Rosie O'Neill*, McCay was also nominated for her performance in the miniseries, *Woman on the Run: The Lawrencia Bambenek Story*. Peggy majored in writing at

Barnard College and earned a B.S. degree from Columbia University. Two weeks after graduation she landed her first professional role in a Kraft Television Theater production.

FRANK PARKER

(Shawn Brady)

Birthplace: Darby, Pennsylvania

Frank has headed the Brady clan since 1985. He made his television debut on the series *Gomer Pyle* and has appeared on such daytime dramas as *All My Children*, *One Life to Live*, *General Hospital* and *The Young and the Restless*. Frank was also in the feature films *Elvis and His Girls* and *Stay Away Joe*. Parker is a graduate of Carnegie-Mellon University. He has three daughters.

MIRIAM PARRISH

(Jamie Caldwell)

Birthplace: Bradenton, Florida

Miriam joined *Days* in 1993 and has also appeared on *Roseanne* and *Step by Step* and performed as a dancer with the Metropolitan Opera in New York City. Miriam enjoys dancing, playing tennis, listening to alternative music, and writing poetry. She's single and has three cats.

AUSTIN PECK

(Austin Reed)

Birthplace: Hawaii

Austin came to Salem early this year. After enjoying a successful, globe-trotting career as a fashion model, Peck was studying acting in New York when he landed this contract role. Austin is single, enjoys working out, boxing, and creating comic book adventure characters.

THAAO PENGHLIS

(Tony DiMera)

Birthplace: Sydney, Australia

The darkly handsome and mysterious Tony DiMera returned to Salem seven years after he disappeared into the fog crying out the name, "Anna!" The part, which Penghlis originated in 1981, earned him Best Supporting Actor in daytime television and ranked him among the top ten male stars by many daytime publications. Thaao also played Victor Cassadine on *General Hospital*. His other television credits are numerous and include the miniseries *Memories of Midnight*, *Sadat*, *Movieola*, *Emma: Queen of the South Seas*, *Under Siege*, and the updated *Mission Impossible*. Among his film credits are *Les Patterson Saves the World* and *Altered States*. He has appeared on the stage in *The Lion in Winter*, *The Balcony*, and *No Exit*. Thaao's first language is Greek. When off-camera, Thaao enjoys world travel or relaxing in his Hollywood hilltop home, which he has filled with antiques and art.

PETER RECKELL

(Bo Brady)

Birthplace: Elkhart, Indiana

Peter brought Bo to Salem first in 1983 and stayed for four years. He visited for a year in 1990 but was busy with other areas of his career and the role went to another actor, until 1995, when Peter returned again. A graduate of the Boston Conservatory, Peter headed for New York and appeared in the Off-Broadway productions *Moonchildren* and *The Fantasticks*. He also played Eric Hollister on *As the World Turns*. Primarily a stage actor who loves to sing and dance, he's done many summer stock productions, including *West Side Story*, *Pippin*, *Camelot*, *Pirates of Penzance*, and *Carousel*. He's also appeared on TV's

Knots Landing. The second oldest of six children, Peter is single. When not working he loves to ride his motorcycle, make furniture, and play softball.

MELISSA REEVES

(Jennifer Devereaux)

Birthplace: Eatontown, New Jersey

Melissa's portrayal of Jennifer began in 1985, and the character has evolved from strong-willed teenage rebel into a divorced (but engaged) mother and career woman. Melissa's first soap role was as Jade Perkins on *Santa Barbara.* Her other television appearances include *Another World,* the HBO movie *Somewhere Tomorrow,* and *The Lakeside High Experiment.* Melissa is married to Scott Reeves, who plays Ryan on *The Young and the Restless.* They reside in the San Fernando Valley with their daughter.

FRANCES REID

(Alice Horton)

Birthplace: Wichita Falls, Kansas

Frances is an original cast member and matriarch of the Horton family. She has appeared on Broadway in such plays as *Hamlet, Cyrano de Bergerac,* and *Twelfth Night.* A graduate of the Pasadena Playhouse, Frances also appeared in the TV movie *Mercy or Murder?*

JAMES REYNOLDS

(Abe Carver)

Birthplace: Oskaloosa, Kansas

Jim became one of Salem's finest in 1981. After a brief stint on daytime's *Generations* in 1990, for which he received an Emmy nomination for his role as Henry Marshall, Jim returned to *Days.* His other credits include *Highway to Heaven, 227, Different Strokes, Hart to Hart,* and the film

Mr. Majestyk. A Vietnam vet, Jim worked as a combat reporter for the *Windward Marine* and as a stateside journalist. He attended Topeka's Washburn University, majoring in pre-law and journalism. He frequently tours colleges in his one-man show *I, Too, Am America,* a commentary on the African-American experience. Jim is married and has one son.

SUZANNE ROGERS

(Maggie Horton)

Birthplace: Lonaconing, Maryland

Suzanne came to Salem in 1974. The former Radio City Rockette has also appeared on *The Ed Sullivan Show, Quincy,* and *Little House on the Prairie.* Her stage performances include *Funny Girl, 110 Degrees in the Shade, Hallelujah Baby, Coco,* and *Follies.* Suzanne, who won an Emmy for her *Days* role in 1979, enjoys golf, horseback riding, and her three cats.

LOUISE SOREL

(Vivian Alamain)

Birthplace: Los Angeles, California

Louise brought devilishly conniving Vivian to town in 1993. She was also on daytime's *Santa Barbara* and *One Life to Live.* Other TV credits include: *The Virginian, Run for Your Life, "Big Valley,* and *Medical Center.* Her stage credits include the Broadway play *The Sign in Sidney Brustein's Window;* films are *Plaza Suite, Airplane II, Where the Boys Are, 1984,* and *Crimes of Passion.* Louise's father, Albert Cohen, was a successful producer of *East of Sumatra, Fighting Seabees, Never Say Good-bye,* and many other films. Louise is currently single and lives with her adorable dog Jiggs in Westwood when she's not traveling the world.

ALISON SWEENEY

(Samantha Brady)

Birthplace: Los Angeles, California

Alison brought Sami to *Days* in 1992 after appearances on *Tales from the Darkside, St. Elsewhere, Webster,* and *Simon & Simon.* Her film credits include *The End of Innocence* and *The Price of Life.* She has appeared in stage productions of *Wedding Band* and *Traveling Lady.* She loves all sports, including Rollerblading and kick-boxing. She is an accomplished equestrienne and plans to direct film and television.

TAMMY TOWNSEND

(Wendy Reardon)

Birthplace: Los Angeles, California

Tammy came to Salem in 1994 after appearances on such TV shows as *In the Heat of the Night, Quantum Leap, Family Matters, Charles in Charge,* and *Crime and Punishment.* An aspiring vocalist, Tammy was featured on the Branford Marsalis release of *Buck Shot LeFonque.* Away from work, Tammy likes to ice-skate, swim, and travel.

MARK VALLEY

(Jack Devereaux)

Birthplace: Ogdensburg, New York

Mark became Jack, the crafty, determined journalist who returns to Salem to reclaim his wife and child, in 1994. A veteran of Operation Desert Storm, Mark attended the United States Military Academy at West Point and graduated with a degree in mathematics. His films include *The Innocent* and *Far Away So Close.* He also played Father Pete on *Another World* and appeared in the TV series *Vanishing Son.* His numerous theater credits include *Hurly-Burly* and *The Crucible.*

Photography Credits

173 *bottom*, © National Broadcasting Company, Inc./
       Paul Drinkwater
173 *top*, Kathy Hutchins/Michelson
174 *above*, Kathy Hutchins/Michelson
174 *top right*, © National Broadcasting Company, Inc./
       Gene Arias
174 *bottom right*, © National Broadcasting Company,
       Inc./Paul Drinkwater
175 © National Broadcasting Company, Inc./
       Gary Null
176 *above left*, Kathy Hutchins/Michelson
176 *below right*, © National Broadcasting Company,
       Inc./Gary Null
177 *bottom right*, © National Broadcasting Company,
       Inc./Gary Null
177 *far right*, Kathy Hutchins/Michelson
177 *top right*, Kathy Hutchins/Michelson
178 *left*, © National Broadcasting Company, Inc./
       Joseph Del Valle
178 *above*, Kathy Hutchins/Michelson
180 *top*, Susan Lakin
180 *bottom*, Susan Lakin
180 *middle*, Susan Lakin
184 Susan Lakin
185 Susan Lakin
186 *above*, Susan Lakin
186 *below*, Susan Lakin
189 Kathy Hutchins/Michelson
191 Susan Lakin
192 *left*, © National Broadcasting Company, Inc./
       Joseph Del Valle
192 *below*, © National Broadcasting Company, Inc./
       Jean Krettler
193 *above*, © National Broadcasting Company, Inc./
       Alice S. Hall
193 *left*, © National Broadcasting Company, Inc.
194 *above*, © National Broadcasting Company, Inc./
       M. L. Miller
194 *right*, © National Broadcasting Company, Inc./
       Gary Null
195 *above*, Susan Lakin
195 *left*, Susan Lakin
196 *above*, Kathy Hutchins/Michelson
196 *above right*, Kathy Hutchins/Michelson
196 *right*, Kathy Hutchins/Michelson
197 Kathy Hutchins/Michelson
198 *below center*, © National Broadcasting Company,
       Inc./Gary Null
198 *left*, © National Broadcasting Company, Inc./
       Joseph Del Valle
198 *below right*, © National Broadcasting Company,
       Inc./Gary Null
198 *below left*, © National Broadcasting Company,
       Inc./Chris Haston
199 *left*, © National Broadcasting Company, Inc./
       Chris Haston
199 *far left*, © National Broadcasting Company, Inc./
       Paul Drinkwater
199 *above left*, © National Broadcasting Company, Inc./
       Gary Null
199 *above right*, © National Broadcasting Company,
       Inc./Joseph Del Valle
200 © National Broadcasting Company, Inc./
       Alice S. Hall
201 *above right*, Kathy Hutchins/Michelson
201 *above left*, © National Broadcasting Company, Inc./
       Alice S. Hall
201 *right*, Kathy Hutchins/Michelson
202 *right*, © National Broadcasting Company,
       Inc./Alice S. Hall
202 *above*, Kathy Hutchins/Michelson
203 *above*, Kathy Hutchins/Michelson
203 *right*, Kathy Hutchins/Michelson

206 © National Broadcasting Company, Inc./
       Alice S. Hall
211 Dana Fineman
214 Dana Fineman
217 © National Broadcasting Company, Inc./Gary Null
221 *below*, Kathy Hutchinson/Michelson
221 *left*, © National Broadcasting Company, Inc./
       Gary Null
222 © National Broadcasting Company, Inc./
       Chris Haston
223 *right*, © National Broadcasting Company,
       Inc./Alice S. Hall
223 *below*, © National Broadcasting Company,
       Inc./Chris Haston
224 © National Broadcasting Company, Inc./
       Chris Haston
225 *above*, The Gannett Company
225 *below*, © National Broadcasting Company, Inc./
       Gary Null
226 *above*, © National Broadcasting Company, Inc./
       Chris Haston
226 *below*, © National Broadcasting Company, Inc./
       Gary Null
227 Kathy Hutchinson/Michelson
228 *top*, Dana Fineman
228 *middle*, © National Broadcasting Company,
       Inc./Lorin Crosby
228 *bottom*, © National Broadcasting Company, Inc./
       Paul Drinkwater
229 *top*, © National Broadcasting Company, Inc.
229 *bottom*, © National Broadcasting Company, Inc./
       Chris Haston
230 Michael Broemer
233 Kathy Hutchins/Michelson
244 Kathy Hutchins/Michelson
252 © National Broadcasting Company, Inc./
       Alice S. Hall
253 © National Broadcasting Company, Inc../Gary Null
254 Susan Lakin
255 © National Broadcasting Company, Inc.
264 *left inset*, Kathy Hutchinson/Michelson
264 *right inset*, © National Broadcasting Company,
       Inc./Chris Haston
264 *below*, © National Broadcasting Company, Inc.

Index

Page numbers in italics refer to photographs.